TEACHER AND STUDENT EVALUATION

Following the recent major school reform of Race to the Top, schools, teachers, and students are increasingly evaluated through high-stakes achievement test scores. In six concise chapters, *Evaluating Teachers and Students* explores the historical rise and modern landscape of accountability in American education, and the current models of teacher evaluation. The authors provide realistic and useful suggestions for responding to current accountability demands.

The authors explore the methodological concerns and policy implications of using value-added and observational measures to make high-stakes decisions. After reaching the conclusion that these contemporary evaluation practices are flawed, Alyson Lavigne and Thomas Good offer possible solutions that inform current and future teacher evaluation. This book is a valuable resource for students of educational assessment as well as policy makers, administrators, and teachers who are currently building accountability plans. The book is written in an accessible but authoritative fashion that practitioners, policy makers, and scholars will find useful.

Alyson Leah Lavigne is Assistant Professor of Curriculum Studies at Roosevelt University, US.

Thomas L. Good is Professor and Head of Educational Psychology at the University of Arizona, US.

TEACHER AND STUDENT EVALUATION

Moving Beyond the Failure of School Reform

By Alyson Leah Lavigne and Thomas L. Good

 Routledge
Taylor & Francis Group
NEW YORK AND LONDON

First published 2014
by Routledge
711 Third Avenue, New York, NY 10017

Simultaneously published in the UK
by Routledge
2 Park Square, Milton Park, Abingdon, Oxon OX14 4RN

Routledge is an imprint of the Taylor & Francis Group, an informa business

Library of Congress Cataloging in Publication Data
Lavigne, Alyson Leah.
   Teacher and student evaluation : moving beyond the failure of school reform / by Alyson Leah Lavigne and Thomas L. Good.
   pages cm
   Includes bibliographical references and index.
   Teachers—Rating of—United States. 2. Students—Rating of—United States.
   3. Teacher-student relationships—United States. I. Title.
   LB2838.L27 2013
   371.14'4—dc23
   2013008364

ISBN: 978-0-415-81052-4 (hbk)
ISBN: 978-0-415-81053-1 (pbk)
ISBN: 978-0-203-07090-1 (ebk)

Typeset in Bembo and Stone Sans
by EvS Communication Networx, Inc.

Printed and bound in the United States of America by Publishers Graphics, LLC on sustainably sourced paper.

CONTENTS

PREFACE

We wrote this book because we believe that teachers make a difference in student achievement. We also know that teacher evaluation and feedback can enhance teaching when done properly. Despite the good intentions and hard work on the part of many educators, we believe that current evaluation practices need to be improved in important ways. In writing the book, we have blended history and current practice with an eye toward improving practice.

Some educators and citizens value lessons from history, but many do not. Those who choose not to examine history seem to take the extreme stance that "we have a problem with student achievement, we have had this problem for a long time, and clearly new strategies must be developed." We reject this position for two reasons. First, much of what we have long known applies in important ways to today's classrooms. Second, yes, many solutions of the past failed, but eerily, many of today's solutions such as improving teachers through the examination of students' standardized test scores and the observation of classroom practice, are repeating, at great cost, the failures of the past.

But learning from history only goes so far so, and accordingly, our book provides much more. It sharply defines the current national concern about teaching effectiveness as expressed in Race to the Top and its mandate as to what constitutes success in American classrooms and what must be done to assure success. Race to the Top (RttT) sees the goal as raising student achievement markedly and reducing the achievement gaps among student groups. The way to achieve this goal is to recognize that good teaching is the key to enhanced student performance. Thus, schools must identify and reward good teachers and identify and dismiss ineffective teachers. In general, when teachers are deemed ineffective they are given limited time to improve or are subject to being weeded out of the profession.

What it means to be a good teacher varies and encompasses a wide range of dispositions and characteristics. To identify good teachers through observation requires that we know what good teachers do in the classroom. We identify with great clarity what is known about good teaching, and what is not known. We illustrate that this knowledge base is used unevenly (and sometimes poorly) in observation systems that claim to find effective and ineffective teachers. Clearly observation systems that are badly flawed will do more harm than good and even the best observation system can be implemented in ways that ruin its effectiveness. We address many of these deficiencies in detail and suggest ways to make observations more useful to classroom teachers.

How different states are conducting teacher evaluations is examined at length and the wide variances in assumptions and procedures across states are illuminated. We discuss the implications of these differences in how states conceptualize good evaluation practices and their consequences for teachers and principals. This examination considers both the intended and unintended effects of these evaluations. We argue that the unintended effects, especially negative ones, have largely gone unexamined, and this is unfortunate as the long-term effects for teachers, teacher education, and their students are considerable.

Our book looks to the future as well. We describe how teacher evaluation can be improved both in the short and long term. Further, we consider and suggest how other players involved in American education can help in improving teaching and learning. Among these possible contributions we suggest ways for teacher education to prepare teachers better for today's schools, and how researchers can help to increase the range of outcomes that are involved in considering good teaching. We also acknowledge that a majority of the observational requirements will fall on the shoulders of administrators. Administrators need adequate preparation in observation—likely beyond the requirements (if any) set by states' certification standards. Although principals have been observing teachers for some time, they likely have never had to conduct as many observations as they will need to now nor in such a high-stakes context. We note that most agree that student achievement on standardized tests is only one of the factors that should be considered in defining good teaching. Yet despite this shortcoming and the frequent attacks on standardized tests, few alternatives or supplements have been put forth. We offer plans that are likely to facilitate the development of a greater knowledge base about what teachers do in the classroom and ways in which learning can occur through observation and analysis of teaching practices. This will not minimize the focus on standardized tests, but will develop a more rigorous understanding and rationale for the ways in which additional strategies and measures can be used to improve teaching and learning outcomes.

This book holds value for teachers and principals and indirectly, but importantly, for students. Teachers and principals will learn what teaching activities are consistently associated with gains in student achievement and allow them to use this knowledge with confidence. We also help practitioners to understand the limitations of this knowledge. Additionally, the book advances some aspects of classrooms that merit consideration for teacher evaluation even though these dimensions have not yet been validated by classroom research. We explain why this is the case. Classroom students will benefit from these teachers because they can plan and provide high quality instruction to their students in environments that are safe, comfortable, and well managed. Below is a summary of the chapters in this book.

In Chapter 1, we provide the history of accountability, laying the foundation for the entire book. We illustrate the concerns of the past remain today. We tell the story of why testing has gained momentum and how it has become a main staple in current teacher evaluation.

In Chapter 2, we provide an overview of education reform in America. Many citizens function under the false perception that reforms build upon one another, which leads to significant improvement. We will review several major reforms (e.g., *Sputnik*, *A Nation at Risk*, the individualization movement, *Prisoners of Time*) and illustrate that this has not been the case.

In Chapter 3, we provide a comprehensive summary on the research on teaching. We will reiterate the circular nature of both reform-based and research-based knowledge. Although this knowledge base has formed an established relationship between classroom practices and student learning as measured on standardized achievement tests, it is limited in its ability to delineate how teachers influence other important student outcomes (e.g., creativity, citizenship, problem solving).

Then, we turn to modern day teacher evaluation. In Chapter 4, we continue to illustrate how past trends are being maintained today. We also describe accountability prior to RttT. We explore how states, under RttT, are evaluating teachers. We raise some important issues regarding the intended and unintended consequences of state plans for teacher evaluation.

In Chapter 5, we provide a more detailed overview of the two primary and popular measures of teacher effectiveness—observation and student achievement data. We explore the knowledge base of various measures of teacher effectiveness with a particular eye towards strengths and limitations.

In Chapter 6, we close by acknowledging that despite a number of challenges and limitations, legislation will continue forward with implementation of high-stakes teacher evaluation. We illustrate the major stakeholders and the ways in which various groups can cope, but also improve upon the situation during this difficult time. High-stakes teacher evaluation may threaten the ways in which teachers, administrators, and teacher educators function, and subsequently, how students learn, and, as noted, we provide a few possible adaptive responses that will create the most amount of good, while limiting harmful consequences.

In sum, we wrote this book with the hopes that a number of groups can be equipped with a deep and broad knowledge base about how it is we have arrived at today's accountability. Schools, teachers, and students are held accountable on the basis of high-stakes achievement test scores; teachers are being fired and students retained and denied graduation. The quality of education continues to be questioned daily in the media, and high-stakes teacher evaluation is being pushed forward despite new and recent protests by teachers and the research community. We believe this book provides an important foundation for understanding both the instructional nature of reforms and knowledge about good teaching. This book equips readers with the ability to ask hard questions about the effectiveness of current teacher evaluation plans. We support this critical and reflective thought process by offering a few solutions to help manage and also improve the trajectory of education reform.

ACKNOWLEDGMENTS

Alyson Lavigne and Tom Good would like to acknowledge the thoughtful and extensive work by Toni Sollars who typed and typed numerous drafts of the manuscript and who was even willing to read and provide feedback on several of the chapters. Her work was indispensable in completing this book. We also thank Candyce Jupiter who helped with formatting the drafts, citations, and references. Also, many thanks to Ganna Sobolevs'ka who assisted in drafting some of the materials as well as providing editorial feedback on some of the work.

1

ARRIVING AT ACCOUNTABILITY

How Did We Come to Be Where We Are?

The nation is in the midst of an accountability addiction. No Child Left Behind (NCLB, 2001) provided a taste of current day accountability, and although it was not successful, the need to document progress in education has made a lasting impression. Today, high-stakes decisions are being made about teachers and students on the basis of test scores. In the 2013–2014 school year under Move on When Reading, Arizona will retain any third grader who falls far below the designated reading standard (Arizona Department of Education, 2012). Using 2012 test scores, an estimated 3,330 students will not progress to fourth grade. Fourteen other states have adopted similar laws (Expect More Arizona, 2012). In just 2 years, the District of Columbia Public Schools (DCPS) has fired 423 teachers for low performance under their new teacher evaluation program, IMPACT; a program that costs the city $7 million a year (DCPS, 2011; Dillon, 2011). In 2012, 45% of teachers eligible for tenure in New York City were denied, as compared to 3% in 2007 (Baker, 2012). As can be imagined, reactions to these new developments have been varied and contentious. On the one hand, there has been considerable teacher resistance to these measures—consider the Chicago teacher strike in September of 2012 (Davey, 2012). And on the other hand, there has been commentary that the consequences have been insufficient and that evaluation systems have identified too few teachers as being unsatisfactory (Badertscher, 2013). Regardless of how these new changes are being perceived, they are not entirely "new." What appears to be a recent addiction to accountability has actually been brewing for some time.

Throughout history, teachers and students have been graded using a variety of methods. In the most recent federal education initiative, Race to the Top (RttT), teachers are evaluated primarily on their ability to demonstrate student achievement gains, and, to a lesser extent on their ratings on observational measures of teaching. This trend has become increasingly popular with new statistical techniques that assess the "value" a teacher "adds" to student learning (aka value-added modeling; see Harris, 2011, for detailed information about value-added techniques). A recent report using such modeling indicated that teachers have a lasting effect on students—students who receive 1 year of instruction with a highly effective teacher are more likely to go to college, less likely to become teenage mothers, and will be more likely to earn higher incomes—an average increase in lifetime earnings of $50,000 (Chetty, Friedman, & Rockoff, 2011). Some, of course, have challenged these claims, but still, this report received significant media coverage (e.g., PBS, *New York Times*, *Harvard Magazine*, *Education Week*, CNN). It also brought value-added and the importance of teachers and teacher evaluation into the homes of those directly or even indirectly interested in schooling in America. The evolution leading up to current approaches to evaluation is complex, changing, and not nearly as modern as perceived (as we will demonstrate that teacher evaluation and assessment methods often appear, disappear, and then return again as newly discovered). In this chapter, we provide a modest historical account of the rise of accountability through the lens of teacher and student evaluation, demonstrating what methods have and can be used, why such methods have gained popularity, and if such methods will yield promising results.

History of Student Testing

The assessment of student learning outcomes dates back long before the time of teacher evaluation, but instead of using student learning as a product of teachers' instruction it was often a reflection of school progress and achievement. In the section below, we document how student achievement shifted to eventually be used as a way of holding others accountable for student learning and as a measure of *teacher* effectiveness.

The Growing Popularity of Student Assessment

Tests are not new. The most early, complex, and best-known forms of testing can be traced back to the Chinese, Greek, and Romans (Odell, 1928). Evidence of student assessment in the United States, often in the form of oral and written examinations, dates as far back as the 1820s (Garrison, 2009; Reese, 2007), however, in these early forms of assessment students usually answered different questions (Odell, 1928). It became clear that some students were given easier questions than others and this called into question if the assessments were fair (of course, issues of fairness and have remained as seen in recent examinations of standardized test questions (Collins, 2012) and cheating scandals (Gabriel, 2010)). Hence, the need for objective measures of student learning quickly emerged. For example, in the Boston Public Schools, committees were called upon to produce "as fair as an examination as possible; to give the same advantages to all; to prevent leading questions; to carry away … positive information, in black and white; to ascertain with certainty what the scholars did not know, as well as what they did know …" (Caldwell & Courtis, 1924, p. 26). As illustrated here, a common, early belief and practice was that students were responsible for their learning and held back if unable to demonstrate so (Ravitch, 2002). A few voices, schools, and school systems opposed examinations, noting the possible negative effects of testing. Odell (1928) summarizes these concerns:

I. Examinations are injurious to the health of those taking them, causing overstrain, nervousness, worry, and other undesirable physical and mental results.
II. The content covered by examination questions does not agree with the recognized objectives of education, but instead encourages cramming, mere factual memorizing and acquiring items of information rather than careful and continuous study, reasoning, and other higher thought processes.
III. Examinations too often become objectives in themselves, the pupils believing that the chief purpose of study is to pass examinations rather than to master the subject or to gain mental power. This objection is more or less similar to the one stated immediately above, but still is probably different enough to warrant separate statement and consideration. At least it has been so considered by unfavorable critics.
IV. Examinations encourage bluffing and cheating. This occurs both because of the premium, which they place on doing so successfully, and because of the frequently prevailing conditions which make bluffing relatively easy and cheating comparatively safe.
V. Examinations develop habits of careless use of English and poor handwriting. This results because they emphasize writing a large amount as rapidly as possible and thus lead to the neglect of good form.
VI. The time devoted to examinations can be more profitably used otherwise, for more study, recitation, review, and so forth.
VII. The results of instruction in the field of education are intangible and cannot be measured as can production in industry or agriculture, physical growth, heat, light, and many other products of human or other activity.
VIII. Examinations are unnecessary. Capable instructors handling classes, which are not too large, are able to rate the work of their pupils without employing examinations. (p. 10)

The Atlanta cheating scandal (Severson, 2010) is just one example that demonstrates these critics were thinking well before their time (see Nichols & Berliner, 2007, for more examples).

Protest over examinations was overshadowed by Horace Mann's Common School movement of the 1840s, a movement that called for common standards and curriculum (Mulvey, Cooper, & Maloney, 2010).[1] This interest has been renewed as demonstrated in The Common Core State Standards, adopted by states beginning in 2010 (www.corestandards.org). Common curriculum and standards meant a common form of assessment of student learning. The purpose of these examinations was two-fold: (a) provide greater supervision of schools by the state; and (b) equalize testing conditions, reduce error and bias, hence, obtain more accurate measurement (Cremin, 1975; Garrison, 2009). Mann believed these tests would assess teaching and more specifically, if students "answer from the book accurately and readily, but fail in those cases which involve relations and applications of principles, the dishonor must settle upon the heads of the teachers" (as cited in Caldwell & Courtis, 1924, p. 244). Testing gained momentum, standardized tests were born, and accountability, as we know it today, made its first mark in history. According to Odell (1928), "A *standardized* test in the most limited sense is any test which has been given to a large enough number of pupils of a given age, grade, or other homogeneous group so that the results are fairly adequate indications of what achievements are actually being attained by such pupils in general" (p. 8). In Boston, students ages 13 and 14 were given written and verbal examinations in six areas of curriculum. It is unclear if and how teachers used such results. Schools, however, were ranked and results reviewed with harsh criticism. The committees provided recommendations for school improvements of what was perceived as dismal student performance (Caldwell & Courtis, 1924); regardless of Horace Mann's approach, teachers were a limited part of this improvement equation. Hence, ideas of holding teachers and schools accountable were beginning to emerge, although consequences were merely suggestions and clearly less severe than they are today.

The early and mid-1800s mark the beginning of adopting tests to assess a large number of students. End of grade and exit examinations soon followed suit. In 1864, the Board of Regents of the State of New York passed an ordinance which required students to take an evaluation at the end of each academic term. Results would signify passing to the next grade. In 1878, high school exit exams were administered in New York State (Folts, 1996). Ironically, these policies are a return to an earlier belief that students should be held accountable for their own learning.

The 1900s is characterized by a swift and widespread adoption of standardized testing. Intelligence testing made its mark in the early 1900s by way of the Stanford-Binet Intelligence Scale (Terman, 1916). At this point in time, standardized intelligence tests were primarily used to diagnose and place children appropriately, but they were not widely used.

The use of standardized tests, at a mass level, began during World War I. The U.S. Army had adopted the use of intelligence tests (e.g., Army Alpha and Beta) to evaluate recruits, assign duties, and select suitable officers (Cronbach, 1975; McGuire, 1994). Army Alpha was modified and released in 1926 under the name Scholastic Aptitude Test (SAT, later the known as the Scholastic Assessment Test; Fuess, 1950). The development of a single test to be used for college admissions served to address the struggles schools were having in preparing students to take a number of college-specific admission tests (Ravitch, 2002). The development and popularization of the ACT and SAT were important in the growing use and application of student testing in higher education and K-12 settings. The ability for the SAT to be adopted on a massive scale was affirmed by its original iteration, the Army Alpha Examination (Cronbach, 1975). William Learned and E. L. Thorndike tested a number of college students during the same period of time (Savage, 1953). This work was followed by the Pennsylvania Study from 1928–1932 that included the testing of both high school and college students and both achievement and learning outcomes (Learned & Wood, 1938). Success and growth quickly trickled down to elementary and secondary settings and manifested in the form of the Iowa Test of Basic Skills in 1935, the California Achievement Test in 1950, and the Metropolitan Achievement Test in 1933.

Below are a few arguments for the growing popularity of testing.

Efficiency, Efficiency, Efficiency.   Criticism of what students were able to demonstrate on the tests described above resulted in a variety of recommendations, one of which was to apply a more business-like or scientific model to the educational system (Rice, 1893, 1913). Scientific management (Taylor, 1911) infected American industry, and schools were not far behind (Ayres, 1918; Bobbitt, 1912). Furthermore, an increase in compulsory attendance laws of the 1900s meant more students in the classroom. Inefficiencies, such as the number of students repeating grades, were noted (Resnick, 1980). Efficiency, thus, came in the form of decreasing the number of students repeating grades by tracking and grouping students of similar intellectual ability (Wigdor & Garner, 1982). Standardized tests allowed such activities to be widely applied, and the infusion of business-like approaches in education continues today (Lavigne, in press; Nichols & Berliner, 2007).

Proving One's Worth.   Continuing criticism of American education changed focus from failing students to *who* or *what* had failed our students. Significant pressure followed the 1957 launching of *Sputnik*, the Coleman Report (1966), and *A Nation at Risk* in 1983. The results eerily echo modern day accountability. For example, Horace Mann believed that teachers were, in part, responsible for student test scores and later, after reviewing the purported low scores of students, argued for teacher selection on merit basis by way of a competitive teacher examination (Caldwell & Courtis, 1924). Although early recommendations to the Boston Public Schools included teachers, a greater emphasis was placed on schools (e.g., organization and resources) and methods of instruction, punishment, and reward as a means of improving student test scores. Early forms of accountability, however, had vaguely established consequences, at best. Instead, it was perceived that schools would be empowered by accountability.

> The school principal who knows in advance where his school is weak and where it is strong, is armed against criticism. But more than that, he is guided in his future efforts. The purely negative results that adverse judgment causes no shock, is of some importance, but the positive result that the school is stimulated to improve itself is a matter of supreme advantage.
>
> *(Judd, 1918, p. 154)*

Greater scrutiny over student performance came with a more government controlled and funded education system. In particular, funding was to be allocated to programs that could document their success. Student performance on tests would indicate if the implemented program was successful or not.

Soon worries were less local and more global. The launching of *Sputnik* in 1957 brought the fear that U.S. students were falling behind their international counterparts, particularly in math and science. Schools were not preparing students enough in these areas. The National Defense Education Act of 1958 was one source of funding that approached the problem in a number of ways. The funding provided low-interest student loans to encourage college attendance. The funding also supported instruction, particularly in the mathematics, sciences, and the foreign languages. The act also included funding for assessments to help better document the progress students were making in these areas. Less than a decade later, the focus turned to poverty in the Elementary and Secondary Education Act (ESEA) of 1965; the achievement gap between more and less affluent students needed to be closed and all students needed to be provided with an equal opportunity to learn. ESEA includes high standards and accountability and school improvement including improvement of low test scores (Popham, 2008). Albeit for different reasons, both of these mid-1900s acts provided funding for standardized testing. Test providers and testing results became more readily available. In the early 1970s, student achievement was measured using the National Assessment of Educational Progress (NAEP). In 1994, state NAEP scores were released in five content areas (Vinovskis, 2012).

This set the stage for versions of accountability similar to what is present today, most notably in California's 1984 education bill. School districts were expected to determine standards for student achievement and evaluate teachers' ability to meet such standards. Similar requirements were present at the federal level in 1988; the amendments to the ESEA Act of 1965 (Augustus F. Hawkins-Robert T. Stafford Elementary and Secondary School Improvement Amendments) included state requirements to establish benchmarks for academic achievement and progress of disadvantaged students receiving aid under Title I. Standards-based reform, which placed standards, tests, and accountability at the crux of quality education, supported state assessment systems that would measure student academic achievement. Similarly, states such as Kentucky and Maryland went forth with high-stakes accountability measures—holding students, educators, and schools responsible for student learning by requiring public reports of progress and administering rewards and sanctions when standards were or were not met.

In sum, standardized testing gained popularity for many reasons and gained momentum fast. In states such as New York, students take a minimum of 33 standardized tests over the course of their schooling (Hursh, 2008). Testing is a booming financial industry and will continue to profit as states transition to the Common Core State Standards (CCSS). Assessment estimates for the CCSS test transition for states range from $1.79 to as much as $34.02 per student; estimates *do not* include the cost of test development. In Texas in 2008–2009, testing cost the state approximately $8 per student—$37 million in total (Murphy & Regenstein, 2012). Clearly, standardized testing has made its mark and is likely here to stay.

What Has Been Measured

We have described the growing interest in assessing students, particularly through standardized testing. A majority of these developments were based within intelligence testing research and development. Below we will illustrate how the growth in student assessment is tied to IQ testing and discuss what other aspects of students and student outcomes have been measured.

Intelligence.　As mentioned earlier, intelligence tests experienced their establishment in the 1900s. Early intelligence tests were administered most often to college students (Cattell, 1890). The most notable start of intelligence testing can be traced back to Alfred Binet. Binet had originally developed intelligence testing to identify children with learning disabilities. His first test to do just that, the Binet-Simon scale, was released in France in 1905 (Siegler, 1992; White, 1977). Binet's test was first popularized in the United States to determine developmental delays and evaluate the intelligence of immigrants (Goddard, 1914, 1917). Eventually, Terman redesigned the test to better apply to education (White, 2000). This redesign, known as the Stanford-Binet Intelligence Scale (Terman, 1916), is one of the most widely used intelligence tests in the United States. It is important to note that many early developments in testing occurred during a time when intelligence was believed to be stable. Hence, early testing was primarily used for classification, predicting, and sorting (Gordon, 2008).

Competence.　Competence can be measured in many forms from state-level standardized tests to classroom work. For decades, report cards have included the measurement of students' knowledge in particular content areas. For example, Odell (1928) commented on appropriate grading and scoring of content area tests, final grades, and distribution of such grades. These include: percentiles, letter grades, pass/fail, and other types of categorizations (e.g., excelling, satisfactory, unsatisfactory). Early forms of classroom assessment were to determine what students had learned and to assign grades (Popham, 2008) rather than to improve instruction and learning (Shepard, 2008). In the 1980s, strands began to appear to assess what skills students were mastering in a particular content area, but more general overarching themes were still present (see Table 1.1).

This pales, however, in comparison to the standards-based report cards that many districts have or are beginning to adopt; parents can expect to now see report cards with content areas with numerous strands and specific skill sets within each strand. For example, on at least one kindergarten report card, under a single content area (e.g., reading), students are assessed on 30 specific skills (e.g., uses pictures, syntax, repetitive language patterns to help predict words, identifies letters) that organize across eight categories (e.g., reading strategies, vocabulary; Middletown Public Schools, 2009). Instead of being scored with traditional grade letters or frequency of behavior, students will now be scored with numbers that align with the standard scale of standards measurement (e.g., meets, exceeds).

Non-Academic Outcomes.   Dating back to the 1920s, report cards have captured non-academic student outcomes, particularly those deemed important for good citizenship such as: health habits, personal habits, social and moral habits, play habits, work and study habits (Hendry, 1929), and attendance (Palmer, 1929). Others have experimented with diagnostic letters written to parents based on teachers' response to a list of questions in three areas: personality development (e.g., Is he emotionally stable or unstable?), methods of study (e.g., Is his work careful or carelessly done?), and academic achievement (e.g., Is he acquiring a genuine reading adaptation?) (Beggs, 1936). Even in the 1980s, non-cognitive outcomes played a substantial role, particularly in the early grades (see Table 1.1). The conversation about the need to assess and develop non-cognitive outcomes continues today in K-12 and higher education (Schmitt, 2012). Students are assessed on categories such as: self-directed learner, quality producer, respectful citizen, and cooperative worker (Middletown Public Schools, 2009).

What Could Be Measured

Many have argued that less and an inadequate amount of time has been spent measuring affective variables. And much has been written about what student outcomes other than achievement could be measured. For example, two special issues in 1999 and 2000, of the *Elementary School Journal* provided a series of papers that discussed and considered multiple outcomes of schooling, particularly non-cognitive ones. Wanlass (2000) has argued for schools to support the development of competence by acknowledging and rewarding students'

TABLE 1.1 Kindergarten Report Card Used in a New Hampshire School*

Kindergarten Report for _____

A = Always   F = Frequently   O = Occasionally   S = Seldom

	Quarters			
	1	*2*	*3*	*4*
SOCIAL DEVELOPMENT				
Can be a friend				
Is sensitive to needs of peers				
Is comfortable with adults				
Plays alone happily				
Cooperates in play				
Shares well				
Initiates play activities				
Is imaginative				
Has the capacity to lead				
Has the capacity to follow				
Uses materials purposely				
Exhibits appropriate sense of humor				
Accepts responsibility for actions				
SKILL DEVELOPMENT				
Is attentive				
Listens in a group				
Contributes to group discussions				
Follows directions				
Works cooperatively				
Completes tasks				
Demonstrates ability to focus on one task				
Respects classroom routines				
Responds positively to constructive criticism				
Is curious				
Is willing to try new activities				
Is a self-starter				
Enjoys new challenges				
Exhibits problem solving abilities				
Expresses ideas well				

(*continued*)

TABLE 1.1 Continued

	Quarters			
	1	2	3	4
PHYSICAL DEVELOPMENT				
Small muscle control and coordination				
Large muscle control and coordination				
Speech development (articulation)				
LANGUAGE DEVELOPMENT				
Speaks in clear sentences				
Uses adequate oral vocabulary				
Relates ideas in sequence				
ACADEMIC DEVELOPMENT				
Recognizes letters presented				
Knows letter sounds presented				
Beginning to blend sounds to make words				
Has feeling for written language				
Beginning to use "inventive spelling"				
Rote counting				
Recognizes relationships and patterns				
Recognizes numbers presented				
Matches numbers to quantity, 1–10				
Recognizes geometric figures presented				
Recognizes colors presented				
Visual discrimination: (likeness & differences in pictures and letters)				
Auditory discrimination: (similarities & differences in common sounds and words)				

* This is the actual form of the kindergarten report card used in Alyson Lavigne's class in her New Hampshire school.

talents and abilities regardless if such competence is academic in nature. Others have noted important nonacademic outcomes such as values education, multicultural education, civics and democratic education, and environmental education (Ladwig, 2010). Rothstein (2000) has deemed similar nonacademic outcomes as important, such as responsible democratic citizenship, sound wellness practices, and teamwork and social ethics. In his proposed composite index of schools, academic outcomes hold the greatest weight (40%). Of lesser weight, but still important, are nonacademic outcomes, such as the development of social, emotional, and moral skills and ethics and the environment and support factors present at the school (e.g., Are students safe? Do students receive individual attention?). For many of the factors presented by Rothstein, schools are not solely responsible—the development of attributes such as morality or citizenship, for example, will and should come from other sources (e.g., home, community).

Importantly, not only have educators argued for the significance of outcomes other than achievement, courts also have had their say about student outcomes that teachers must address. For example, in *Rose v Council for Better Education* (1989) the court ruled that schools must provide sufficient: (a) oral and written communication skills to function in a complex and rapidly changing civilization; (b) knowledge of economic, social, and political systems to enable students to make informed choices; (c) understanding of governmental processes to enable the student to understand the issues that affect his or her community, state or nation; (d) self-knowledge and knowledge of his or her mental and physical wellness; (e) grounding in the arts to enable each student to appreciate his or her cultural and historical heritage; (f) training or preparation for advanced training in either academic or vocational fields so as to enable each child to choose and pursue life work intelligently; (g) levels of academic or vocational skills to enable public school students to compete favorably with their counterparts in surrounding states, in academics or in the job market.

Despite considerable and long-standing interest in non-cognitive outcomes, this has not resulted in any significant form of accountability. Even prior to new techniques in teacher evaluation (e.g., value-added), students' scores on achievement tests have been the preferred outcome measure of student learning and evidence of program effectiveness (Popham, 2008). Under NCLB this was true, and this continues in RttT and large teacher evaluation studies such as the Measures of Effective Teaching (MET) Project. Ironically, teachers grades remain a better predictor for success in college than do standardized tests, and this is true for both American and foreign students who attend American universities (Fu, 2012; Soares, 2011). The growing emphasis on holding teachers accountable in combination with placing weight on standardized tests rather than teachers grades demonstrate that teachers are valued, but not trusted.

Who Is Accountable for Student Learning?

As noted above, historically students have been held accountable for their own learning. A noted emphasis was placed on schools and teachers in the 1800s, but these beliefs failed to materialize in any meaningful way. More apparent accountability systems emerged in the 1990s, but the responsibility of student learning appeared to be a shared one between schools and teachers. With the arrival of NCLB, policy shifted to a clearer focus on school effects. Meanwhile, research shifted to a broader approach that would help identify which variables explained variation in student performance. More modern statistical techniques, such as hierarchical linear modeling and structural equation modeling honor this body of research and the importance of acknowledging effects at multiple levels (e.g., individual, classroom or teacher, school). Furthermore, recent legislation that holds schools accountable for student learning continues to support the premise that schools matter. In addition there is evidence that schools influence student achievement just as teachers do. For example, students with similar backgrounds have been found to register higher achievement in some schools (Brookover et al., 1978; Rosenholtz, 1985; Rutter, 1982). However, this research is correlational and not experimental. It should also be noted that school effects are notably weaker than teacher effects (Kane & Staiger, 2008; Rivkin, Hanushek, & Kain, 2005). According to Nye, Konstantopoulos, and Hedges (2004), teacher effects explain 7%–21% of the variance in student achievement outcomes.

No Child Left Behind reform efforts rewarded and punished schools, placing the blame and the solution primarily on the school rather than the student, teacher, parent, or a variety of other possible factors. Under RttT state plans, the emphasis has now shifted to show that teachers do matter, leaving them with the responsibility to demonstrate their value, and, hence, to fight for their position to gain entry into or remain in the classroom. This shift in locus of responsibility for student learning has an interesting and evolving history.

History of Teacher Evaluation

Teacher evaluation is often bound by how teaching is conceptualized. As noted elsewhere (Darling-Hammond, Wise, & Pease, 1983; Mitchell & Kerchner, 1983), the work of teaching often falls into four categories: labor, craft, profession, or art. A definition of *labor* assumes teaching as systematic, planned, organized, routine, and requires an amount of adherence to and implementation of the prescribed curriculum. This differs substantially from the conception of teaching as a *craft* where teaching is seen as knowledge of techniques and rules of application and is less prescribed. If one considers teaching as a *profession*, one includes elements subsumed under craft, but also includes judgment about when particular techniques should be applied. Teaching as an *art* is the least prescriptive and standardized definition indicating that teaching may be innovative, unconventional, and unpredictable. This definition emerges out of the understanding that classrooms are unpredictable learning environments.

Conceptually-Based Evaluations. Evaluations, then, may vary based on the abovementioned conceptualizations—or the many other conceptions of good teaching that have been developed. Teachers' work as defined as *labor* warrants an evaluation of lesson plans, classroom performance, and performance outcomes (e.g., Did the teacher follow the designated curriculum?). A definition of teaching as a *craft* would result in a more indirect evaluation (e.g., Did the teacher use appropriate techniques when explaining concepts?). In teaching as *profession*, teacher evaluation may be peer-designed and assess a teacher's ability to problem solve (e.g., Was the teacher able to address student misconceptions? How so?). Finally, utilizing a teaching as *art* definition would require individualized evaluations that honor a teacher's ability to be resourceful and intuitive in an unpredictable setting (Darling-Hammond et al., 1983). Conceptions of teaching, however, are rarely measured in a pure form. Observation instruments usually reflect a blend of conceptual approaches or measure good teaching, as defined by research.

Effective Teaching.   What is a good teacher? What do good teachers do? Of course, the answer to this is, in part, driven by how teaching is conceptualized. Each individual and stakeholder may vary widely on what aspects of a teacher and teaching are important. For example, Ryans (1949) notes that:

> Most of us have in mind, nebulous as our concept may be, some idea of what constitutes effective teaching. But we may well remind ourselves here of the old and familiar fable of the blind men who perceived the elephant in widely varying manners depending upon the part of the elephant's body with which each came in contact. Many of us are equally blind professionally when it comes to describing competency in teaching. Some of us believe good teaching to be a function of having enrolled in certain courses, some believe it to be a matter of a pleasing personality, and some that it is revealed in the discipline a teacher may be able to maintain in the classroom.
>
> *(p. 691)*

These struggles continued into the 1980s and today. Wise, Darling-Hammond, McLaughlin, and Bernstein (1985) note that indeed what teachers do in the classroom matters and that effective teaching behaviors vary based on student characteristics. The authors argue:

> … this [is] problematic because if markedly different teaching behaviors lead to divergent results that can be deemed equally desirable, one cannot identify a single, unidimensional construct called "effective teaching," much less limit its component parts.
>
> *(p. 57)*

Teachers have an all-encompassing role. For example, Raths (1971) argues that teachers' roles include at least the following:

1. Explaining, informing, showing how
2. Initiating, directing, administering
3. Unifying the group
4. Giving security

5. Clarifying beliefs, attitudes, and problems
6. Identifying learning problems
7. Making curriculum materials
8. Evaluating, recording, and reporting
9. Enriching community activities
10. Organizing and arranging classrooms
11. Participating in school activities
12. Participating in professional and civic life

And, of course, readers can readily add to this list. The number of outcomes that teachers are expected to address in their students is so vast as to be overwhelming (see Rothstein, 2000). Smylie, Miller, and Westbrook (2008) concisely summarize these diverse expectations:

> Teachers are expected to promote students' intellectual development and academic achievement as well as their personal, social, and moral development. Teachers are to prepare students for citizenship and economic productivity. Teachers are also to perform a socialization function, passing along ways of life and culture to future generations.
>
> *(p. 4)*

The wide expectations held for teachers may exacerbate the difficulty in defining good teaching. As Good (in press) notes, these wide expectations about what teachers could and should do mitigates a consensus of what schools should be accountable for other than student achievement. Regardless of the academic or policy communities' inability to reach consensus on what good teaching is and looks like, we have measured "it" (teaching) for years.

Methods of Evaluating Teachers

An extensive discussion of methods of teacher evaluation is presented in Chapter 5, with a discussion of strengths and limitations. Below is a brief historical account of the emergence of some of these methods. We provide this review because a grounding in history often leads to an understanding that we have tried many things earlier that are related to today's problem issue(s) and that we can learn things that were done well previously as well as things that were done poorly. Unfortunately, as we will see in Chapters 2 and 3, many things done in education are forgotten only to be rediscovered at a later date and a great expense.

Observation. Rating scales (also in the form of checklists, score cards, and appointment blanks) first appeared in 1915. Rating scales allowed individuals, most often administrators, to rate the presence, absence, or quality of traits that were deemed important for effective teaching (e.g., voice, grasp of subject matter, attention and response of the class); many of these scales were deemed as highly subjective. High-inference observational instruments, those based on more global, subjective measures, emerged in the 1920s (Good & Mulryan, 1990). Research in the 1950s and 60s was dominated by quantitative forms of observation that reduced classroom activities to low-inference, discrete, countable, and highly objective descriptions (Brophy, 2006; Good & Mulryan, 1990). Low-inference measures were preferred because of purported (Medley & Mitzel, 1963) and documented (Remmers, 1963) issues of reliability and validity with high-inference measures. However, Rosenshine and Furst's review (1973) found that some high-inference measures of teaching were related consistently to student achievement and in the 70s and 80s both high and low inference observation instruments were used (Brophy & Good, 1970; Evertson & Green, 1986; Flanders, 1970; Soar & Soar, 1979; Simon & Boyer, 1970a, 1970b; Stallings & Kaskowitz, 1974; Withall, 1960). As we will demonstrate in Chapter 4, a renewed interest has emerged in the observation of teaching.

Student Ratings.   Student course evaluations and ratings are common practice in higher education and, because they are considered in tenure and promotion decisions, a significant amount of research, most notably work by Wilbert McKeachie (1997), has been done on how college students rate their instructors. To a lesser extent, research has explored how younger students rate their teachers. Research on student ratings has identified numerous aspects about a teacher or good teaching that matters to students. For example, students may rate affective or affiliation-based elements (e.g., My teacher gives me praise. My teacher likes me.). Students may also rate cognitive and instructional elements about a teacher (e.g., My teacher explains school work so that I can understand it.).

Students have also been asked to respond to open-ended questions about characteristics that define good teaching. An examination of 12 studies from 1896 (Butsch, 1931) reveals that pupils believe the following qualities embody an effective teacher (in order of most frequently reported):

1. Fairness (noted in 7 studies)
2. Kindness (noted in 6 studies)
3. Instructional skill (noted in 6 studies)
4. Good-natured/pleasant (noted in 5 studies)
5. Good disciplinarian (noted in 5 studies)
6. Knowledge of subject matter (noted in 5 studies)
7. Sense of humor (4 noted in studies)
8. Strong character (4 noted in studies)

The following characteristics were less important and noted in three or fewer studies: personal appearance, inspiring, sociability, interest in work, personality, sympathetic, ability to make class interesting, politeness, neatness, serious and dignified, interest in pupils, broad educational interest, efficiency in use of class time, intelligent, and broad-minded. In 1947, Witty conducted a similar study asking students to identify the attributes that capture "the teacher who has helped them the most." Students noted: cooperative and democratic attitude, kind, considerate of the individual, patient, and interest in pupils' problems.

Historically, pupil ratings have shown strong reliability ($r = .64-.96$; Della Piana & Gage, 1955; Follman, 1992), and, these methods have gained renewed interest (Bill & Melinda Gates Foundation, 2013). As we will see, much of this current work is done without any awareness of previous work on pupil assessment. It is important to note, however, that pupils' ratings of teachers do not exist in isolation—they are a function of an interaction between pupils' values and teachers' attitudes (Della Piana & Gage, 1955).

Other forms of teacher evaluation include self-report measures, student achievement measures (as discussed earlier), and peer ratings. A more extensive discussion of these measures and others is available in Chapter 5.

Uses and Applications

Most early methods of observing teachers were focused on evaluation for administrative purposes; even a few of the early coding systems were developed by supervisors (Horn, 1914; Puckett, 1928). However, observational data were rarely used to inform or improve teaching practices. This may be partially due to the fact that up until the 1970s few studies sought to identify what teaching practices were linked with particular student outcomes (Dunkin & Biddle, 1974). Process-product studies of the 1970s and 80s changed this trend. Even still, process-product findings have not been applied widely and are often rediscovered in research. It has been noted that in the 1980s teacher evaluation has resulted in removal or "counseling out" and remediation and reinstatement of teachers in some districts (e.g., Salt Lake City, Lake Washington, Toledo; Wise et al., 1985), but historically, teacher evaluation hasn't had as severe consequences as those prescribed in today's teacher accountability plans.

As noted earlier in this chapter, in just the last decade the spotlight has turned to teachers. Hence, the history of holding teachers accountable is brief. As we will demonstrate in Chapter 4, merit pay is one piece of evidence that supports the belief that teachers matter. Although such policies have a well-established history, consequences for teachers for low performance, historically, have been minimal. Eliminating a teacher for poor performance is an involved, complicated, and a time-consuming process, particularly if the effectiveness of a tenured teacher is in question. Because of this, the profession has been criticized for using tenure as a means of protecting poor teachers. As a result, tenure policies are under fire and many states, such as Florida, have moved to eliminate tenure altogether or make tenure a less attainable status (e.g., New

York). Others have argued that change in the quality of the teacher workforce needs to come at the point of entry (Gabriel & Dillon, 2011). Given that developments in holding teachers accountable for student learning (in a high-stakes environment) is recent, we provide a more comprehensive discussion of this evolution in Chapter 4.

Conclusion

The history of student assessment and teacher evaluation is essentially a perfect storm. The continuation of business-like mechanisms, an increasing belief that standardized assessments are the best measure of student outcomes, a shift towards an interest in teacher effects, and a greater emphasis on the importance of teachers leads to a system that primarily holds teachers accountable for student testing outcomes. What we will illustrate in this book is that history indicates this new development is likely here to stay (and if not, will return again as a "new" idea in future education reforms).

History Repeats Itself. Unfortunately, the "history repeats itself" disease plagues education reform. It is unlikely that these new efforts will be successful because many of them are only old efforts repackaged as the latest and greatest reform. These new reforms often move forward without addressing past reforms or illustrating how the new reform incorporates lessons from failed reforms. For example, current issues with testing and teaching evaluation can be traced back in history. Student testing as a good measure of a teacher's worth was challenged in the 1970s. Furthermore, in the 1980s unintended consequences of high-stakes testing such as teaching to the test and a reduced emphasis of teachers' effects on other desirable student outcomes were addressed (Centra & Potter, 1980; Darling-Hammond & Wise, 1985; Popham, 1983). However, these warnings fell on deaf ears—an important issue that will be discussed in later chapters.

The circular nature of approaches to education reform supports the idea that education reform is ahistorical. This idea that nothing is new was voiced over 30 years ago:

> One of the paradoxes of American education is how little, and yet how much, our schools have changed over the past two decades of unprecedented ferment, turbulence, and systematic efforts at reform. In many of their most obvious features, schools have scarcely changed at all … [despite] a virtual revolution in authority relations in schools; a sense of crisis about the normative order of schools; a serious decline in public confidence in, and support for, the schools, and substantial change in how schools are governed.
>
> *(Boyd & Crowson, 1981, pp. 311–312)*

Ironically, the same message was noted 20 years later (Tyack & Cuban, 1997) and continues to stand today. Lack of change, may be due, in part, to the recycling of ideas to solve newly conceptualized "crises" of education. As a result, one should not be entirely surprised at where we have arrived today—teachers, schools, and teacher education under fire and on the brink of elimination or closure. This was forecasted, in one way or another, in a plethora of articles from the 1980s onward. For example, in noting a shift towards middle-class acceptance of the failure of public schools, Boyd and Crowson (1981) noted that the educational crisis outlined in the Coleman report, "...could conceivably contribute to the adoption of policies that could transform or even dismantle public education" (p. 313).

We will demonstrate in Chapter 5 that even new methods that purport to account for past problems may face other issues not accounted for. For example, one of the reasons why accountability has not placed a heavy emphasis on teachers is because researchers have not been able to partition out the variance that teachers explain in student outcomes as compared to other important variables (e.g., school and/or home factors). One of the purported advantages of value-added modeling is the ability to control for a number of variables that are related to student achievement outcomes (e.g., race, socioeconomic status), although value-added scores have shown significant instability (Darling-Hammond, Amrein-Beardsley, Haertel, & Rothstein, 2012), with some arguing that many exogenous variables (e.g., peer effects) cannot be accounted for in such models (Berliner, in press). Hence, even in cases in which history lessons are incorporated, challenges remain.

Missing the Target. Many have commented that past reform failure and the likelihood of future reform failure is a result of (a) overly ambitious goals, (b) inadequate funding, and (c) incomplete implementation (Vinovskis, 2012). For example, unrealistic goals can put teachers, schools, districts, and states in positions that result in cutting corners; some of these corner-cutting examples from NCLB (e.g., cheating, teaching to test) were mentioned earlier. We also add that reforms are plagued by problem solutions that are too broad, too narrow, or too simple. For example, student outcomes on standardized tests only captures a small part of the wide set of beliefs that citizens, policy makers, educators, and parents hold about important schooling outcomes. Further, we believe that some of the problems of value-added modeling are due, in part, to its inability to fully capture the complex nature of teaching and learning.

In the upcoming chapters we will elaborate upon these points. In Chapter 2, we will address the history of school reform. We will illustrate the circular nature of reform furthering supporting our doubt that current efforts will be successful in improving student learning. We continue with history in Chapter 3 as we explain what is known about teachers' impact on student learning. We explore how this knowledge can and cannot be used to improve student learning. After establishing a historical foundation, in Chapter 4, we turn to current teacher evaluation. We describe in detail Race to the Top and current trends in teacher evaluation. Next, we take a closer examination of the knowledge base around methods of teacher evaluation as a means of assessing the success of teacher evaluation under RttT. In Chapter 5, we will demonstrate the complex nature of evaluating teachers and illustrate how even sound observation instruments pale in comparison to the rich interactions that occur in classrooms. In Chapter 6, we assess the roles of particular players in the movement to hold teachers accountable for student learning. We acknowledge that current teacher evaluation is here to stay. We offer some solutions to improve upon the present situation.

Note

1 Similar issues were noted in higher education at about the same the time (College Entrance Examination Board, 1926).

References

Arizona Department of Education. (2012). *Move on when reading homepage*. Retrieved from http://www.azed.gov/k12-literacy/move-on-when-reading-home-page/

The Augustus F. Hawkins-Robert T. Stafford Elementary and Secondary School Improvement Amendments of 1988. Public Law 100-297, April 28, 1988.

Ayres, L. P. (1918). History and present status of educational measurements. In G. M. Whipple (Ed.), *The measurement of educational products* (Part II, pp. 9–15). Bloomington, IL: Public School Publishing Company.

Badertscher, N. (2013, January 7). New evaluation pilot 'skewed,' with too few unsatisfactory teachers, officials say. *The Atlanta Journal-Constitution*. Retrieved from http://www.ajc.com/news/news/new-evaluation-pilot-skewed-with-too-few-unsatisfa/nTpKN/

Baker, A. (2012, August 17). Many New York City teachers denied tenure in policy shift. *New York Times*. Retrieved from http://www.nytimes.com/2012/08/18/nyregion/nearly-half-of-new-york-city-teachers-are-denied-tenure-in-2012.html?pagewanted=all

Beggs, V. L. (1936). Reporting pupil progress without report cards. *Elementary School Journal, 37*(2), 107–114.

Berliner, D. C. (in press). Exogenous variables and value-added assessments: A fatal flaw. *Teachers College Record*.

Bill & Melinda Gates Foundation. (2013). *Ensuring fair and reliable measures of effective teaching: Culminating findings from the Met Project's three-year study*. Retrieved from http://www.metproject.org/downloads/MET_Ensuring_Fair_and_Reliable_Measures_Practioner_Brief.pdf

Bobbitt, J. F. (1912). The elimination of waste in education. *The Elementary School Teacher, 12*, 259–271.

Boyd, W. L., & Crowson, R. L. (1981). The changing conception and practice of public school education. *Review of Educational Research, 9*, 311–376.

Brookover, W. B., Schweitzer, J. H., Schneider, J. M., Beady, C. H., Flood, P. K., & Wisenbaker, J. M. (1978). *American Educational Research Journal, 15*(2), 301–318.

Brophy, J. (2006). Observational research on generic aspects of classroom teaching. In P. A. Alexander & P. H. Winne (Eds.), *Handbook of educational psychology* (pp. 755–780). Mahwah, NJ: Erlbaum.

Brophy, J., & Good, T. (1970). Teachers' communication of differential expectations for children's classroom performance: Some behavioral data. *Journal of Educational Psychology, 61*(5), 365–374.

Butsch, R. L. C. (1931). Chapter VII: Teacher rating. *Review of Educational Research, 1*(2), 99–107.

Caldwell, O. W., & Courtis, S. A. (1924). *Then and now in education 1845–1923: A message of encouragement from the past to the present.* New York, NY: World Book Company.

Cattell, J. M. (1890). Mental tests and measurements. *Mind, 15,* 373–380.

Centra, J. A., & Potter, D. A. (1980). School and teacher effects: An interrelational model. *Review of Educational Research, 50*(2), 273–291.

Chetty, R., Friedman, J. N., & Rockoff, J. E. (2011). *The long-term impacts of teachers: Teacher value-added and student outcomes in adulthood.* Retrieved from http://obs.rc.fas.harvard.edu/chetty/value_added.pdf

Coleman, J., Campbell, E., Hobson, C., McPartland, J., Mood, A., Weinfeld, F., & York, R. (1966). *Equality of educational opportunity.* Washington, DC: U.S. Department of Health, Education, and Welfare, Office of Education.

College Entrance Examination Board. (1926). *The work of the college entrance examination board, 1901–1925.* Boston: Ginn & Co.

Collins, G. (2012, April 27). A very pricey pineapple. *New York Times.* Retrieved from http://www.nytimes.com/2012/04/28/opinion/collins-a-very-pricey-pineapple.html?_r=0

Common Core State Standards. (n.d.). Retrieved from http://www.corestandards.org

Cremin, L. A. (1975). *The republic and the school: Horace Mann on the education of free men.* New York, NY: Bureau of Publications.

Cronbach, L. J. (1975). Five decades of public controversy over mental testing. *American Psychologist, 30*(1), 1–14. doi:10.1037/0003-066X.30.1.1

Darling-Hammond, L., Amrein-Beardsley, A., Haertel, E., & Rothstein, J. (2012). Evaluating teacher evaluation. *Phi Delta Kappan, 93*(6), 8–15.

Darling-Hammond, L., & Wise, A. E. (1985). Beyond standardization: State standards and school improvement. *Elementary School Journal, 85*(3), 315–336.

Darling-Hammond, L., Wise, A. E., & Pease, S. R. (1983). Teacher evaluation in the organizational context: A review of the literature. *Review of Educational Research, 53*(3), 285–328.

Davey, M. (2012, September 10). Teachers' strike in Chicago tests mayor and union. *New York Times.* Retrieved from http://www.nytimes.com/2012/09/11/education/teacher-strike-begins-in-chicago-amid-signs-that-deal-isnt-close.html?pagewanted=all&_r=0

Della Piana, G. M., & Gage, N. L. (1955). Pupils' values and the validity of the Minnesota Teacher Attitude Inventory. *Journal of Educational Psychology, 46*(3), 167–178.

Dillon, S. (2011, June 27). Teacher grades: Pass or be fired. *New York Times.* Retrieved from http://www.nytimes.com/2011/06/28/education/28evals.html?pagewanted=all

District of Columbia Public Schools. (2011). *DCPS continues to strengthen workforce.* Retrieved from http://dc.gov/DCPS/About+DCPS/Press+Releases+and+Announcements/Press+Releases/DCPS+Continues+to+Strengthen+Workforce

Dunkin, M., & Biddle, B. (1974). *The study of teaching.* New York, NY: Holt, Rinehart and Winston.

Elementary and Secondary Education Act (ESEA) (1965). (Pub.L. 89–10, 79 Stat. 27, 20 U.S.C. ch.70).

Evertson, C., & Green, J. (1986). Observation as inquiry and method. In M. C. Wittrock (Ed.), *Handbook of research on teaching* (3rd ed., pp. 162–213). New York, NY: MacMillan.

Expect More Arizona. (2012, September 25). *Tag archives: Move on when reading. A strong foundation in reading for all Arizona students.* http://www.expectmorearizona.org/blog/tag/move-on-when-reading/

Flanders, N. (1970). *Analyzing teacher behavior.* Reading, MA: Addison-Wesley.

Follman, J. (1992). Secondary school students' ratings of teacher effectiveness. *High School Journal, 75*(3), 168–178.

Folts, J. D. (1996). *History of the University of the State of New York and the state education department, 1784–1996.* Albany, NY: Author.

Fu, Y. (2012). *The effectiveness of traditional admissions criteria in predicting college and graduate success for American and international students* (Unpublished doctoral dissertation). University of Arizona. Tucson.

Fuess, C. M. (1950). *The college board: Its first fifty years.* New York, NY: Columbia University Press.

Gabriel, T. (2010, June 10). Under pressure, teachers tamper with tests. *New York Times.* Retrieved from http://www.nytimes.com/2010/06/11/education/11cheat.html?pagewanted=all

Gabriel, T., & Dillon, S. (2011, January 31). G. O. P. govenors take aim at teacher tenure. *New York Times.* Retrieved from http://www.nytimes.com/2011/02/01/us/01tenure.html?_r=0

Garrison, M. J. (2009). *A measure of failure: The political origins of standardized testing.* Albany, NY: State University of New York Press.

Goddard, H. H. (1914). *Feeble-mindedness: Its causes and consequences.* New York, NY: Macmillan.

Goddard, H. H. (1917). Mental tests and the immigrant. *The Journal of Delinquency, 2*(5), 243–277. doi:10.1037/h0067047

Good, T. L. (Ed.) (1999). Non-subject-matter outcomes of schooling [Special Issue]. *Elementary School Journal, 99*(5).

Good, T. L. (Ed). (2000). Non-subject-matter outcomes of schooling [Special Issue]. *Elementary School Journal, 100*(5).

Good, T. L. (in press). What do we know about how teachers influence student performance on standardized tests, and why do we know so little about other student outcomes? *Teachers College Record.*

Good, T. L., & Mulryan, C. (1990). Teacher ratings: A call for teacher control and self-evaluation. In J. Millman & L. Darling-Hammond (Eds.), *The new handbook of teacher evaluation* (pp. 191–215). Newbury Park, CA: Sage.

Gordon, E. W. (2008). The transformation of key beliefs that guided a century of assessment. In C. A. Dwyer (Ed.), *The future of assessment: Shaping teaching and learning* (pp. 3–6). New York, NY: Erlbaum.

Harris, D. N. (2011). *Value-added measures in education: What every educator needs to know.* Cambridge, MA: Harvard Education Press.

Hendry, F. (1929). Report cards of the Royal Oak public schools. *Elementary School Journal, 29*(8), 603–609.

Horn, E. (1914). Distribution of opportunity for participation among the various pupils in classroom recitations. *Contributions to Education, 67.*

Hursh, D. (2008). *High-stakes testing and the decline of teaching and learning: The real crisis in education.* Lanham, MD: Rowman & Littlefield.

Judd, C. H. (1918). A look forward. In G. M. Whipple (Ed.), *The measurement of educational products* (pp. 152–160). Bloomington, IL: Public School Publishing Company.

Kane, T. J., & Staiger, D. O. (2008). Estimating teacher impacts on student achievement: An experimental evaluation. Retrieved from http://www.dartmouth.edu/~dstaiger/Papers/WP/KaneStaiger NBER wp 14607 2008.pdf

Ladwig, J. G. (2010). Beyond academic outcomes. *Review of Research in Education, 34,* 113–141.

Lavigne, A. L. (in press). Exploring the intended and unintended consequences of high-stakes teacher evaluation on schools, teachers, and students. *Teachers College Record.*

Learned, W. S., & Wood, B. D. (1938). *The student and his knowledge: A report to the Carnegie Foundation on the results of the high school and college examination of 1928, 1930, and 1932.* No. 29. Boston, MA: The Merrymount Press.

McGuire, F. (1994). Army alpha and beta tests of intelligence. In R. J. Sternberg (Ed.), *Encyclopedia of intelligence* (Vol. 1, pp. 125–129). New York, NY: Macmillan.

McKeachie, W. J. (1997). Student ratings of faculty: A reprise. *American Psychologist, 65*(6), 384–397.

Medley, D., & Mitzel, H. (1963). Measuring classroom behavior by systematic observation. In N. Gage (Ed.), *Handbook of research on teaching* (pp. 247–328). Chicago, IL: Rand McNally.

Middletown Public Schools. (2009). Kindergarten report card. Retrieved from http://www.

mpsri.net/uploaded/documents/central_office/asstsuper/academictech/sbreportcards/revised_sb_report_cards_09/grk_reportcard.pdf

Mitchell, D., & Kerchner, C. (1983). Labor relations and teacher policy. In L. Shulman & G. Sykes (Eds.), *Handbook of teaching and policy* (pp. 214–238). New York, NY: Longman.

Mulvey, J. D., Cooper, B. S., & Maloney, A. T. (2010). Ethnically-based charter schools and racial separation: The aims of education. In L. Cohen-Vogel, B. S. Cooper, & B. Fusarelli (Eds.), *Blurring the lines: Charter, public, private, and religious schools coming together* (pp. 73–89). Charlotte, NC: Information Age.

Murphy, P., & Regenstein, E. (2012). *Putting a price tag on the Common Core.* Retrieved from http://edexcellencemedia.net/publications/2012/20120530-Putting-a-Price-Tag-on-the-Common-Core/20120530-Putting-a-Price-Tag-on-the-Common-Core-FINAL.pdf

National Commission on Excellence in Education. (1983). *A nation at risk: The imperative for education reform.* Washington, DC: U.S. Department of Education, National Commission for Excellence in Education.

National Defense Education Act of 1958, P.L. 85-864; 72 Stat. 1580.

Nichols, S. L., & Berliner, D. C. (2007). *Collateral damage: How high-stakes testing corrupts America's schools.* Cambridge, MA: Harvard Education Press.

No Child Left Behind Act of 2001, Pub. L. 107-110, 20 U.S.C. § 6301 et. seq.

Nye, B., Konstantopoulos, S., & Hedges, L. V. (2004). How large are teacher effects? *Educational Evaluation and Policy Analysis, 26,* 237–257.

Odell, C. W. (1928). *Traditional examinations and new-type tests.* New York, NY: The Century Company.

Palmer, J. T. (1929). Rating of pupils and report cards. *Elementary School Journal, 29*(5), 373–379.

Popham, W. J. (1983). Measurement as an instructional catalyst. In R. B. Ekstrom (Ed.), *Measurement, technology, and individuality in education* (pp. 19–30). New directions for testing and measurement, no. 17. San Francisco, CA: Jossey-Bass.

Popham, W. J. (2008). Classroom assessment: Staying instructionally afloat in an ocean of accountability. In C. A. Dwyer (Ed.), *The future of assessment: Shaping teaching and learning* (pp. 263–278). New York, NY: Erlbaum.

Puckett, R. C. (1928). Making supervision objective. *School Review, 36,* 209–212.

Raths, J. (1971). Teaching without specific objectives. *Educational Leadership, 28*(7), 714–720.

Ravitch, D. (2002). Testing and accountability, historically considered. In W. M. Evers & H. J. Walberg (Eds.), *School accountability* (pp. 9–21). Stanford, CA: Hoover Institute Press.

Reese, W. J. (2007). *History, education, and the schools.* New York, NY: Palgrave Macmillian.

Remmers, H. (1963). Rating methods in research on teaching. In N. Gage (Ed.), *Handbook of research on teaching* (pp. 329–378). Chicago, IL: Rand McNally.

Resnick, D. P. (1980). Minimum competency testing historically considered. *Review of Research in Education, 8,* 3–29.

Rice, J. M. (1893). *The public-school system of the United States.* New York, NY: The Century Co.

Rice, J. M. (1913). *Scientific management in education.* New York, NY: Hinds, Noble, & Elderedge.

Rivkin, S. G., Hanushek, E. A., & Kain, J. F. (2005). Teachers, schools, and academic achievement. *Econometrica, 73,* 417–458.

Rose v Council for Better Education. (1989). 790 S.W. 2d 186, 60 Ed. Law Rep. 1289

Rosenholtz, S. J. (1985). Effective schools: Interpreting the evidence. *American Journal of Education, 94,* 352–358.

Rosenshine, B., & Furst, N. (1973). The use of direct observation to study teaching. In R. Travers (Ed.), *Second handbook of research on teaching* (pp. 376-391). Chicago, IL: Rand McNally.

Rothstein, R. (2000). Toward a composite index of school performance. *Elementary School Journal, 100*(5), 409–442.

Ryans, D. G. (1949). The criteria of teaching effectiveness. *Journal of Educational Research, 42,* 690–699.

Rutter, M. (1982). *Fifteen thousand hours: Secondary schools and their effects on children.* Cambridge, MA: Harvard University Press.

Savage, H. J. (1953). *Fruit of an impulse: Forty-five years of the Carnegie Foundation.* New York, NY: Harcourt, Brace, and Company.

Schmitt, N. (2012). Development of rationale and measure of noncognitive college student potential. *Educational Psychologist, 47*(1), 18–29.

Severson, K. (2010, December 12). Scandal and a schism tattle Atlanta's schools. *New York Times.* A36(L).

Shepard, L. A. (2008). A brief history of accountability testing, 1965–2007. In K. E. Ryan & L. A. Shepard (Eds.), *The future of test-based educational accountability* (pp. 25–46). New York, NY: Routledge.

Siegler, R. S. (1992). The other Alfred Binet. *Developmental Psychology, 28,* 179–190. doi:10.1037//0012-1649.28.2.179

Simon, A., & Boyer, E. (Eds.). (1970a). *Mirrors for behavior: An anthology of observation instruments.* Philadelphia, PA: Research for Better Schools.

Simon, A., & Boyer, E. (Eds.). (1970b). *Mirrors for behavior: An anthology of observation instruments continued, 1970 supplement* (Volume B). Philadelphia, PA: Research for Better Schools.

Smylie, M. A., Miller, C. L., & Westbrook, K. P. (2008). The work of teachers. In T. L. Good (Ed.), *21st century education: A reference handbook* (pp. 3-11). Thousand Oaks, CA: Sage.

Soar, R. S., & Soar, R. M. (1979). Emotional climate and management. In P. Peterson & H. Walberg (Eds.), *Research on teaching: Concepts, findings, and implications.* Berkeley, CA: McCutchan.

Soares, J. A. (2011). *SAT wars: The case for test-optional college admissions.* New York, NY: Teachers College Press.

Stallings, J., & Kaskowitz, D. (1974). *Follow through classroom observation evaluation 1972–1973* (SRI Project URU-7370). Stanford, CA: Stanford Research Institute.

Taylor, F. W. (1911). *Scientific management.* New York, NY: Harper & Brothers Publishers.

Terman, L. M. (1916). *The measurement of intelligence: An explanation of and a complete guide for the use of Stanford revision and extension of the Binet-Simon intelligence scale.* Boston, MA: Houghton Mifflin.

Tyack, D., & Cuban, L. (1997). *Tinkering toward utopia: A century of public school reform.* Cambridge, MA: Harvard University Press.

Vinovskis, M. A. (2012). The past is prologue? Federal efforts to promote equity and excellence. In F. M. Hess & A. P. Kelly (Eds.), *Carrots, sticks, and the bully pulpit: Lessons from a half-century of federal efforts to improve America's schools* (pp. 15-36). Cambridge, MA: Harvard Education Press.

Wanlass, Y. (2000). Broadening the concept of learning and school competence. *Elementary School Journal, 100*(5), 513–527.

White, S. (2000). Conceptual foundations of IQ testing. *Psychology, Public Policy, and Law, 6*(1), 33–43. doi:10.1037//1076-8971.6.1.33

White, S. H. (1977). Social implications of IQ. In R. Houts (Ed.), *The myth of measurability* (pp. 23–44). New York, NY: Hart Publishing.

Withall, J. (1960). Research tools: Observing and recording behavior. *Review of Educational Research, 30,* 496–512.

Wigdor, A. K., & Garner, W. R. (Eds.). (1982). *Ability testing: Uses, consequences, and controversies.* Washington, DC: National Academy Press.

Wise, A., Darling-Hammond, L., McLaughlin, M. W., & Bernstein, H. (1985). *Teacher evaluation: A study of effective practices.* Santa Monica, CA: Rand Corporation.

Withall, J. (1949). The development of a technique for the measurement of social-emotional climate in classrooms. *Journal of Experimental Education, 17,* 347–361.

Witty, P. (1947). An analysis of the personality traits of the effective teacher. *The Journal of Educational Research, 40*(9), 662–671.

2
REFORM DE JOUR

Introduction

Chapter 1 discussed the increasing pressure for accountability for schools, teachers, students, and we noted that accountability had focused primarily upon student achievement on standardized performance tests. We argued that, at least in relative terms, the development of new accountability plans has not been resisted in any serious systematic fashion by professional educators. In part, this relative passivity may be explained by the fact that an attack at any one point in time typically was focused upon schools, or teachers, or students … and occasionally parents. This is not necessarily to suggest that there was ever an explicit divide and conquer plan, but that was essentially the effect.

The history of the testing–accountability movement is paralleled by a history of school reform. There have been many reforms attempting to change schools and classrooms, and many have written the story of these reforms, especially over the past 50 to 70 years. The story is rich and complex, and in dealing with this history authors have to choose how to frame the part of the story they tell. Not only are there many accounts of school reform in America, there are many accounts of school reform and all in one way or another High Cost-Limited Return. These stories report but little effect on practice.

Readers have many good choices to make as they study school reform. For example, Labaree (2010) examines reform at a level we would describe as more macro, including the effects of broad social movements on conceptions of societal goals that society suggests for its schools. Where did the common school and school choice movements come from? Although aspects of his book do overlap with our effort, they can be distinguished by a micro versus a macro comparison—his book has a broader or more macro, approach including political and social influences on schooling. Our focus is a more micro and focuses on the classroom and the human interactions of teacher and students that occur there.

In this chapter we describe five of these reform efforts and cover a few others in passing. As most readers know, the number of reforms in American education over the past 70 years has been pronounced, and several reviews are available (Good & Braden, 2000; Payne, 2010; Ravitch, 2010). Here, as noted, we address five of the arguably most important reforms. We also discuss how these reforms developed, how they differed, how they quickly disappeared, and provide an analytical framework to assess the lack of productivity across these reforms. Finally we end, with a brief discussion of what we should learn from these reforms as we move toward new efforts to improve teaching and learning in American schools.

Sputnik: The Math-Science Crisis

The Soviets launching of the satellite *Sputnik* in October 1957 produced profound concerns about U.S. military and scientific capacity. Critics contended that the public schools of the 1940s and 1950s had lost their vigor and America was vulnerable because of this general educational decline and especially its inadequate science and mathematics curriculum. This crisis and the conception of the problem led to what in time became known as new math. The advocates of new math firmly believed that the mathematics and science curriculum should become more formalized, more rigorous, and more abstract. Many of these advocates believed that the mathematics curriculum should be based on set theory. Barker, Curran, and Metcalf (1964) reported that one aspect on new math was to bring content taught in junior high to the elementary school curriculum such as geometry, coordinates, and integers. As the authors noted "teachers must reorient their thinking about mathematics" (p. iii). Along these lines, Willoughby (1968) noted that set theory, at least in its most general form, has been known since the late 1800s, and at one point it had been taught in mathematics graduate courses prior to 1950.

Willoughby (1968) provided a reason why some advocated for the inclusion of set theory in new math: "The hope of those who introduce set notation and language into the curriculum was that it would help to unify mathematics and also help children to understand the structure of mathematics. Unfortunately, there is considerable doubt that this lofty goal has been achieved" (p. 8).

However, these claims were based upon beliefs and there were no data to suggest that set theory would enable students to master mathematics and science more fully or use it more productively. There were some critics of new math. One of these, Professor Kline, contended that mathematics should be presented in ways that helped students to understand the physical world. Accordingly, he suggested that mathematics should be organized around real-world problems that would cause students to think and to explore mathematic topics, rather than abstract thought:

> Students are asked to learn operations with sets and the notion of subset, finite and infinite sets, the null set (which is not empty because it contains the empty set), and lots of other notations which are abstract and in fact rather remote from the heart and essence of arithmetic. Yet on this abstract basis, students are required to learn arithmetic. The whole theory of sets should be eliminated. On the elementary and high school levels it is a waste of time.
>
> *(Moise, Calandra, Davis, Kline, & Bacon, 1965, p. 14)*

One of the reasons that set theory was problematic was because it was poorly defined and meant different things to different people. Willoughby (1968) aptly expressed the irony of this situation:

> The vastly divergent opinions about the new mathematics come at least partially from the fact that the term means so many different things to so many different people. One of the ironies of the new mathematics phenomenon is that many programs described as new mathematics emphasize careful definition of terms, but this term itself is not well defined.
>
> *(p. 4)*

For our purpose, it is sufficient to note that new math emerged and disappeared very quickly despite the fact that vast sums of money were spent publishing textbooks and changing teacher education. As Hummel-Rossi and Ashdown (2002) have argued, it is exceedingly difficult to estimate the cost of any reform, but clearly the number of mathematics books that were rewritten to include new math content only to be rewritten to exclude the content was itself a huge amount. Good and Braden (2000) noted that it was instructive (if not ironic) that those American scientists who eventually addressed and won the space challenge were products of a school system that had emphasized a traditional form of mathematics teaching. Clearly, exposure to this outdated curriculum did not prevent scientists educated in the 1940s and 50s from making notable progress in the 1960s.

Transition

Individualized and Humanistic Learning. Between *Sputnik* and *A Nation at Risk*, there was an era of reform during the 1960s and early 1970s that can be generally characterized as reforms urging individualized and humanistic reforms. In general, these reforms stood in opposition to traditional classroom instruction in which teachers lectured or held large group instruction and then students worked individually on common tasks. The individualized curriculum was designed to allow students to move at their own pace. The open and humanistic movement challenged traditional instruction as well but in a different way. Here the challenge was to give students more choice in content and how it was studied.

Individualization took many forms including the mastery learning approach developed by Benjamin Bloom (see Block and Anderson, 1975, for a thorough discussion). In 1960, much work on computerized instruction teaching students with computers was occurring, and many believed that this technology (and related ones) could improve learning. Lundgren (1972) and others had found that teachers taught to the steering group—roughly the average student in their classes. As a result, the putative charge/belief was that slower students did not get the attention/structure that was believed to be needed and that faster students did not receive sufficient challenge. However, implementing these programs was problematic for several reasons. The technology was not advanced, and it was relatively expensive, and, typically, there was limited user capacity in the classroom. How many students could use the technology at one time? Individualized plans that did used less advanced technology—such as self-paced text books or materials—were hampered by several factors. Allowing students to go at their own pace appeared to widen the curriculum knowledge of students, some students fell farther and farther behind and some teachers found the lack of common learning time to lower the opportunities for learning from peers.

Following the individualization movement was a distinct humanistic move to make schools more personable and more child or student oriented than discipline driven. Much of the writing of the humanistic tradition was influenced by the open education movement in England (see Barth, 1971, for more information). Within the United States, humanistic concerns were expressed in different ways, but perhaps the most important reform within this genre was the open education/open classroom movement. For an examination of the tenets of open education, see Appendix 2.1, and for a discussion of the reform itself see Good, Biddle, and Brophy (1975) and Good and Braden (2000).

For the purposes of this chapter, we note only that the call for open education and individualized learning occurred without any research evidence that it would work, and the ensuing data that were collected describing the effects of the reform were varied leading Good et al. (1975) to conclude that this "innovative reform" included some of the worst forms of teaching and also some successful instances of teaching. Extant data suggested that the "innovative reform" was not a panacea, and some concluded that it was ineffective in improving students' understanding and use of important academic concepts. Independent of its degree of success, this reform did not build on previous reform—instead it rejected it.

As noted, new reforms often occur without any realization that the reform has been previously implemented and, for whatever reason, discarded in the past. Old solutions often reappear in new names. For example, the Progressive Era that sought to bring reform to government and society in the 1920s and 1930s was reflected again in the open education movement in the 1970s. Reschly and Sabers (1974) found that attitudes and practices recommended in the open education movement were correlated .50 with attitudes and practices recommended by advocates of progressive education.

A Nation at Risk

In 1983 the National Commission of Excellence in Education boldly asserted in *A Nation at Risk* that American education was in terrible shape and the country was vulnerable militarily and economically due to inadequate American education.

> Our Nation is at Risk. Our once unchallenged preeminence in commerce, industry, science, technology, and innovation is being overtaken by competitors throughout the world ... If an unfriendly foreign power had attempted to impose on America the mediocre educational performance that exists today, we might well have viewed it as an act of war. As it stands, we have allowed this to happen to ourselves. We have even squandered the gains in student achievement made in the wake of the sputnik challenge.
>
> *(p. 1)*

Just as reformers in the *Sputnik* era argued that the schools of the 1940s and 50s had failed us, *A Nation at Risk* lamented the failure of the public schools of the 1960s and 70s. Open education was no longer a panacea—it was now a problem to overcome. *A Nation at Risk* drew a plethora of headlines and created serious and widespread concerns in the United States about the quality of American education. It was also translated into various languages including Arabic, Greek, and Japanese. Apparently, bad news travels rapidly; the whole world quickly knew about the demise of the American public school system. For a vivid and extensive account of the wide media coverage of *A Nation at Risk,* see Tomlinson, 1986. It is sufficient here to say that the media coverage for an educational reform was unprecedented and to note that numerous reports were published in leading newspapers, including the *New York Times* and the *Washington Post* and other popular media sources such as *Time, Newsweek, US News and World Report, Better Homes and Gardens,* and many more.

So what was the new prescription for improving schooling? Among the various recommendations were longer school days, longer school years, and more homework. This took place in many schools and in different states, however most of the evidence on this is anecdotal or media reports. Most of the coverage about the effects of implementing *A Nation at Risk* was limited to descriptive newspaper articles (see, for example, Berger, 1989; Celis, 1994; Fiske, 1986;

Macfarquhar, 1995; Purnick, 1985). In general these articles tell the story of states or school districts trying to add more hours to the school calendar with teachers and/or unions pushing back. There is no data to illustrate that more time spent in the classroom increases student learning. Still despite any clear evidence that longer school days or longer school years have any impact on student learning, Race to the Top (RttT) legislation has expressed, once again, a renewed interest in increased learning time (including a longer school day, week, or year) in order to increase the total number of school hours in which students receive instruction (Federal Registrar Department of Education, 2010).

A *Nation at Risk* (1983) suggested that crisis was not centrally embedded in curriculum and instruction, but rather the central concern was that students and teachers needed to work harder. Although there were recommendations in the report broader than this (e.g., more school business partnerships, one half year of computer science in high school, better preparation of teachers, and more fiscal support), the attention in the popular media focused on the need for youth (especially) and teachers to renew their commitments to work hard. For example, the suggestion of the need for increased compensation to attract more qualified teachers was not commonly included in media releases. A brief synopsis of five major recommendations from *A Nation at Risk* appear in Table 2.1.

What problem(s) were these recommendations addressing? The commission reported numerous indicators of risk and problems with American education.

- The amount of homework for high school seniors had decreased and grades had risen at a time when average student achievement declined.
- Average achievement of college graduates was lower than in the 1970s.
- Military and business leaders complained that they were spending vast amounts of money on remedial education.
- In 13 states, 50% or more of the units required for high school graduation could be electives chosen by the student (including less demanding personal service courses, such as bachelor living!). Clearly, the movement for more open education, including student choice as recommended in the 1960s and 70s was rebuked by *A Nation at Risk*.
- It was noted that in many industrialized countries it was not unusual for high school students to spend 8 hours a day at school, and 220 days per year. The report stated that in the United States the typical school day was only 6 hours, and the school was open for 180 days.
- A California study was cited to note that some elementary students received one fifth of the instruction that others received in math and reading. The reason reported for this fluctuation in time allocated for classroom instruction was due to poor management of classroom time.

So what did *A Nation at Risk* accomplish? Certainly it stimulated many schools that had abandoned a core curriculum to reestablish one and it encouraged some states to increase graduation requirements; some states and school districts

TABLE 2.1 Five Major Recommendations from *A Nation at Risk**

Recommendation A: Content
We recommend that State and local high school graduation requirements be strengthened and that, at a minimum, all students seeking a diploma be required to lay the foundations in the five New Basics by taking the following curriculum during their 4 years of high schools: (a) 4 years of English; (b) 3 years of mathematics; (c) 3 years of science; (d) 3 years of social studies; and (e) one-half-year of computer science. For the college-bound, 2 years of foreign language in high school are strongly recommended in addition to those taken earlier.

Recommendation B: Standards and expectations
We recommend that schools, colleges, and universities adopt more rigorous and measurable standards, and higher expectations, for academic performance and student conduct, and that 4-year colleges and universities raise their requirements for admission. This will help students do their best educationally with challenging materials in an environment that supports learning and authentic accomplishment.

Recommendation C: Time
We recommend that significantly more time be devoted to learning the New Basics. This will require more effective use of the existing school day, longer school day, or a lengthened school year.

Recommendation D: Teaching
This recommendation consists of seven parts. Each is intended to improve the preparation of teachers to make teaching a more rewarding and respected profession. Each of the seven stands on its own and should not be considered solely as an implementing recommendation.

Recommendation E: Leadership and fiscal support
We recommend that citizens across the Nation hold educators and elected officials responsible for providing the leadership necessary to achieve these reforms, and that citizens provide the fiscal support and stability required to bring about the reforms we propose.

* From National Commission for Excellence in Education. (1983, April). *A nation at risk: The imperatives of educational reform.* Washington, DC: U.S. Department of Education.

did extend the school day. However, there is no evidence that these changes improved student learning or the quality of teaching that students received in core high school classrooms that made their college work more successful. Unfortunately, arguments about the need for harder subject matter or more time went without careful experimental studies. Finally, it signaled (for better or worse) an emerging interest in education from the federal government.

A Nation at Risk was in part a response to the belief that economically America was in trouble, especially in contrast to the Japanese economy. As history has shown, the American economy rebounded so there is clear evidence that the businesswomen, bankers, and educators who contributed to this successful economic revival were composed primarily of students who had been educated in those American public schools that *A Nation at Risk* had condemned. And, as before, this reform did not build on the previous reform in any way.

Prisoners of Time

The sequel to *A Nation at Risk* was the National Education Commission on Time and Learning 1994 report *Prisoners of Time,* which provided prima facie evidence that policy makers believed that American education was still in crisis. The *Prisoners of Time* report offered a highly critical account of American education, but it recommended a new solution for the crisis. Now more of the same was not recommended (e.g., longer school days or more homework) but rather structural changes were demanded such as longer school periods to provide students with extended time for inquiry, exploration, and discussion. It called for flexible use of time and more thematic and integrated approaches to subject matter instruction, including inner-disciplinary inquiry. Although there were a few studies of thematic instruction (teaching math and science together) and the like but these studies followed the reform thus as with previous reforms, these solutions were not based on research evidence, and when research was finally conducted it did not provide support for thematic teaching. Eight recommendations from the *Prisoners of Time* report were:

- Reinvent schools around learning not time.
- Fix the design flaw: use time in new and better ways.
- Establish an academic day. We recommend that schools provide additional academic time by reclaiming the school day for academic instruction.
- Keep schools open longer to meet the need of children and communities.
- Give teachers the time they need. We recommend that teachers be provided with the professional time and opportunities they need to do their jobs.
- Invest in technology.
- Develop local action plans to transform schools … that offer different school options and encourage parents, students, and teachers to choose among them.
- Share the responsibility. We recommend that all of our people shoulder their individual responsibilities to transform learning in America.

As in previous reforms, the media ran with some recommendations and ignored or downplayed others. For example there was not a ground swell of support for giving teachers more professional time to think and reflect. With regard to the recommendation to share the responsibility for the problem, some might feel that the very act of releasing the National Education Commission on Education and Learning (1994) was in itself an act of finger pointing.

One particularly attractive call was for establishing an "academic day." The report noted that American schools spent only 1,460 hours on core subjects, whereas in Japan students spent 3,170 hours. In France students spent 3,280 hours and in Germany students spent 3,528 hours. Clearly, the commission felt that these differences in subject matter time allocations generated a crisis and that American schools must spend more time on core subject matter instruction.

Across the nation numerous editorials were written in which arguments called for local public schools to increase their commitment to teaching important subject matter. For example, an editorial entitled "Wasted Days" appeared in the *Arizona Daily Star* (1994) which provided enthusiastic support for the commission's recommendation. "The traditional school day must now fit in a whole set of requirements for what has been called the 'the new work of the schools' —Education about personal safety, consumer affairs, AIDS, conservation and energy, family life, and drivers' training" (p. 18A).

Not all citizens agreed with this analysis. For example, one of the authors of this volume, Tom Good, responded to the indiscriminate cry to markedly increase school time on core subject matter:

> If the curriculum includes some study of family life, it is because some political constituency and citizens thought this content would improve the curriculum. Perhaps educators and citizens were concerned because children were having children and children were killing children. They may have thought that information about family life and personal safety might allow sixth graders to make it to high school so they could receive extra instruction in history. Were these citizens and policymakers wrong?
>
> *(Good, 1996a)*

Many have written on the value of a pluralistic curriculum, and the debates on the purpose of American education are rich and complex. There is the struggle between equity and excellence. There is the curriculum dilemma of breadth versus depth and a diverse versus well-focused curriculum. Clearly, *Prisoners of Time* was a plea for a core curriculum. However, generally parents have been found to want a more diverse curriculum and want schools to address nonsubject matter outcomes of schooling and the business community generally wants more technical knowledge to be taught. Below is one argument for a more diverse curriculum from Berliner and Biddle (1995).

> Americans are also profoundly committed to breadth of education. Primary students in our country not only study the three Rs, but they also paint, play musical instruments, debate, and complete in chess tournaments in their schools. American high schools offer a huge range of courses, and students are encouraged to sample these courses as electives and to participate in a host of extracurricular activities. This commitment to breadth shows up also in the concept of a four-year, liberal-arts undergraduate education, a concept unique to the United States; students elsewhere begin their professional training as doctors, lawyers, or licensed psychologists when they *enter* the university at 18. Our system works well because students stay in school longer than they do in other countries. By comparison then, at any given age American students are likely to be more broadly educated than are students elsewhere though they may not yet have as much detailed knowledge of specific academic

subjects. They will acquire this knowledge over time, of course; and they should, on average, end up with a knowledge base that is uniquely broad as well as deep.

(p. 53)

And more recently, Labaree (2010) aptly expressed the wide public expectations for what schools should accomplish.

We Americans have long penned our hopes on education. It's the main way we try to express our ideals and solve our problems. We want schools to provide us with good citizens and productive workers; to give us opportunity and reduce inequality; to improve our health, reduce crime, and protect the environment. So we assign the social missions to schools and educators gamely agree to carry them out.

(p. 1)

Prisoners of Time received considerable media attention, but it had its detractors as well. We suspect that some scholars who study reform would not describe the report as prominently as we do and might even give it transitional status. However, we base our argument on the fact that subsequent reforms and federal initiatives have focused almost exclusively on the importance of student achievement learning as measured by standardized tests. Arguments of the past, including those of the Progressive Era, humanistic, and open education, do not survive in more recent reforms such as No Child Left Behind and Race to the Top—which we will discuss later.

In retrospect, it is clear that *Prisoners of Time* and before it *A Nation at Risk* did not comment on many factors that were associated with the performance of youth in public schools. Unexplored were issues of poverty, abuse, inadequate physical plants, and uneven funding across states and within states. As in other reforms, the problem definition pursued by *A Nation at Risk* was relatively narrow and it focused on a narrow set of problems (even though these were potentially important). Clearly, this reform created many future problems by its focus on narrowing the school curriculum. As a result of this, many school programs were eliminated or sharply reduced, and in an era now in which childhood obesity and its potential for diabetes is truly a national crisis, we might reflect on the wisdom of moving physical education from the curriculum.

Transition

After the *Prisoners of Time* report and before *A Nation at Risk*, there were several other reforms, including two National Education Summits (1989, 1996) and various subject matter standards that were pursued by various professional organizations, including the National Council of Mathematics Teachers and the American Chemical Society. For more information on subject matter reforms, see Good and Braden (2000) and a very brief synopsis appears in Appendix 2.2. However, it is sufficient here to say that the reforms of the professional group also proposed a radical shift from the status quo (teacher centered instruction) to a student centered focus. And these arguments were not based upon pilot research studies—they were simply asserted.

Educational Summit 1989   In 1989 President George H. W. Bush held a meeting with 49 of the 50 state governors. Initially, the summit was proposed to focus on examples of good educational practice from different states. However, eventually the conference was used as an opportunity to involve governors in a new focus on educational standards and goals. The participants at the summit included many business leaders and members of the Bush administration. Notably there were *no* professional educators. President Bush made it clear that his intention and that of the federal government was to stimulate and coordinate improvement efforts, but he made it clear that solutions would be found at the state and local levels. The significance of this meeting arises from the fact that this was the first meeting of the president and governors that focused on education since the depression. Governor Bill Clinton played a leading role at the summit in articulating these goals and subsequently led efforts to create the goals for the year 2000. President Bush announced these goals in his 1990 State of the Union Address. These goals appear in Appendix 2.3. An examination of these goals including that by the year 2000 U.S. students will be first in the world in science and mathematics achievement seemed to be ridiculously unattainable in a period of 10 years. It would seem that the governors, while lamenting a public education system in trouble, believed that the solutions were simple. Ipso facto raise standards and they will be met!

Educational Summit 1996.   The 1996 Educational Summit took place at IBM's Executive Conference and included 44 executives of major businesses from various states, including Eastman Kodak, Boeing, and Proctor and Gamble, in addition to 41 governors and some educational experts. The conference was convened by Governor Tommy Thompson of Wisconsin and Louis Gerstner, the CEO of IBM. The purpose of the summit was to address standards, assessment, and technology. The goal was to move past current goals and to create higher and more rigorous goals for students. The call was for individual states assume the responsibility for creating and using the standards. Consistent with the 1989 summit, the putative intent was to limit federal responsibility to a coordinating role. Educational researchers who were left out of the summits had plenty to say about the summit proposals and little of it good. Tom Good edited two special issues of the *Educational Researcher* (Good, 1996a, 1996b) in which educational researchers responded to policy makers' narrow conceptions of educational goals.

Goals 2000: Educate America Act. Signed into law by President Clinton on March 31, 2004, the intent was to improve learning and teaching through the creation of a strong national framework to promote, among other things, research and consensus building designed to produce equitable and high standards for all students. The call was to develop and adapt a voluntary national system to identify skill and certification standards.

No Child Left Behind

In January 2001 President George W. Bush signed into law No Child Left Behind Act. The executive summary is provided in Appendix 2.3. President Bush wrote, "these reforms express my deep belief in our public schools and their mission to build the mind and character of every child, from every background, in every part of America." He further noted that the law was "the cornerstone of my administration."

The legislation noted that, despite the nearly $200 billion that the federal government had spent since the passage of the Elementary and Secondary Education Act of 1965 (ESEA), too many children were still being left behind. It is important to understand that the reform articulated in the No Child Left Behind Act (NCLB) was notably different than the other reforms that we have discussed. This was not a panel or a commission report, this was federal law. This law reauthorized the ESEA and included increased responsibility for states, school districts, and schools. It further provided greater choice for parents particularly those whose children attended low-performing schools. It also provided more flexibility for states and local agencies in how they spent federal dollars.

Most importantly the law called for increased accountability for all public schools and students. This accountability called for the development of challenging state standards in reading and mathematics. It required annual testing of all students in grades 3 to 8 and required that assessments (and progress objectives) must be broken out by poverty, race, ethnicity, disability, and limited English proficiency. The intent was the disaggregation of data so that each group of students' scores could be examined separately. These accountability measures were used to create adequate yearly progress (AYP) goals for schools and school districts. School districts and schools were required to make AYP and those that did not, over time, were to be subjected to improvement corrective action, and restructuring measures that could involve radically changing school staffs and even leading to closure. Another aspect of NCLB was to increase the choices available to parents of students who attended Title I schools that failed to meet state achievement standards. Local education authorities were required, if standards were not met, to provide students attending schools identified for improvement corrective action, or restructuring, the opportunity to attend a better public school (including a public charter school) within the school districts. Districts were required to provide transportation to the new schools. Further, students who attended persistently failing schools (those failing to meet state standards for at least 3 of the 4 preceding years) had the right to monies for supplementary educational services. The Executive Summary made clear that the motivation was a stick and not a carrot. "Schools that want to avoid losing students—along with a portion of their annual budgets typically associated with those students—will have to improve or, if they fail to make AYP for five years, face the risk of reconstitution under restructuring plan." NCLB also provided more flexibility for states, school districts, and schools. For example, the new program gave states and school districts the opportunity to decide those instructional strategies that they would use to improve teaching and to raise student achievement. Further, states had some flexibility in designing performance measures in math and science upon which AYP would be determined.

Comprehensive School Reform. The Comprehensive School Reform (CSR) program was signed into law in 2002. It was an important aspect of NCLB. Essentially, the CSR program was to provide funds so that schools could coordinate whole school reform rather than changes that were less comprehensive. Despite these lofty goals, the funds provided were limited. Schools could obtain funding grants of $50,000 for three consecutive years or $150,000 total. Even though these funds were limited, they were seen as having the potential for organizing thoughtful planning that involved all school personnel and outside constituencies including parents. The criteria for obtaining funds were initially based upon 11 components. These appear in Appendix 2.4. The impact of the CSR program has been summarized by Mary McCaslin, Tom Good, and their colleagues in a special issue of *Teachers College Record* (2008).

No Child Left Behind was politically important because at least initially it drew bipartisan support from both parties and it initially received general, if not considerable support from professional educators. Clearly, NCLB moved the federal government into public education in a central and powerful way never seen before.

Race to the Top

The lack of success of NCLB can perhaps best be reflected by the fact that the Obama administration and the Department of Education initiated a new funding program entitled Race to the Top established to improve student achievement. We will discuss this more fully later in the book. Here we simply note that now the focus was more than math and science, it expanded the reform agenda to include a focus on science, technology, engineering, and mathematics. Under RttT students, even though many had not met the math and reading standards, now must meet even higher standards in more subjects.

RttT offered states a chance to compete for new federal dollars, and only the states with the best proposals for reforming education were to receive funding. States were given clear criteria for how their success would be scored.

These criteria follow:

- Creating standards and assessments that prepare students to succeed in college and the workplace.
- Building data systems that measure student growth and success, and inform teachers and principals how to improve instruction.
- Recruiting, developing, rewarding, and retaining effective teachers and principals where they are needed most.
- Turning around persistently lowest performing schools.

We will delay comments on RttT for now as we will cover it in greater detail and provide our prognosis of its success in Chapter 4.

What Is the Problem?

School reforms can be viewed from various perspectives. First, as we have done, they can be examined in terms of recommended actions. Second, they can be considered in terms of the problem. Third, although it is beyond our purpose to do so here, they can be analyzed in terms of motivational dynamics—how can we impact those who are responsible? For information on motivational analyses, see McCaslin (2009) and McCaslin and Lavigne (2010).

Given the reforms that we examined, the core problem generally seems clear—but shifting over time. The new math reform saw the problem in terms of the curriculum. Students, teachers, and schools were not blamed in any serious way—the math curriculum needed to be changed for everyone. The *Nation at Risk* report saw the problem in terms of students not working hard enough, especially those from low-income schools. The problem discussion in *A Nation At Risk* was a bit richer and more textured than the new math. Schools, teachers, and parents were given a little nudge—pay for longer school days, assign more homework, and supervise it more closely. Some concern about teachers and teaching practice emerged including recognition that teachers varied in how they managed time (more on this in Chapter 3). Still, in full analysis, the core problem was effort and those students with less ability needed to pull up their socks and work harder.

The *Prisoners of Time* report provided an interesting segue in the direction of school reform. At the simplest level it also focused on time, but in ways that differed importantly from *A Nation at Risk*. Now it was not just more time but more time for core subjects. The previous reform had at least implicitly allowed that the general school curriculum was okay, but we needed more time if we were to accomplish everything. *Prisoners of Time* boldly asserted that some subjects were more important than others and thus time for some subjects or activities could be sharply reduced or eliminated. Further use of time was recommended to allow for more ambitious forms of learning (e.g., teach math and science together, lengthen class periods so students would have more time to explore, discover and organize data, generate conclusions, and so forth).

No Child Left Behind sharply ramped up performance expectations and imbedded those expectations in federal law, hence giving this reform more power than those that preceded it. The floor was increased—higher standards for all. But the target became primarily those schools serving a large numbers of students from low-income homes. Increased student performance was mandated, and schools that did not increase student achievement in time faced loss of students and money, restructuring efforts, and even closure. Oddly (if one expects any continuity over reforms), the recommendations for an ambitious curriculum receded, and schools were left to their own devices to design learning experiences that equated to higher student achievement. Presumably what good teaching entailed was widely known and results would be achieved if schools, teachers, and students worked hard enough. The locus of the problem can be argued, but the focal point to us seems to be the school. Schools were to be restructured or closed (with obvious consequences for teachers, administrators, and students), but the unit of analysis was failing schools.

Race to the Top was designed with full knowledge of the problematic results of No Child Left Behind. Clearly, NCLB had failed in its mission to free children from failing schools, because when RttT surfaced, the number of failing schools was larger than ever before. Part of the issue was a clear recognition that no one knew how to turn around failing schools. Despite the promise of help, state agencies did not have the resources or sufficient knowledge to help schools improve. Clearly, the focus on schools and to some extent school districts had not solved the problem. Thus it is not surprising that states became the unit of analysis in RttT. States were now seen as needing more power and having more incentive to improve student, teacher, school, and now statewide performance. If states were to receive vast new resources, they had to show that all constituents in the state were pulling together to implement high standards and to build strong data systems for tracking students, teachers, and schools. Rigorous standards for teachers were to be built requiring that teachers performed well in preparing students for exam success and demonstrating good teaching to observers.

In its simplest form, the core problem of each major reform can be seen in Table 2.2. Obviously, there is much detail in each reform, but we believe the table captures the central problem.

TABLE 2.2 The Core Problem in Five Major Reforms

Sputnik Launch/ New Math 1957	CURRICULUM	Math/science needed major reform.
A Nation at Risk 1983	STUDENTS	Students need to work harder.
Prisoners of Time 1994	CORE SUBJECTS NEGLECTED	Allocate more time to core subjects and use more ambitious strategies.
No Child Left Behind 2001	SCHOOLS	Identify failing schools—correct or close.
Race to the Top 2011	STATES	Provide states with incentives to encourage high-stakes evaluation.

What Have We Learned From This?

First, each crisis is a concern for lack of achievement on standardized tests (and only occasionally a concern about other outcomes such as ability to use technology). Second, each crisis is typically based not on goals that the educational community has set, but from a comparison of student performance in other countries or from the cries of the U.S. business world or military that our high school graduates are not prepared well by their needs. Third, the solution in general is based on a complete rejection of the status quo and a call for something sharply new and that has not even been piloted in small-scale research. Fourth, in time, data suggest that the new reform has not resolved the problem. Fifth, the professional community has not been active in systematically speaking against problematic reform until after their deficiencies have become known. Sixth, when professional groups do become active in asserting reform agendas, they exhibit most of the same weaknesses embedded in the reforms created by policymakers.

Perhaps the largest lesson that we have learned is that we are willing to embark on costly new endeavors without even defining what the movement means. The independent variable or the essence of what an innovative reform should be is not presented. Earlier we quoted Willoughby (1968) on the specious lack of definition for new math. Unfortunately, we could make the same lament for virtually any new reform movement. For example, Kliebard (1986) reported his frustration with the progressive education movement this way. "The more I studied this, the more it seemed to me that the term encompassed such a broad range, not just a different, but of contradictory ideas on education as to be meaningless" (p. IX).

So we are left with a puzzlingly, complex question. What can explain this continuing support for a repeated cycle of failed reforms? Each reform invests large sums of money which are soon dissipated. These reforms emerge quickly like hurricanes, waste human and fiscal resources, and then quickly disappear only to return in a new form. We will try to address this later in the book, but first, other parts of the story need to be told.

Chapter 3 explores a different but related topic. Here we address what is known about good teaching. And, again, we will see that beliefs about how teachers should teach and organize learning also change rapidly. New ways to teach that do not flow from data but rather are based on belief, often as simple as out with the old—in with the new. Research follows reform and typically informs us that the reform is problematic.

References

Barker, C., Curran, H., & Metcalf, M. (1964). *The new math: For teachers and parents of elementary school children*. Belmont, CA: Fearon.

Barth, R. S. (1971). So you want to change to an open classroom. *The Phi Delta Kappan, 53*(2), 97–99.

Berger, J. (1989, October 14). New York's new school chief visits city and faults system. *New York Times*. Retrieved from http://www.nytimes.com/1989/10/14/nyregion/new-york-s-new-school-chief-visits-city-and-faults-system.html

Berliner, D., & Biddle, B. (1995). *The manufactured crisis: Myths, fraud, and the attack on America's public schools*. New York, NY: Addison-Wesley.

Block, J., & Anderson, I. (1975). *Mastery learning in classroom instruction*. New York, NY: Macmillan.

Celis, W. (1994, March 19). 15 Massachusetts public schools are entrusted to private managers. *New York Times*. Retrieved from http://www.nytimes.com/1994/03/19/us/15-massachu-setts-public-schools-are-entrusted-to-private-managers.html?pagewanted=all&src=pm

Editorial. (1994, May 7). Wasted days. *The Arizona Daily Star*, p. 18A.

Federal Registrar Department of Education. (Part 3, April 14, 2010). *Overview information; Race to the Top Fund; Notice inviting applications for new awards for fiscal year (FY) 2010; notice*. Retrieved from http://www2.ed.gov/programs/racetothetop-district/resources.html

Fiske, E. (1986, April 27). Effort to improve U.S. schools entering a new phase. *New York Times*, p.32.

Good, T. L. (Ed.). (1996a). Educational researchers comment on the Educational Summit and other policy proclamations from 1983–1997. *Educational Researcher, 25*(8), 4–6.

Good, T. L. (Ed.). (1996b). Talking "truth" to power: The conversation continues [Special issue]. *Educational Researcher, 25*(9).

Good, T. L., & Braden, J. S. (2000). *The great school debate: Choice, vouchers, and charters*. Mahwah, NJ: Erlbaum.

Good, T., Biddle, B., & Brophy, J. (1975). *Teachers make a difference*. New York, NY: Holt, Rine-hart, & Winston.

Hummel-Rossi, B., & Ashdown, J. (2002). The state of cost-benefit and cost-effectiveness analyses in education. *Review of Educational Research, 72*(1), 1–30.

Kliebard, H. (1986). *The struggle for the American curriculum: 1893–1958*. New York, NY: Routledge.

Labaree, D. (2010). *Someone has to fail*. Cambridge, MA: Harvard University Press.

Lundgren, U. (1972). Frame factors and the teaching process. Retrieved from http://hdl.handle.net/2077/12809

Macfarquhar, N. (1995, July 22). 2 Trenton schools begin an experiment with year-round classes. *New York Times*. Retrieved from http://www.nytimes.com/1995/07/22/nyregion/2-tren-ton-schools-begin-an-experiment-with-year-round-classes.html?pagewanted=all&src=pm

McCaslin, M. (2009). Co-regulation of student motivation and emergent identity. *Educational Psychologist, 44*(2), 137–146.

McCaslin, M., & Good, T. (2008). School reform matters [Special issue]. *Teachers College Record, 110*(10).

McCaslin, M., & Lavigne, A. L. (2010). Social policy, educational opportunity, and classroom practice: A co-regulation approach to research on student motivation and achievement. In T. Urdan & S. Karabenick (Eds.), *The decade ahead: Applications and contexts of motivation and achievement* (*Advances in motivation and achievement*, Vol. 16, pp. 211–249). London, England: Emerald Group.

Moise, E. E., Calandra, A., Davis, R. B., Kline, M., & Bacon, H. M. (1965). *Five views of the "new math."* Washington, DC: Council for Basic Education.

National Commission on Excellence in Education. (1983). *A nation at risk: The imperative for education reform.* Washington, DC: U.S. Department of Education, National Commission for Excellence in Education.

National Education Commission on Time and Learning. (1994). *Prisoners of time.* Washington, DC: U.S. Government Printing Office.

No Child Left Behind Act of 2001, Pub. L. 107-110, 20 U.S.C. § 6301 et. seq.

Payne, C. (2010). *So much reform so little change.* Cambridge, MA: Harvard Education Press.

Purnick, J. (1985, March 12). Raises of new teachers must wait, mayor says. *New York Times*, p. 3.

Ravitch, D. (2010). *The death and life of the great American school system: How testing and choice are undermining education.* New York, NY: Basic Books.

Reschly, D., & Sabers, D. (1974, June). Open education: Have we been there before? *Phi Delta Kappan, 5*(10), 675–677.

Tomlinson, T. M. (1986). A nation at risk: Background for a working paper. In T. M. Tomlinson & H. J. Walberg (Eds.), *Academic work and educational excellence: Raising student productivity* (pp. 3–28). Berkeley, CA: McCutchan.

Willoughby, S. (1968). What is the new mathematics?. *NASSP Bulletin, 52*(327), 4–15. doi:10.1177/019263656805232704

3

HOW TEACHERS INFLUENCE STUDENT LEARNING

Historical and Contemporary Considerations

Introduction

Here, we discuss the history of research and the current evidence describing how teaching affects student achievement. In doing so, we will describe how the knowledge base linking teacher behavior to student achievement was established. As we will see, studies of teaching attempting to understand how teachers impacted student achievement reached its apogee in the late 1980s, followed by an era that discarded and even forgot about this research. Yet, in the last several years, interest in discovering how teachers obtain student achievement has reemerged and is now a dominant policy issue. This intense interest is driven both by federal law (Race to the Top) and many foundations (including the prestigious Bill and Melinda Gates Foundation). Ironically, and disappointingly, this renewed interest in and funding of research on teaching has yielded findings that replicate but do not extend what was known in the mid- to late-80s. And it could be argued that current value-added scores, and the achievement test they are based on, tell us even less about student achievement because at least with tests in the 70s and 80s you could look within particular content areas to obtain some notion about students' learning of particular content.

As noted, this chapter presents the literature that describes how teachers influence student achievement. Mostly this research explores how teachers influence students' learning of concepts and skills measured on standardized achievement tests. Important teaching behaviors associated with increases in student achievement include active teaching, proactive classroom management systems, appropriate expectations for student learning, ample opportunity to learn, and supportive classrooms that allow and encourage student effort. We then note that "modern" research has recently rediscovered results that were summarized years earlier (Brophy & Good, 1986). After reviewing this literature, we argue that unlike many current observation and evaluation systems now used to identify more and less effective teachers, the current focus on checklists of individual teaching skills is misguided. We suggest that a better strategy for describing and improving teaching is to look at teaching as a system rather the delivery of individual instructional behaviors.

Research on Teaching: Brief History

Research on teaching has a long history. We start our review in the mid-1960s and early 1970s, because this is the time when more systematic attempts to describe what teachers do in the classroom occurred. Prior to this time, there had been many descriptions of what teachers should do. These accounts were largely based on armchair analysis and occasionally on the basis of some theory. However, it is important to stress that even then there was a tremendous number of articles on teaching. Dunkin and Biddle in their book—*The Study of Teaching*—estimated in 1974 that over 10,000 studies were available but that only a few involved the observation of teaching. Not until the mid-60s had observational work really started in earnest, and in the 1970s and throughout the 1980s, educational researchers moved into the classroom and began to describe teachers' interactions with students in various ways (see our discussion of observational methods in Chapter 5, and for extensive coverage see Evertson & Green, 1986).

Historic Disinterest in Classroom Observation

Why was interest in describing classroom instruction so limited prior to at least the mid-1960s? There are many reasons including the amount of time and cost involved in training observers, obtaining permissions from teachers to collect data, traveling to schools, and the difficulty of analyzing collected data. Perhaps the most important reason that teachers and instruction were given limited attention is because prior to the 1960s teachers were seen as relatively unimportant influences on student learning. So, if teachers and teaching had similar (and little) impact on students, why bother to study it? At that time, most of the variation in student achievement was largely attributed to variables such as students' IQ and family backgrounds.

Research by educators was also unable to show that teachers or teacher education influenced student learning. A committee appointed by the American Educational Research Association (AERA) reached a dismal conclusion:

> The simple fact of the matter is that, after 40 years of research on teacher effectiveness during which a vast number of studies have been carried out, one can point to few outcomes that a superintendent of schools can

> safely employ in hiring a teacher or granting him tenure, that an agency can employ in certifying teachers, or that a teacher-education faculty can employ in planning or improving teacher-education programs.
>
> *(AERA, 1953, p. 657)*

In 1975, Good, Biddle, and Brophy wrote *Teachers Make a Difference* and contended that teachers make a definite contribution to student achievement and that social scientists, educators, and the media regularly, and erroneously, had underestimated the importance of classroom teachers. In doing so, they presented a review of the available evidence and provided a coherent synthesis of this information and suggested guidelines for how this research might be enhanced.

> Just as data suggesting that teachers do not make a difference frequently have been over generalized and accepted uncritically, there is a danger that the same mistakes can be made with the kinds of data cited in this chapter. While these data do establish that certain teachers consistently outperform others and that particular kinds of teaching behavior are almost always preferable to contrasting kinds, the present state of research in the area does not allow for the use of process-product findings for accountability purposes. Ultimately, findings of this type might be usable for making decisions about teacher tenure or pay issues, but at present they are too sparse and unsophisticated to be used for such purposes legitimately. We believe that officials charged with making accountability decisions must base them on reasonable and appropriate criteria. In our belief, such criteria do not exist at this time. Thus, before prematurely committing time and money to an imperfect accountability system, time and money should be allocated to the basic research needed to identify appropriate and inappropriate teacher behavior clearly and unambiguously.
>
> *(Good et al., 1975, p. 85)*

Thus, in over 20 years the field had made notable progress from the AERA committee's conclusion in 1953 that there was *no* evidence about teacher effectiveness to the assertion that teachers *did* make a difference. In 1975 there was sufficient data to argue, plausibly, that teachers influence students' learning. Now, we further consider why so many (including leading social scientists) in 1970 believed that teachers made little difference, if any, on students' school achievement. Then, after discussing the dismissal of possible teacher effects on achievement prior to the 1970s, we examine the literature that proceeded and led to Good et al.'s (1975) strong conclusion. In particular, we identify some of the important pioneering work upon which they built their case for the importance of teachers.

Why Were Teachers Believed to be Unimportant?

Why were teachers seen as unimportant determinants of students' learning? First of all, as noted, there was a prevalent belief that students' background largely explained students' school achievement. Further, this belief was greatly reinforced by research studies (Coleman et al., 1966; Jencks et al., 1972) that concluded that the level of school resources had little effect on student achievement. That is, these research findings further strengthened societal beliefs that teacher effects on student achievement were minor.

The Coleman et al. (1966) study attempted to relate school expenditures to student achievement. This huge study involved a national sample that examined responses from 4,000 public schools and 645,000 students. The report concluded that increased spending did not lead to any incremental increases in achievement. These data were widely disseminated and incorrectly interpreted to mean that money made no difference in student achievement. Yet, the data could not support these popular but inaccurate conclusions because school expenditures and students' socioeconomic status (SES) in schools were woefully compounded. Then, most students attended neighborhood schools and, as school funding was highly related to local property taxes, schools serving low-income students had less money to spend than those schools enrolling high or middle SES students. It was not possible to separate school achievement from the social background of the students who attended them.

Yet another and highly related misconception about the Coleman et al. study (1966) was that schooling made no difference in student learning. This error occurred because Coleman et al. only measured school inputs (like budgets, teachers' highest level of training, and so forth) and outputs (student achievement). This study and others like it were typically called black box studies because they only studied the resources that went into the "box" and the student products that came out. Importantly, what happened inside the box was not studied. Research since then has made it abundantly clear that the variation in schools serving students of similar SES is very wide. Some teachers in high SES schools obtain more achievement than other teachers in their school and it is also the case that some teachers in low SES schools obtain more student achievement than do other teachers. For example, the number of books in a high or low SES school library may vary widely, but so does teachers' use of the library. Thus some students in high or low SES schools may access library books more than others because some teachers assign work that requires a library visit and others do not. Hence, many variables measured by Coleman et al. were confounded—schools that have fewer books per se may have some teachers who assign more books to their students to read.

Further, and most important, it was possible—if not likely—that some teachers were more effective than others in the same school. Since Coleman et al. (1966) used a study design based on school means, their research strategy guaranteed that any within school variation in teacher effects on students would be missed. The mean school average—how much did fourth-grade students learn in Longfellow Elementary School during the year—did not allow for the possible discovery that some fourth-grade teachers had important effects on students while others had little. Thus, it seems clear how these data, which masked the effects of individual teachers, may have helped to maintain the belief that teachers were relatively unimportant influences on student achievement. Coleman et al.'s work was seen as evidence that schools were ineffective, and other research analyses conducted around that time provided even more negative claims to imply that student achievement was primarily explained by social background and pupil ability (Jencks et al., 1972).

In the 1960s it was evident that students from high SES families did better, and often considerably better, in schools than did those from less affluent homes. However, social scientists of the era failed to consider that factors other than hereditary might explain the success of these students. For example, many students from more affluent homes often enjoyed advantages that those from less affluent homes did not, including books, magazines, TV, and opportunities to join after school clubs, visit museums and libraries, and attend summer camps.

However, there were other sources of data to support the belief that hereditary heavily determined students' level of school learning. For example, despite the large investment in Project Head Start and other compensatory programs, there were no data then to show that students in these programs benefitted consistently in ways that differed from control children (those who did not receive the program). These data led some citizens, policy makers, and researchers to conclude that early education efforts had failed, and some, such as Jensen (1969), concluded that these failures occurred because student learning was determined largely by students' heredity. Thus, these disappointing results reinforced the belief in many citizens that social class and hereditary were intractable forces.

At a policy level, the Head Start investment (spearheaded by President Lyndon Johnson) was an effort intended to show that young children, although hindered by conditions of poverty, if given adequate nutrition and educational support, could achieve at notably higher levels than many believed. Although initial results were not strong, the investment in Head Start provided evidence and symbolic support that some policy makers and citizens were beginning to reject long-held assumptions that student potential was fixed at birth. Some societal beliefs were shifting.

Teacher Training

Despite the symbolic gains of Head Start funding, other data continued to suggest that teachers and teaching were not important, and other evidence came from the study of teacher training programs and their effects. Popham (1971) conducted several studies suggesting that teacher training did not enhance teachers' ability to make measureable differences in student learning. In several studies, Popham compared the effects on learning when students were taught by experienced certified teachers and when they were taught by individuals who had knowledge of the skills being taught, but no formal training as a teacher. For example, Popham compared experienced teachers and auto mechanics teaching content about auto repair. He found that trained teachers achieved no more student learning of auto repair than did auto mechanics.

These results were interesting (and distressing) but far from compelling as the findings were compounded by training and experience. Obviously, auto mechanics had much more experience in diagnosing and repairing cars than did teachers. Moody and Bausell (1971, 1973) used an improved design to avoid compounding teacher training and teacher experience. Still, their results were the same as Popham's—teacher training was not associated with improved student learning. These findings were reinforced by Dembo and Jennings (1973), who studied experienced teachers and inexperienced teacher interns presenting mini-lessons. Again, teaching experience did not lead to better student learning or in the quality of teaching as measured by observational ratings or in an ability to solve simulated classroom situations. The only sign of the favorable impact of teaching experience was an ability to achieve more positive student attitudes toward education.

Some Evidence That Teacher Behavior Could Be Related to Student Learning

Despite this large and consistent literature suggesting that teachers made little difference in student learning, some researchers continued to explore the topic. Perhaps the single most important effort to demonstrate the possibility that teachers influenced student achievement came from a review by Rosenshine and Furst (1973). In part these researchers made progress because they, and the research of those they reviewed, actually observed teaching.

Rosenshine and Furst (1973) reviewed several correlational studies that related instructional behavior and student learning. They found students learned better when teachers exhibited the following behaviors: clarity, variability in teaching methods, enthusiasm, task-oriented behavior, indirectness, student opportunity to learn, teachers' use of structuring comments and multiple levels of questions. And, teacher criticism was consistently shown to have a negative effect on student learning.

To reach these conclusions, Rosenshine and Furst (1973) examined about 50 process (what happens in the classroom) and product studies (outcomes like student achievement). Most of these studies centered their observational research on process that occurred naturally in the classroom, but in most of these studies the amount of time observed was limited—1 hour or less. Further, measurement of classroom process was done primarily with high inference rating scales, and observers were largely left to their own judgment for separating and rating inferences such as high from moderate or low enthusiasm. Still, their review revealed that five teacher behaviors consistently correlated with student achievement. Rosenshine and Furst's five most important variables merit discussion not only for their historical value but also because these variables remain important for understanding classroom learning now over 40 years later. These variables relating teaching to student achievement follow.

Teacher Clarity.   Most studies of clarity involved high inference variables. When low inference measures were used, they included measurements— questions were answered without additional information or teachers spent less time answering student questions that called for interpretation. All seven teacher clarity studies reviewed yielded significant and positive correlations (.37–.71).

Variability.   Variety was studied in different ways using both high and low inference measures. Further, a range of events were considered to show variability including instructional procedures, materials, and level of cognitive discourse. Positive and significant correlations ranged from .24–.54.

Enthusiasm.   Teacher enthusiasm was measured in various ways including observer ratings on paired adjectives (stimulating–dull; alert-apathetic), of teacher energy, and student ratings (teacher involvement or excitement). Positive and significant correlations ranged from .36–.62.

Task-Oriented.   This variable and a related one called "businesslike" were combined. Definitions included—stimulation of thoughts not information or skills, focus placed on student learning not enjoyment, teachers encouraged students to work hard, creatively, and independently. Positive and significant correlations ranged from .42–.61.

Student Opportunity to Learn Content.   Opportunity to learn was measured in diverse ways. In two of the studies reviewed by Rosenshine and Furst (1973), the researchers examined lesson transcripts to see if test items had been covered. In a related study, a researcher examined the amount of time spent on various topics across four hour-long lessons. In another study a researcher asked teachers to rate the extent to which students had an opportunity to learn the type of problems on the achievement test. Positive and significant correlations ranged from .16–.40.

This research yielded promising results, but as Rosenshine and Furst (1973) noted, this literature had several limitations. For example, typically the class mean was used as the unit of analysis so it was not possible to determine if different types of students benefitted more or less from these instructional behaviors. That is, would some students need or benefit from more teacher enthusiasm or clarity than would other students? Further, they noted that the data were only correlational and that follow up experimental studies were needed.

Kounin

At roughly the same time Rosenshine and Furst (1973) published their integrative work, Kounin (1970) published his seminal work on classroom management. Kounin's findings were important. However, they failed to receive the notoriety they merited at that time for two reasons. First, Kounin did not include student achievement measures, and second, the zeitgeist of the era was changing. Some educators seemingly reasoned, "perhaps education could not make up for social class, in terms of achievement, but schools could become more interesting to and supportive of children." Books appearing in the early 70s like Silberman's (1970) *Crisis in the Classroom* and Barth's (1972) *Open Education and the American School* were highly critical of the structured and joyless learning environments that schools imposed on students. And some reform movements of the era called for less whole class instruction and advocated for the use of learning stations where students' interests could be accommodated and where students could move at their own pace. Thus, some educators may have concluded (we feel incorrectly) that management variables relevant to traditional classrooms had no place in modern classrooms.

Whether Kounin's (1970) findings were sufficiently appreciated then, or not, we contend that they were important then and now. Why? First, Kounin provided correlational data to describe how teachers with well-managed classes differed from teachers who managed classrooms less well. Kounin had a long record of studying what he called "the ripple effect." In various settings, he explored how students intervened in management situations in ways that stopped the misbehavior and did not lead to other students to lessen their involvement (e.g., to see who was being reprimanded) because then teachers would have to bring these students' attention back to the assigned task. Kounin conducted many inquiries, but the results for clarity, firmness, and specificity, for example, varied from study to study. He could find no way, for example, that teachers could respond to misbehavior in a way that consistently and quickly restored order.

Ironically, Kounin (1970) subsequently designed and conducted a study that showed that good classroom behavior was strongly related to what teachers did to prevent misbehavior. After student inattentiveness or misbehavior occurred, teachers lost instructional time. Kounin demonstrated that proactive management was far superior to reactive managements. Three general classes of management were identified in this work: movement management, maintaining

TABLE 3.1 Proactive Management Variables: Kounin (1970)*

---

1. Withitness and overlapping. These dimensions deal with a teacher's communicating that he/she knows what is going on regarding children's behavior and by attending to two issues simultaneously when two different issues are present.

2. Smoothness and momentum. These measures describe how the teacher manages movement during recitations and at transition periods.

3. Group alerting and accountability. These aspects of teachers' technique deal with the extent to which they maintain a group-focus during recitations in contrast to becoming immersed in dealing with a single child.

4. Valence and challenge arousal.

5. Seatwork variety and challenge. This dimension deals with the teachers' planning learning activities with variety and intellectual challenge, especially in seatwork settings.

---

* This table is adapted from Kounin, J. (1970). *Discipline and group management in classrooms*. New York, NY: Holt, Rinehart and Winston.

group focus, and avoiding satiation. Table 3.1, provides definitions of some of Kounin's key variables.

The behaviors that Kounin (1970) uncovered were highly correlated with student involvement in both whole class and seatwork activity. Table 3.2 presents the correlation between these teaching behaviors and student behaviors. Two types of information are presented. First, correlations between teacher actions and student attention during whole class activities are provided. Second, the table also includes information about the relationship between teacher management variables and student behavior during seatwork activity.

Other Promising Classroom Research

Research on classroom teaching flourished in the 70s, and other interesting variables emerged. For example, the steering group concept set forth by Lundgren (1972) was a teacher expectation variable as it focused on the small group of students that the teacher used to make instructional decisions, i.e., at what level to present instruction and to decide when material had been sufficiently understood to allow moving to new content. The higher the achievement level of the steering group, the higher the learning for the class as a whole. That is, teachers who aimed higher generally obtained higher achievement from students than teachers who chose a lower achieving group of students as the steering group. Although these data were correlational, they pointed to the distinct possibility that teachers affect student achievement.

Similarly, Brophy and Good (1970) studied teachers interactions with students that teachers believed to be more or less capable and found that some teachers behaved markedly differently toward students believed to be more or

TABLE 3.2 Correlations between Teacher Behavior and Students' Behavior in Recitation and Seatwork Settings: Kounin (1970)[1,2,3]

	Recitation		Seatwork	
	Work Involvement	Freedom from Deviancy	Work Involvement	Freedom from Deviancy
Momentum (Freedom from Slowdowns) (b)	.656	.641	.198	.490
Withitness	.615	.531	.307	.509
Smoothness (Freedom from Thrusts, Dangles, Stimulus – Boundedness)	.601	.489	.382	.421
Group Alerting	.603	.442	.234	.290
Accountability	.494	.385	.002	−.035
Overlappingness	.460	.362	.259	.379
Valence and Challenge Arousal	.372	.325	.308	.371
Seatwork Variety and Challenge	.061	.033	.516	.276
Overall Variety and Challenge	.217	.099	.449	.194

(1) This table is adapted from Kounin, J. (1970). *Discipline and group management in classrooms.* New York, NY: Holt, Rinehart and Winston.
(2) N = 49 classrooms (r = of .276, p < .05)
(3) Intercoder agreements for the various measures of children's behavior and teacher styles ranged from 79% to 99% agreement, with an average intercoder agreement of 92%.

less able. For example, they found that students who teachers believed to be more able received more favorable instructional opportunities than did students believed to be less capable. Other studies also illustrated the importance of teacher expectations in influencing student achievement. Pidgeon (1970) reported a positive relationship between teachers' expectations, the pace of instruction, and students' learning. He noted that in part, teachers' expectations were based on the curriculum used as it conveyed what was appropriate for students to learn at a particular grade level. Pidgeon compared elementary school students in England and in California (students were of similar age and achievement) and reported that British students had learned much more mathematics than did students in California. Good et al. (1975) commented on the value of the Pidgeon study.

However, an additional analysis comparing the percentage of students in each group who passed each specific item showed no difference between groups on items which had been taught in *both* school systems. The advantage to the British students was due solely to the fact that they had been taught more during the year than the students in California. Apparently expectations for mathematical learning in this grade were higher for the British schools (appropriately so, judging from the test scores), so that British children learned more than the American children even though there was no difference in student ability.

(p. 66)

Chang and Raths' (1971) research supported Pidgeon's work. They studied achievement scores of fourth- and fifth-grade students from seven low-SES and seven middle-SES urban schools. As expected, students in higher-SES schools performed better than those in lower-SES schools. Teacher interviews helped to explain *why* students performed differently. Chang and Raths reported that middle-SES schools' teachers placed emphasis on most of the test items, whereas teachers in lower-SES schools only emphasized some of the items. Students in lower-SES schools generally performed well on those items that they were taught. Clearly, this differential opportunity to learn material was a part, perhaps an important part, of the differences in student achievement in high- and low-SES schools. It seems reasonable to conclude that students are unlikely to learn material that they are not taught.

In addition to work on achievement outcomes, there was also research in the 1970s relating instruction to various affective outcomes. For example, St. John (1971) reported based on her study of 36 White, urban, sixth-grade teachers that warmer and more student-oriented teachers were more successful with Black children. Black children experience more growth in reading when teachers were rated high on traits such as kindliness, adaptability, and optimism. Similarly, Kleinfeld (1972) found that teacher warmth and student orientation were especially important to minority students in Alaska. Further, Aspy (1973) also illustrated the importance of a teacher affective variable which Aspy called "interchangeable responses"—a concept adapted from the writings of Carl Rogers, a noted psychologist who made the non directive method popular in psychology. Interchangeable responses were teachers' reactions to or summaries of student statements which could be seen as interchangeable with what the student had actually said. That is, the teacher response presumably indicated that he or she had heard and understood the student accurately. In one study Aspy found that students' reading achievement scores were positively related to teacher scores on providing interchangeable responses. A follow-up study indicated that reading teachers who were provided with training in how to make interchangeable responses were twice as successful in increasing reading achievement during a summer session than were untrained teachers. Yet, another study provided fascinating data showing that when elementary teachers increased their frequencies of interchangeable responses, it was associated with good student attendance resulting in the lowest levels of student absences in the schools' 45-year history. As provocative as Aspy's data were, it is important that they were correlational studies, and as far as we know, never replicated.

Although, as we noted earlier, most research on teaching concerned itself with the effort to relate teaching to student achievement, the study of affective outcomes of schooling was also popular in the 1970s and early 1980s (movements such as open classrooms and humanistic schools were notably concerned about affective outcome of schooling). This brief review suggests that teaching may be related to important outcomes of schooling other than achievement such as student attendance. We return to this issue later.

Dunkin and Biddle

Dunkin and Biddle (1974) writing soon after Rosenshine and Furst (1973) noted that over 10,000 studies had appeared on teacher effectiveness and that studying this literature was overwhelming. Why then had this large literature yielded so little useful knowledge? First, they noted was the failure to observe in classrooms. Dunkin and Biddle were aware that observational research was already gaining some ascendency in the field and they referred to the need for more observational research (Flanders, 1970; Medley & Mitzel, 1963; Nuthall, 1968; Withall, 1960). Following Gage (1963), they concluded that most previous research was black box studies that ignored what happened inside of classrooms. Second, the limited research yield was also due to what Dunkin and Biddle called theoretical impoverishment. They contended that many variables seem to be added with little or no rationale as to why they were measured "… and in many cases, there seemed to be no justification for even suspecting a relation between a particular item and teacher effectiveness. Thus, studies have appeared in which nearly all conceivable teacher characteristics have been examined for their relationships to effectiveness. Among these have been, for example, teachers' eye color, voice quality, clothing style, musical ability, and even strength of the teachers' grip!" (pp. 13–14). Third, they noted the inadequate criteria of effectiveness used in previous research. Studies of teacher effectiveness rarely measured student learning but rather relied on principal and students rating of teachers. Fourth, they noted that good teaching may well be highly related to teaching context and that previous research had too little concern for contextual effects. For example, they hypothesized that some variables like teacher warmth may be more important in some settings such as first-grade classes than say in 12th-grade classes. Further, they noted that impact of teaching variables may be more or less important not only in terms of students' age, but also in terms of subject matter and school context (e.g., inner city or suburban).

Dunkin and Biddle (1974) felt that teaching effectiveness would be sharply defined by the particular context in which teaching occurred. Still, they were open to the possibility that some general effects might cut across specific contexts. "It is possible of course that some qualities may make for effectiveness of teaching regardless of context. But others, perhaps the majority, will be context related" (p. 15).

Dunkin and Biddle (1974) clearly depicted and expanded the conception and complexity of classrooms that others had commented upon (e.g., Jackson, 1968; Waller, 1961). Their model for the study of teaching provided an overview of the variables that they believed influenced teaching and student learning. See Figure 3.1 for a modified version of the model. Several classes of variables are included in their model. Presage variables include things associated with the teacher—formative experiences, teacher characteristics, and type of teacher training. Process variables are what teachers and students actually do in the classroom. Product variables address the outcomes of schooling—changes that occur in students because of their experiences in classrooms. Product variables may be both short-term (students attitudes toward subject matter taught) or long-term (college admission).

As observed under process variables, the classroom is the center of their model. Dunkin and Biddle (1974) noted that several classes of knowledge can be arrived at from an analysis of classroom behavior, including the rate which

PRESAGE Variables	PROCESS Variables	PRODUCT Variables
Teacher Formative Experiences	Teacher Classroom Behavior	Short Term Pupil Growth
Social Class	Pupil Classroom Behavior	Changes in Student Behavior
Gender	Classroom Activities	Subject Matter Learning
Age	Classroom Discussion	Student Attitudes
		Toward Peers
Teacher Training Experiences		Toward Subject Matter
Student Teaching Experiences		
Traditional or Alternative/		Long Term Pupil Effects
Teacher Education		Admission to College
Quality of Institution		Professional Skills
		Professional Occupation
Teacher Characteristics		Adult Civic Behavior
Teaching Ability		
Motivation		
Dispositions		
Intelligence		

FIGURE 3.1 A model for the study of classroom teaching: Proposed by Dunkin and Biddle, 1974. This table is adapted from Dunkin, M., & Biddle, B. (1974). *The study of teaching*. New York, NY: Holt, Rinehart and Winston.

teaching processes occur, what kinds of teaching processes are typical in class-rooms, the relationship between presage and processes of teaching, the relationship among processes occurring in the classroom, and how teaching affects student development.

Improvements in Classroom Research

Based upon the research literature that we have just reviewed, Good et al. (1975) suggested some important considerations for improving the research base. These recommendations appear in Table 3.3.

TABLE 3.3 Suggestions for Improving Research on Teaching: Good, Biddle, and Brophy, 1975*

Naturalistic settings. The recommendation that research on teaching be conducted in actual classrooms may seem obvious. However, prior to the mid-1970s much of the research on teaching came from microteaching experiments and as such had little generalizability to real classrooms. The advice was simple, if you want to generalize about first grade classrooms, study first grade classrooms.

Use a variety of classroom measures. Most studies of classroom research typically study only one or two student outcomes. This is unfortunate because it makes it impossible to understand if improvements on one measure come at the expense of another outcome. For example, do increases in student attitudes toward learning come at the expense of achievement gains?

Use both high and low inference measures. High inference measures are rating scales that involve a high degree of deduction on the observer's part. For example, after observing for 15 minutes or longer, the observer is asked to arrive at a judgment about the extent to which the teacher has exhibited warmth or not. Low inference measures do not rely on subjective judgments and call for the observer to code only the frequency or type of a specific behavior exhibited within a clearly defined range (e.g., how many open-ended questions were asked in five minutes). Using both measures makes it possible to capture specific information about particular behaviors and to also make higher order judgments about the meaning or implications of those behaviors.

Use adjusted achievement gain rather than raw gain scores. Simple gain scores (post-score minus pre-score) should not be used because they can be influenced by many factors other than instructional behavior. When done appropriately, adjusted scores (taking into consideration differences in students before the treatment) enable researchers to compare teachers' comparative effects even if they are teaching students who differ in some way at the beginning of the experiment.

Match classrooms. Even when adjusted or residual scores are used to compare teachers, the results may provide misleading conclusions when the differences in students in the classrooms vary greatly from teacher to teacher. Thus to the extent possible, it is important to match classrooms so that pre-achievement scores are similar and that student demographics (for example, the number of special learners) are also comparable across classrooms. Such matching helps to assure that the differences, if any, that are obtained are due to instructional behavior and not to some extraneous variable (e.g., such as one teacher having more special learners than another).

(continued)

TABLE 3.3 Continued

Analyze the distribution of achievement gains. The concern here is whether or not the gains in achievement—or whatever is being measured—are general and common across all students or whether the gains occur more for some students than others. For example, is it possible that girls benefit more from the treatment than do boys; or that high achieving students benefit more than low achieving students?

Use a large sample of teachers. Defining large or small obviously is a relative concept. However, at a minimum, the number of teachers used in a study should be large enough so that the sample can be divided in half so that teachers are high or low on some variable (e.g., the emphasis they place on conceptual development of the content being studied) to see if these teacher differences are associated with differences in achievement.

Use selected (purposeful) rather than random samples. At first glance this suggestion might appear to be counterintuitive to some readers. After all, many students of research have been encouraged to use random samples rather than purposeful samples so that they may generalize the findings more broadly. However, including a random sample of teachers in most instances would likely lead to including some, if not many teachers who have no large effect on the many student outcomes being studied or teachers who were highly inconsistent in their effects on students from one year to another. Using samples that are selected rationally can lead to selecting teachers who are more consistent in producing either high or low effects on the student outcomes being studied. Studies designed with selected or purposeful samples are likely to have more variance in teacher effects on students than would a random sample of teachers.

Analyze data for nonlinear as well as linear relationships. A linear relationship suggests that the instructional variable has a direct and proportionate effect on the student outcome. For example, the more warmth or greater clarity that a teacher projects in a classroom leads to more student achievement. However, it is likely that many relationships between instructional process and student outcomes have a nonlinear relationship. For example, there may be an optimal level of a certain behavior—for example, up to a point more teacher clarity increases student achievement, but after that point no additional increases in student achievement occur or that beyond that point decreases in student achievement occur. For example, one way a teacher exhibits clarity is by giving additional examples as requested by students. However, after providing a couple of examples, 90% of the students may understand the point, and if teachers keep responding to new questions, there is no reason to believe that most of the students will benefit from new examples.

Collect enough data to ensure reliability and validity. To collect sufficient data to address reliability and validity concerns may vary from study to study depending upon many factors such as the frequency with which instructional behaviors of interest occur and the stability of those behaviors from lesson to lesson. Further, certain types of instructional behaviors may be more relevant to some lessons than to others. Hence, in order to measure both the teacher's general style and the variability of teacher's behavior (within that style), it is useful to visit the classroom on multiple occasions so that contextual effects can be considered. To take but one example, teachers may behave differently depending on the time of the day, whether they are introducing new ideas or whether they are reviewing ideas, and so forth.

Measure teachers' values, goals, and perceptions. Teachers' beliefs are often highly similar to their behavior (for example, teachers who believe that it is more important to call on low achieving more frequently than high achieving students may do so).

However, in some instances, there may be large discrepancies between what teachers believe and what they do (teaching involves quick decisions in a fast moving classroom and some types of classroom interactions are very difficult for teachers to monitor while engaging in instruction). Thus when teachers have different values and goals, it may be reasonable for their classroom instruction to differ as well. It is only possible to obtain information describing how teachers' beliefs and goals influence their classroom behavior if we measure teachers' beliefs and behaviors.

---

* This Table is adapted from Good, T., Biddle, B., & Brophy, J. (1975). *Teachers make a difference.* New York, NY: Holt, Rinehart and Winston.

Good and Grouws

Good and Grouws (1977, 1979) built upon the guidelines presented above, and in doing so, illustrated that instructional behavior could be linked to student achievement in both correlational and experimental studies. For example, they studied a large sample of teachers and found a subset of teachers who were differentially effective in influencing student achievement. Over 100 third- and fourth-grade teachers were initially sampled, and their students' scores on the Iowa Test of Basic Skills were analyzed. From this sample, it was possible to identify nine teachers who were relatively effective on total mathematics scores over 2 consecutive years. And, it also identified nine relatively ineffective teachers who also were stable across 2 consecutive years. Stability in this case implied that teachers stayed in the top third or bottom third of the distribution of achievement scores. They used this sample of teachers to explore through observational research how more effective teachers differed from less effective teachers. One important consideration in this research was that they did not select teachers randomly as is traditionally recommended. Building upon the literature review described earlier, these researchers reasoned that many teachers were not consistently differentially effective, and that if one wanted to study effective teachers it was important to assure that the sample included such teachers. Obviously, finding a purposeful sample of teachers who made a difference in student achievement took much time and money. But then, if one is trying to find effective teachers, why study a convenient or random sample of teachers?

Good and Grouws (1977, 1979) brought at least three new dimensions to this research. First, they were convinced that teachers made a difference in student learning based upon their own experience in K-12 classes. They knew that some of their teachers were more motivating, challenging, and interesting than were others and they believed these teachers influenced their own learning in important ways; and they believed that it was likely that other public school students had had similar experiences. Second, they knew that teaching was not an isolated set of skills, but a system of communication that provided goals, motivation, instruction, and feedback to students. Thus they believed that previous studies of isolated behavior needed to be explored as a system. Third, on the basis of experimental work in mathematics education, they knew that both meaning and practice review were important lesson components.

In building an observation system, these researchers built programmatically upon research that had previously related instructional behavior to student achievement (Kounin, 1970; Pidgeon, 1970, Rosenshine & Furst, 1973). Four types of observational measures were collected. First, descriptions of how mathematical instructional time were collected, as well as, the ratio of time spent in developing mathematical ideas versus practice. Second, low inference measures were collected to describe interactions with individual students using the Brophy-Good Dyadic System (1970). Third, high inference variables were drawn from the work of Emmer (1973) (which in part was based upon the research of Rosenshine and Furst, 1973) and various observational systems (e.g., Kounin, 1970). Fourth, various checklists were used to describe classroom materials and homework assignments. After the system was developed, observers were trained to code target variables reliably, and they did not know if the teachers were more or less effective when they made classroom observations. For complete details of the observational procedures and extended discussion of the rationale and findings, see Good and Grouws (1975, 1977). Teachers were observed on several occasions and analyses of data collected during these observations provided a number of positive correlations between instructional behavior and student achievement that consistently differed between the two groups of teachers. In general, this work confirmed previous research that had been conducted under various conditions. What was notable about the study was that the research was conducted during regular classes (teachers were not teaching special units) and that teachers were observed teaching multiple lessons.

The findings of how relative effective and ineffective teachers taught mathematics are presented in Appendix 3.1. Both groups of teachers taught mathematics using whole-class procedures. And, as Good and Grouws (1977) noted, teaching the class as a whole is not a poor or good strategy categorically. "If the teacher possesses certain capabilities, it may be an excellent strategy; if not, the whole class instructional mode may not work well" (p. 52). The researchers noted that effective teachers introduced and explained material more fully and clearly than did less effective teachers. And more effective teachers presented students with a clear focus of what was to be learned and provided feedback and structure as appropriate. Good and Grouws commented upon two other patterns that differentiated the two groups of teachers. First, more effective teachers communicated higher performance expectations, assigned more homework, and covered more of the curriculum (a faster pace) than did less effective teachers. The second pattern of effectiveness was the provision of opportunities to students for immediate and non-evaluative feedback.

Experimental Study

These correlational results were interesting and potentially important, but because they were only correlational data many other possibilities might explain the differences in student achievement. For example, perhaps the more effective teachers were more knowledgeable about mathematics or spent more time planning for instruction and reflecting on student performance in class or on exams. Good and Grouws (1979) then developed a teacher training program that articulated the system of instruction (see Table 3.4) that was derived from their correlational study and provided teachers with detailed examples of key variables such as development, controlled practiced, distributed review, and so forth. Their previous findings were summarized in a 45-page manual, and this manual, along with two 90-minute in-service workshops, composed the treatment that provided teachers with information about previous research and

TABLE 3.4 Missouri Mathematics Effectiveness Project

Summary of Key Instructional Behaviors
Daily Review (first 8 minutes except Mondays)
  a. Review the concepts and skills associated with the homework
  b. Collect and deal with homework assignments
  c. Ask several mental computation exercises
Development (about 20 minutes)
  a. Briefly focus on prerequisite skills and concepts
  b. Focus on meaning and promoting student understanding by using lively
     explanations, demonstrations, process explanation, illustrations, etc.
  c. Assess student comprehension
     1. Using process/product questions (active interaction)
     2. Using controlled practice
  d. Repeat and elaborate on the meaning portion as necessary
Seatwork (about 15 minutes)
  a. Provide uninterrupted successful practice
  b. Momentum—keep the ball rolling—get everyone involved, then sustain
     involvement
  c. Alerting—let students know their work will be checked at end of period
  d. Accountability—check the students' work
Homework Assignment
  a. Assign on a regular basis at the end of each math class except Fridays
  b. Should involve about 15 minutes of work to be done at home
  c. Should include one or two review problems
Special Reviews
  a. Weekly review/maintenance
     1. Conduct during the first 20 minutes each Monday
     2. Focus on skills and concepts covered during the previous week
  b. Monthly review/maintenance
     1. Conduct every fourth Monday
     2. Focus on skills and concepts covered since the last monthly review

suggested ways of teaching. Good and Grouws in summarizing the key aspects of their treatment noted the importance of:

1. The program is a system of instruction.
2. Instructional activity is initiated, discussed, and reviewed in the context of meaning.
3. Students are prepared for each lesson stage in order to enhance student involvement and to minimize student errors.
4. The principles of distributed and successful practice are built into the program.
5. Active teaching presentations and explanations are emphasized.

The sample for the Good and Grouws (1979) experimental study involved 40 classrooms and teachers from 27 schools. At an initial workshop all 40 teachers were told that the program was largely based upon an earlier study of relative effective and ineffective fourth-grade mathematics teachers. The researchers indicated that they thought the program would lead to better achievement, but they noted that the present project was a test of those ideas. After a brief introduction, the teachers (and their principals) were divided into two groups (treatment and control) using schools as the unit for random assignment. Control teachers were told that they would not get the details of the instructional program until later in the year, and were informed that this information might be especially useful to them as they would get information not only about the program but also about their own classroom behavior. Control teachers were told that their role in the project was to instruct students as they had done in the past. Treatment teachers were given the manuals and in-service training describing the rationale for the instructional program. After the workshops were completed, observers collected data in both control and treatment classrooms.

The results indicated that treatment teachers generally implemented the program. Also control teachers implemented some of the programs, as would be expected, because the treatment was derived from what teachers did in classroom instruction. These results appear in Appendix 3.2, and, as can be seen, treatment teachers consistently implemented more of the program than did control teachers. The program effects on student achievement were very large. Although the experimental teachers started the project with lower student achievement than did control teachers, the raw gain score of students' in the experimental teachers' classes was much higher on the SRA achievement test than for control teachers two and a half months after the treatment was administered. These results appear in Table 3.5.

It is beyond our purpose to discuss details of this research program further. Interested readers can obtain detailed descriptions elsewhere (Brophy & Good, 1986; Good & Brophy, 2008; Good, Grouws, & Ebmeier, 1983). However, a few summarizing points merit consideration. First, this program of research

TABLE 3.5 Missouri Mathematics Effectiveness Project

Preproject and Postproject Means and Standard Deviations for Experimental and Control Classes on the SRA Mathematics Achievement Test[*]

Group	Preproject Data			Postproject Data			Pre-Post Gain		
	Raw Score	Grade Equivalent	Percentile	Raw Score	Grade Equivalent	Percentile	Raw score	Grade Equivalent	Percentile
				All treatment and all control teachers					
Experimental									
M	11.94	3.34	26.57	19.95	4.55	57.58	8.01	1.21	31.01
SD	3.18	.51	13.30	4.66	.67	18.07			
Control									
M	12.84	3.48	29.80	17.74	4.22	48.81	4.90	.74	19.01
SD	3.12	.48	12.43	4.76	.68	17.45			

[*] This table is reprinted from Good and Grouws (1979).

provided compelling data that instruction could be linked to student achievement in actual classrooms. Second, the study provided clear evidence that correlational information about effective teaching could be shared with other teachers in ways that improved their ability to influence student learning in an experimental study. This provided strong evidence that these teacher behaviors provided a direct impact on student learning. Third, Good and Grouws (1977, 1979) demonstrated that the guidelines provided earlier by Good et al. (1975) could be used to identify effective teachers; and, fourth, this successful demonstration suggested that these guidelines might be useful in identifying teachers who were effective in achieving other student outcomes (e.g., written compositions).

Although these main findings received considerable attention for the reasons we noted earlier, subsequent research qualified these results in important ways. Consistent with the guidelines suggested by Good et al. (1975), Ebmeier (1978), and Ebmeier and Good (1979) explored various beliefs and values that teachers and students held about mathematics and formed teacher and student typologies. An analysis of achievement results with these typologies indicated that the treatment program benefited some combinations of teachers and students more than others. Importantly, this finding qualifies the Good and Grouws (1979) experimental study as it suggests that modifications in this instructional program might have important benefits for student learning. Although the effects of the treatment were generally positive, it was clear that teachers and students beliefs, cognitions, and preferences mediated the instructional behavior in some ways.

Despite these promising results, the investigators noted the limitations of their research both at the time they completed it and subsequently. For example, Good (2011) wrote about the value/limitations of this program.

> There is nothing shabby about this—it provided a clear illustration that teachers affect student achievement. But can this format be improved? Most likely it can be. Could a different format be as effective? Most likely it could. Can the MMP format be used in the ninth grade or in social studies classes? These are good research questions. The MMP study was based on an intervention with teachers—is it likely that a treatment centered on curriculum or students could be as effective? Yes, most likely it could.
>
> *(p. 12)*

This research was a solid beginning that linked instructional behavior and student achievement—but far from a finished story. Alas and alack, the story essentially ended there. As we saw in Chapter 2, reformers often abandoned one reform for another, and then another. In this case as well, classroom researchers largely abandoned the process-product research approach. The field of research on teaching moved on to new questions and new opportunities. In moving on, the field generally dismissed these findings such that the new research was literally that—*new*. Aspects of the process-product research tradition were not a part of what followed.

Lack of Programmatic Research in Research on Teaching

As noted, in the 1970s and 80s a considerable amount of research was generated exploring the relationship between instructional behavior and student achievement as measured by standardized achievement tests. Oddly, despite these gains, the field abruptly headed in a new direction and after a few years changed direction again, then again, and so forth. The change in focus among the research community was not absolute. For example, Floden (2001) noted that some large process-product research continued, however the reduction in large scale quantitative research in classrooms declined dramatically after 1986, and in the ensuing years, until very recently when it emerged with new energy and resources—more on this later.

The movement to new areas was due to many reasons and there was no single compelling reason. Among the possible reasons for the decline of large-scale research in the 1980s was the fact that, comparatively, educational funding for these studies was very expensive. Further, the number of researchers involved in this area of inquiry was very small in part because this research required outside funding and advanced expertise in methodology research and measurement (or the ability to pay consultants for this expertise). Many teacher educators, at the time, did not possess large funding or access to methodological resources/expertise, but nonetheless. wanted to voice their insights about research on teaching, hence new directions provided a large number of individuals with opportunities to initiate different research traditions. Further, there were some, if not many teacher educators at the time who felt that process-product representations of teaching were narrow and failed to represent fairly the complexity of what teachers needed to do in the classroom.

So process-product research was abandoned for various reasons including differences in how teaching and learning were conceptualized, shifting research proclivities by government and foundation agencies and politics. As shown in Table 3.6, the rejection of process-product research summarily was not an isolated event in the history of classroom research. Many traditions have been rejected (including teacher personality, teacher behavior, and more recently student understanding), and some many years later have been embraced anew (teacher behavior). This table provides a brief overview of work undertaken between 1960 and 1995.

As shown in Table 3.6, prior to the process-study era, there had been considerable emphasis upon teacher characteristics including teachers' knowledge of subject matter, teachers' personality (open minded, nondogmatic), and teaching experience. See Getzels and Jackson (1963) and Ryans (1960), for example,

TABLE 3.6 Observational and Interview Research Classrooms: 1960–1995*

1. Teacher Personality
   a. General teacher characteristics (Getzels & Jackson, 1963; Ryans, 1960)
   b. Classroom interaction and climate (Amidon & Flanders, 1961; Flanders, 1965)
2. Program Implementation (Gallagher, 1970; Taba, Levine, & Elzey, 1964)
3. Classroom Ecology and Classroom Teaching
   a. Teacher expectations (Brophy & Good, 1970, 1986; Rosenthal & Jacobson, 1968)
   b. Teachers and classroom cultures (Barker, 1968; Dreeeben, 1973; Jackson,1968; Philips, 1983; Smith & Geoffrey, 1968)
4. Teacher Behavior
   a. Specific behaviors, such as clarity, enthusiasm, questioning, and so on (Gage, 1963; Rosenshine & Furst, 1973; Wright and Nuthall, 1970)
   b. Management behavior toward the whole class (Gump, 1960; Kounin, 1970)
   c. Wait time (Rowe, 1969)
   d. Process-product, naturalistic (Brophy, 1973; Brophy & Good, 1986, Dunkin & Biddle, 1974; Gage, 1963)
   e. Time and academic learning time research (Berliner, 1979; Bloom, 1980; Carroll, 1963, 1993)
   f. Process-product, experimental (Clark et al., 1979; Evertson, Anderson, Anderson, & Brophy, 1980; Good & Grouws, 1979)
   g. Instructional pace content coverage (Barr & Dreeben, 1983; Freeman & Porter, 1989; Lundgren, 1972)
5. Subject Matter Research (e.g., Stodolsky, 1988)
6. Teacher Cognition Research
   a. Teacher expectations (Good & Brophy, 2008)
   b. Teacher decision making, planning (Borko, Cone, Russo, & Shavelson, 1979; Borko & Shavelson, 1983; Clark & Peterson, 1986; Shavelson, 1976, 1983)
   c. Teaching as task engineering (Doyle, 1979, 1983)
   d. Student grouping as task engineering (Slavin, 1980)
   e. Teachers' conceptions of lessons (Leinhardt & Putnam, 1987)
   f. Teacher conceptions of subject matter (Shulman, 1986, 1987)
   g. Teacher progress; Novices to expert (Berliner, 1992)
   h. Teacher responsibility, morality, ethics (Jackson, Boostrom, & Hansen, 1993; Noddings, 1984; Oser, 1994; Philips, 1983; Shulman, 1992; Tom, 1984)
7. Student Mediation
   a. Student social cognition (Blumenfeld, Hamilton, Bossert, Wessels, & Meece, 1983; Marx, 1983; Rohrkemper & Corno, 1988; Rosenholtz & Simpson, 1984; Weinstein, 1983)
   b. Student leaning in small groups (Cohen, 1994; Webb, 1983)
   c. Student task literature (Alton-Lee, Nuthall, & Patrick, 1993; Anderson, 1981; Blumenfeld, 1992; Leinhardt & Putnam, 1987; Mergendoller, Marchman, Mitman, & Packer, 1988; Winne & Marx, 1982)
   d. Student passivity (Good, Slavings, Harel, & Emerson, 1987; Goodlad, 1984; Newman & Goldin, 1990; Sizer, 1984)
   e. Students' self-regulated learning (Corno & Mandinach, 1983; Pressley & Levine, 1983; Zimmerman & Schunk, 1989)
   f. Teaching for understanding (Blumenfeld, 1992; Newmann, 1992)
   g. Student volition (Corno, 1992, 1993; Snow, Corno, & Jackson, in press)
   h. Goal co-regulation (McCaslin & Good, in press a, in press b)
8. An Emerging Paradigm; Teaching for Student Understanding (e.g., Bluemenfeld & Marx, in press)

---

* This table is adapted from Good (1996)

for reviews of this. However, this literature failed to provide any consistent relationship between teacher characteristics, classroom teaching, and student outcomes. But as noted, some of the researchers who were advancing the study of general teaching process also suggested that context would sharply limit the generality of teaching effects (Dunkin & Biddle, 1974; Rosenshine & Furst, 1973). And, as can be seen in Figure 3.1 from Dunkin & Biddle (1974), classrooms are complex and many pathways merit examination.

Teacher Thinking—Teacher Beliefs—Teacher Cognition

When the process-product research tradition was at its apogee, some researchers began to explore teacher cognitions and teacher beliefs. This paradigm has been called various things, perhaps the most consistent label has been "teacher thinking." The important aspect of this movement was that many classroom researchers rejected an image of teaching based upon instructional behavior. After all, teachers thought, felt, and processed information. From this perspective, teaching variables like pace, controlled practice, and alerting, seem rather pedestrian, in contrast to a view that teaching was a complex cognitive activity based on thought, analysis, and other forms of thinking.

Clark and Peterson (1986) wrote a comprehensive review of this literature:

> The thinking, planning, and decision making of teachers constitute a large part of the psychological context of teaching. It is within this context that curriculum is interpreted and acted upon; where teachers teach and students learn. Teacher behavior is substantially influenced and even determined by teachers' thought processes.
>
> *(p. 255)*

Later, in their chapter, Clark and Peterson (1986) noted that "Much research on teaching has been devoted to identifying the behaviors of effective teachers with the intent of using the findings to increase teachers' effectiveness. [See, for example, Brophy & Good, this volume; Dunkin & Biddle, 1974; Peterson & Walberg, 1979.] Thus, one might ask the question, 'What kinds of interactive decision making do effective teachers engage in?' or 'What constitutes effective interactive decision making by a teacher?' although, as we shall see, little empirical research has been directed toward answering these questions, several researchers have attempted to conceptualize the interactive decision making of an effective teacher" (p. 278).

Clearly, teachers think and make decisions in the classroom, and the exploration of teacher cognition seemed a logical and useful extension of research on what teachers do. However, despite the rich research on instructional behavior and achievement, this new research on teacher thinking preceded in a different and largely unrelated direction. For example, given earlier research showing that some teachers influenced student achievement more others, it might seem reasonable to ask if it is possible that those teachers who obtained higher achievement thought differently about teaching, classrooms, or students than did less successful teachers. Even Clark and Peterson (1986) acknowledged that logically it made sense to relate the emerging teacher thinking tradition to the earlier process-product paradigm. Yet, the research they reviewed, and the research that followed generally made no attempt to establish a relationship between teaching behavior and teacher thinking.

The teacher thinking literature not only ignored process-product research but also rejected research in the teacher expectation tradition and in the classroom management tradition. For example, research on teacher expectations, which was highly visible and controversial in the late 1960s and a research tradition that carried on into the 1980s and beyond (e.g., Cooper & Good, 1983; Rosenthal & Jacobson, 1968; Weinstein, 2002) would have seemed a natural topic of inquiry for those interested in teacher thinking. For example, do teachers who sharply differentiate in the behavior toward students they believed to be high or low achieving, also differ in their conception of equality, student potential and/or other philosophical dimension that could be brought to bear on issues of classroom learning?

Along the same lines, as noted earlier, Kounin (1970) had radically changed conceptions of appropriate classroom management. Given Kounin's seminal work most educational researchers thought about proactive management (how to prevent misbehavior and to involve students meaningfully in assigned work). For example, it might have been instructive to explore more explicitly how those teachers who exhibited proactive behavior thought about issues such as student involvement and learning. Yet, these potentially interesting linkages were not explored.

One research tradition within the teacher thinking paradigm focused upon how teachers planned for instruction. This research focused primarily on teacher interviews and think aloud protocols. Although this and related research traditions raised some interesting questions and provided rich data, the overall value of this research was limited due to small sample sizes and the teachers studied were chosen primarily because they were available. Hence, we do not know what these teachers were representative of or how typical their thinking was. Further, this literature was not productive in linking teacher thinking research to teacher behavior research and provided no linkage to student achievement.

Clearly researchers in the teacher thinking tradition had every right to pursue their conceptions of good research. However, the decision to pursue a notably different issue was not consistent with a programmatic orientation. Second, the decision not to study standardized measures of achievement largely rendered the work as of no value to policy makers.

Subject Matter Context

At about the same time teacher thinking research was reaching its peak, subject matter research became popular. It was not entirely clear why subject matter was chosen to follow the teacher thinking paradigm. After all, many other contexts also merited study. For example, might student age be at least an interesting research topic as subject matter? Is it possible that students who were preoperational in their thinking might have different instructional needs than students functioning at the level of formal operations? Might students who identify with teachers more than peers benefit from different instruction than those students who are more consumed with peers and/or social networking? We believe that subject matter captured research attention largely because most teacher educators were considerably more oriented to subject matter considerations than to psychological, developmental, or organizational variables. This is not to suggest that subject matter research was unimportant, as indeed, it was extremely important. Our point here is that although important, other context variables could just as easily have been studied and, to note that programmatic concerns were not a prevalent consideration in selecting the new direction.

Thus, many researchers felt, and understandably so, that teaching needed to be studied within the context of subject matter. One line of research that commanded considerable attention was the work by Susan Stodolsky (1988; Graybeal & Stodolsky, 1985). Stodolsky believed that teachers would teach subjects differently because subject matter shapes knowledge itself, the structures of subject matter disciplines vary, and because of potentially different instructional goals in teaching these subjects. She wrote an important book that provided new information about an interesting issue. She focused on subject matter teaching in elementary schools, compared mathematics and social studies classrooms, and remarked upon the importance that subject matter had on classroom activities: "This book demonstrates that what is being taught profoundly shapes instructional activity" (p. 1). "A major finding of this research is that individual teachers varied instructional arrangements as a function of the subject they teach" (p. 131).

Although there were many good reasons to study subject matter (then and now) and how it influenced teaching and learning, it was unclear as to why the guidelines provided by Good et al. (1975) were not used as part of this new research tradition. For example, Good and colleagues argued for the advantages of using purposeful samples of teachers who were distinguished either because of some process or some outcome that they had achieved. That is, they argued that random samples of teachers were unlikely to contain more and less effective teachers (no matter what the affective or cognitive measure was) because of restricted variation in teachers' actions or effects. Obviously, this was only their opinion, but an opinion that was grounded in awareness of much history on the study of teaching.

Stodolsky's (1988) sample involved volunteer teachers and included 20 math classes and 19 social studies classes. She primarily emphasized findings from the study of 15 teachers who taught both math and social studies. In each class she selected eight students at random for observation (however, in some classes the poor response rate was so low that virtually all children were selected). Hence, we can see that the sample was one of convenience, and, clearly, those teachers studied were not selected for any purposeful reason (i.e., because the teachers possessed high levels of subject matter knowledge, had distinguished impact on student achievement, or who had students that were highly engaged during instruction). Further, this sample was not a random sample, and there is no way to determine the extent to which these teachers were representative of any other group of teachers.

Stodolsky (1988) reported that the average student involvement in mathematics classes and math achievement test scores correlated (.62), but reported that there was no correlation in social studies classes between reading test performance and average involvement. (Unfortunately, there was no detailed discussion of the achievement test used.) Finally, of the 15 teachers who taught the same students in both mathematics and social studies, 10 teachers taught these subjects differently and five taught both subjects basically the same way. These are interesting differences and point to the fact that subject matter data added to an ability to understand classrooms, but they did not suggest the utility of abandoning the study of general teaching behaviors that cut across subject matter.

Given the inroads garnered in relating general teaching behaviors to student achievement, it would have seemed logical and important to study subject matter teaching in terms of its impact on student achievement. Social studies teachers not only taught differently than did mathematics teachers, but also had different styles of teaching social studies (or math) and had more or less impact on students' learning of social studies (or math) content or in students' attitudes about the value and importance of learning this material.

Some social studies and mathematics teachers taught similarly, but others did not. And, given that only 15 teachers were included in the study, and that it was unclear what these teachers were representative of, it was not clear if there were consistent differences in how teachers generally taught social studies and mathematics. In addition to the small and undistinguished sample, the newness of the approach (observing teachers during social studies instruction) seemed to narrowly, and unprofitably, focus research attention only on the differences observed when teachers taught social studies and mathematics. Stodolsky's (1988) data showed that there were differences in how teachers taught subject matter, and she primarily discussed extensively these subject matter differences. She concluded that mathematics teachers taught more consistently alike than did social studies teachers and that instruction in mathematics was typically teacher centered. She noted that social studies teachers included more diversity and used more small group work, project activities, student reports, and other strategies that allowed for more student control of instruction. Further, student involvement rates varied notably in social studies and mathematics classes even when taught by the same teacher. She concluded, "A surprising result was that the average involvement level of students in the teacher's math class and the same teacher's social studies class were completely uncorrelated" (p. 74).

Given the high correlation between student involvement in math classes and student achievement (.62), it would have been instructive to have explained how math teachers that had high involvement differ from those who did not.[1] Were the math teachers who obtained higher involvement in math more likely to change their methods when teaching social studies or not? Were teachers with higher achieving students or with more involved students more likely to use Kounin (1970) variables well or not?[2] Clearly, the movement to a subject matter paradigm successfully resisted any impulse to relate the "new" to previous research conditions.

The findings can also be criticized on several grounds. For example, decisions about use of non-teacher-centered methods reported by Stodolsky (1988) may be due to factors other than inherent subject matter differences. A belief in the need for variety may have motivated some teachers to vary instruction of style. Or perceived physical needs of students may have led teachers to use variety—perhaps because they thought students' attention spans were shorter later in the day when social studies was taught. Still we grant that some of the findings reported are likely subject matter differences, but there are rival hypotheses that merit consideration. There is no explanation of how these teachers were classified as "same or different" nor is there any discussion of how student involvement rates varied in "same vs. different" teachers' classrooms.

Research on subject matter took other forms as well. Perhaps the most salient example was that provided by Shulman (1987), where he wrote about pedagogical content knowledge. This was an important distinction as earlier researchers had studied teachers' content knowledge (Can they pass a test on ratios?), but Shulman's argument focused not on knowledge (e.g., of ratios), but on knowledge of how to teach that content meaningfully to their students. This was exciting and potentially important for at least two reasons. First, the existing literature linking teacher content knowledge to student achievement and very weak relationships, if any, were typically found between teacher content knowledge and student achievement. Second, this new paradigm might help to explain this weak relationship. After all, most researchers (as well as citizens) had long known from their personal experiences that smart teachers were not always successful in the classroom and that good teaching involved more than content knowledge. Thus, Shulman's concept resonated favorably with teacher educators (most of whom had a background in teaching some subject matter).

It is beyond our purpose here to review this literature, but we direct the reader to Good & Brophy (2008), and their chapter describing teachers' subject matter specific knowledge and its effects on students. In brief, unfortunately, this literature has little relevancy to policy maker's current concerns that are focused on raising student achievement as by and large this research tradition ignored considerations of teacher effects on students' achievement as measured by standardized tests. Again, this illustrates the non-programmatic effects of the research on the teaching field.

As noted earlier in reviewing Stodolsky's (1988) work, the focus on subject matter was exclusive. The same argument applies to Shulman's (1987) work on pedagogical content knowledge. Although it is perfectly reasonable to assume that teachers may possess some information about how to teach content that uniquely comes from their content knowledge, it seems equally true that teachers' knowledge of students as learners, their understanding of motivation, and indeed their understanding of the broader society, may also enable them to more effectively teach subject matter concepts. For example, consider the teaching of a math concept such as percents. How might teachers make this meaningful? For example, in asking students to name their most popular song, favorite Web site, baseball player, type of phone, and so forth. In involving students in such activities and asking them to make graphs and to share their knowledge with the class and to see if females and males have different preferences and if their preferences are similar to national surveys (that the teacher directs students to find on the Internet), is this not psychological pedagogical knowledge that is useful in involving students in constructing and applying information about percents? This is not to suggest that pedagogical content knowledge has not generated useful information as the study of misconceptions has yielded abundant and rich insights about how students struggle with unique subject matter content and has provided strategies for helping teachers to address these misconceptions. Our arguments here may appear a bit strident; however, the topic we address here is the general evaluation of teachers and we feel that teacher educators have often paid too little attention to the aspects of instruction that cut across subject matter.

In describing research since the mid-1980s that ignored process-product research, we have used two examples. Subject matter research and teacher cognition are but two of the many research of teaching paradigms that appeared and disappeared. However, it is hoped that these examples capture the spirit of research on teaching as a field. This research area has not been problematic and researchers move from topic to topic without any integration of what was learned into the new paradigm. In general the field rejects or ignores the past and confidently moves on to something new.

As we noted in Chapter 2, reform movements appear and rapidly disappear and sometimes reappear again. That is something that was popular many years earlier reemerges as something that is new and important. This is now happening with process-product research as many prominent researchers and foundations are embracing this paradigm. Once again, and for the most part, those who are supportive and involved in the new research do not realize that these issues have been addressed previously and that many efforts are simply reinventing the past.

New Knowledge

In this section, we describe that knowledge obtained in the 1980s, discarded for many years, was then *rediscovered* in the 2000s. We show that this knowledge is not new and that such claims to that effect are at best misleading. We then discuss the useful knowledge base that links teaching and student achievement, and its relationship to current efforts to evaluate teachers.

Current Pressures to Identify Effective Teachers

In the time immediately preceding and following federal law Race to the Top (RttT), there was a tremendous interest in identifying teachers who were successful in raising student achievement. In part the new interest in teacher evaluation was created by advances in methodology in separating the specific effects of teaching in a given year from the more general effects of many other variables including student aptitude, home factors, previous instruction, cohort effects and the like. The method of identifying more and less effective teachers is commonly called "value-added" (VA). VA suggests how much value a teacher adds to student achievement compared to other teachers teaching similar students under similar circumstances. Arguments abound about the adequacy and limits of the method (Berliner, in press; Harris, 2011). However, despite considerable debate, the method has gained credibility among many policy makers and some researchers. Teachers' VA effects on student achievement along with classroom observational measures of good teaching (more on this in Chapter 4) are the primary ways that teachers are evaluated currently (and sometimes sharply rewarded or punished) under RttT mandates.

Given this context, research on teaching behavior that relates classroom teaching to student achievement has become popular and valuable. After all, it seems that teacher education programs should graduate teachers who have these skills. Further, if teachers in place do not have these skills, they should obtain them, and clearly if principals or others who rate teachers and give them poor scores, should have knowledge that will help low scoring teachers to improve. Thus, this opportunity has created much interest and attention in relating observational measures to code teaching acts that influence student achievement.

All the new knowledge studies were accompanied by considerable fanfare upon their publication. For example, Michael Fullan, a noted educator and author, wrote *"Visible Learning* is a definitive book for sorting out the effectiveness of teaching strategies—a must-read for those who want to improve teaching and learning." Similarly, in the Times Educational Supplement, Hattie's book is described as one that "reveals teaching's Holy Grail." High praise indeed!

Steven Farr's book, *Teaching as Leadership* (2010), was greeted with similar enthusiasm. Kati Haycock, president, Education Trust, "from its very beginnings, Teach For America has invested more energy in understanding effective teaching than any teacher preparation program I know … With this book, they have distilled what they are learning—along with relevant research—into a guide that is at once both fabulously readable and highly practical. If I had three thumbs, they would all be pointed up."

Marian Wright Edelman, president, Children's Defense Fund, noted "… and this new book is a terrific resource that shares the valuable lessons learned from studying highly effective teachers and successful classrooms across the country."

Although we understand that statements accompanying the publication of a book are always presented with notable accolades, it is clear that these books received distinguished, if not excessive, praise. For example, it would seem that many teacher educators would take exception with Haycock's statement "… Teach for America has invested more energy in understanding effective teaching than any teaching preparation program I know."

We briefly comment upon these two books later, but first we give careful attention to the work by Strong (2011). We chose to carefully examine Strong's book because it explicitly attempted to study and link classroom observations of teaching to student achievement. Strong described four experiments that he conducted in order to describe how effective teachers performed in the classroom. In the end, he concluded that his results produced "new information" that links teaching to student learning. How did he reach this conclusion?

Experiment One. He studied fourth-grade mathematics teachers from a medium-size California school district whose value-added scores associated with students' math achievement and were consistently higher or lower compared to others teaching comparable students over the past 3 years. Then, he randomly selected teachers from high- and low-effective groups and obtained their approval for participation.

Subsequently, he contacted 10 volunteer teachers, and these 10—all White females—agreed to be filmed. One teacher withdrew from the study, and the quality of the video tapes was of insufficient quality to be used in two classrooms. Thus, the final sample was seven classroom teachers.

Classroom lessons were videotaped, and 2-minute segments were selected from the seven lessons "using a commercial computer digital editing program" (Strong, 2011, p. 92). Each video segment depicted the teacher presenting part of a lesson on fractions to the whole class (generally, the first two consecutive minutes at the beginning of the lesson). The tapes were then viewed by 100 judges drawn from various backgrounds including school administrators, math educators, undergraduate students taking education courses, elementary school students, and adults that were unconnected to any educational role. The findings showed that the judges could not successfully identify those teachers who had obtained high, and those who had obtained low student achievement. The correlational agreement across judges was low (.24). Further, there was no relationship between type of judge and accuracy of judgment. Strong concluded "there appeared to be no benefit from expertise in education, since the elementary school children had the best accuracy record (about equal to chance). Whatever was driving the systematic nature of the judgments and the inaccuracy, it was something to which educational experts were not immune" (p. 93).

Experiment Two.   Strong (2011) provided six explanations to explain the poor results: biased VAM scores; too small a contrast in student achievement between more and less capable teachers; inadequately trained judges; non-representative video clips; changes in the student population; and idiosyncratic local context issues.

In order to rule out some possible explanations for why judges were inaccurate in experiment one, Strong repeated the experiment with several planned differences that included a new sample of teachers (this time teachers came from Tennessee, as opposed to California in study one), different film clips, and different judges. Twenty teachers of fourth and fifth grade were used in the experiment, and, as before, the teachers were selected on the basis of their high or low ability to influence student-achievement in mathematics consistently and the video lessons were again collected.

Despite differences in the studies, the results were highly similar to those obtained in experiment one. Indeed, the correlations for inter-judge agreement were only (.27). Even with the differences in experiment two including a more experienced and larger group of judges, different teachers who were further apart in their effects on students' achievement (in comparison to study one); and a more rigorous set of value-added calculations, the ability of judges to separate teachers into high and low groups was not improved.

Experiment Three.   The third experiment varied yet other study aspects utilized in the first two experiments. The major changes in this study were that judges were fully trained, they used an established observational protocol, and they viewed full-length videos of teaching. This study was conducted in collaboration with researchers at the University of Virginia, Center for the Advanced Study of Teaching and Learning. There, trained observers used the CLASS observational instrument (Pianta, La Paro, & Hamre, 2008) and coded eleven aspects of classroom climate and interactions within three broad areas—emotional support, classroom organization, and instructional support. Strong noted that "to everyone's surprise, judges using the CLASS protocol correctly categorized only fifty percent of the teachers" (p. 97). Thus, trained observers using an explicit observation system on which they were well trained essentially did not produce any results better than those obtained in the first two experiments. These findings were no better than chance.

Next, the observers scored lessons of twelve teachers who were not included in experiment two. Using these teachers and eight teachers coded in experiment three, the researchers found that a small subset of observational items accurately and consistently identified teachers who were more and less effective. Interestingly, these items were all from the instructional domain on the CLASS. Thus, items related to classroom organization and classroom emotional support were not related to teaching effectiveness.

Experiment Four.   In experiment four, the researchers used the new instrument (those that had been related to teacher effectiveness in the follow-up activities after experiment three) and called this instrument the Rapid Assessment of Teacher Effectiveness (RATE). The RATE consisted of 11 items—all related to instruction—and eight items of these appear in Table 3.7.

Given the present interest in identifying effective teachers, these results hold considerable potential, if they can be replicated in new research. However, we have some reservations about the system. Although the RATE may appear attractive to policy makers, its orientation toward teacher evaluation is counterproductive to us, if not, simplistic. Strong (2011) incorrectly assumes that these eight instructional behaviors are predictive of teacher effectiveness as a summary across behaviors. This logic seems inadequate, as, in our opinion, the absence of some of these behaviors would render teaching less effective if

TABLE 3.7 The RATE Instrument: Those Eight Items Used in Experiment Four*

1.	*Lesson Objective*—express verbally or visually, students are conscious of the goal(s) and are able to explain the purpose of the activity in which they are engaged.
2.	*Student Background*—teacher demonstrated knowledge of where students are in the instructional process, relates current concepts to previously mastered material and students are told to reach the learning objective in a way that conveys confidence and support.
3.	*Multiple Examples*—teacher provides/elicits from students multiple examples of the math concept being presented.
4.	*Pace*—neither too slow nor too fast.
5.	*Process*—teacher feedback is more than just correctness; the teacher explores the thinking behind a student's response.
6.	*Guided Practice*—meaningful and timely opportunities for students to work with the concepts that were discussed in the lessons; students provided with corrective feedback (if needed) before they work independently.
7.	*Clarity*—teachers' explanations are clear and accessible to all students.
8.	*Student Engagement*—most time is spent on task and students are engaged in content work throughout most of the lesson.

* Two of the items from the RATE system were not included because of missing data. These two were: teacher provides a variety of instructional delivery approaches and teacher uses non-examples to provide students with a clear comparison of what is and is not an exemplar.

not ineffective. For example, if a teacher receives high marks in seven of the behaviors, but is woefully unclear—this fact alone—would seemingly reduce the effectiveness of the teaching considerably. In our view, teaching is better seen as a system of communication rather a checklist of isolated behaviors.

It is also important to consider the frequency which these instructional activities should occur. We use but one example to make this point. Consider the appropriate use of *nonexamples*, one of the eight criterion behaviors recommended by Strong (2011). Consider the scoring system that he used to rate teachers in terms of their appropriate use of nonexamples:

3 = Teacher uses nonexamples or mistakes in clarifying a concept; teacher regularly provides explanation or clarification for incorrect answers
2 = Teacher does one or other element from 3
1 = Teacher rarely or never uses non-examples and rarely or never explains incorrect answers.

In examining these items, one wonders about the validity of the scoring. For example, if the teacher provides two or more examples of nonexamples, the teacher would be scored as a 3. However, if the teacher provides one example (even a very clear, stellar example), the teacher will only be scored as a 2. It seems that a teacher who provides, say, three or four examples in a very short period of time might confuse students more than a teacher who provides one very clear example. Further, consider that teachers, in this experiment, were teaching fractions. Even *if* it was the first lesson introducing fractions, it is hard to understand why the provision of multiple examples of "non-fractions" would be desirable.

We could provide additional comment on each observational item, but hopefully this one example illustrates our major objection to this scoring system. Specifically, there is no theory of instruction (formal or informal) or data that provides clear evidence that multiple examples of nonexamples are important in a given lesson and that the use of more nonexamples (especially in a very brief time period) facilitates learning.

In summary, the first three experiments illustrate that trained or untrained observers were not able to differentiate more and less successful teachers from small clips of instructional behavior, and that when given longer segments of instruction of teachers who differed more notably in their achievement effects, raters were still unreliable. Finally, even well-trained observers using a recognized instrument to code full lessons produced problematic results. Only when a subset of these items was used was it possible for observers to differentiate more and less effective math teachers.

Table 3.8 presents those instructional activities that Strong (2011) associated with student achievement. Ironically, despite the vast amount of resources and time invested in these four experiments, the results obtained are essentially identical to those obtained in the correlation data by Good and Grouws (1977)

TABLE 3.8 Effective teaching practices as reported by Strong (2011)

Lesson objective is clearly expressed to students
- Teacher understands student background and prior knowledge
- Teacher and/or students demonstrate consideration of the topic in more than one way
- Teacher provides/elicits students' multiple examples
- Teacher uses appropriate non-examples
- The pace of the lesson is not too slow or too fast
- Feedback to students is about the process—not just correctness
- Teacher uses guided practice—students practice and immediate feedback is provided
- Teacher explains the math concepts with good clarity
- Teachers are actively engaged—most time spent on task

TABLE 3.9 Effective teaching practices as reported by Good and Grouws (1979)

Teacher provides a review of material previously presented, collects homework, and asks students to engage in mental computation work
- Teacher conducts development lesson where the teacher focuses on meaning and promoting student understanding through discussion and demonstration
- Development also includes the assessment of student understanding the asking of both process and product questions and controlled practice where teachers elaborate upon the meaning as necessary
- Teacher conducts homework using appropriate pace and alerting and accountability
- Students are given 15–20 minutes of uninterrupted time for successful practice
- Seat work involves momentum—keeping the ball rolling—get everyone involved;
- Seat work also involves appropriate alerting (e.g., their work will be checked and accountability, the work is actually checked)
- Homework assignment if students have done seat work well
- Homework should include review problems

and experimental data reported by Good and Grouws in 1979. Their data are presented in Table 3.9.

Although it is useful to know that results obtained decades earlier still have application in today's classroom, it is extremely disappointing that the field of research on teaching has made but such little progress. Further, the results presented by Strong (2011) do not include some of the variables that Good and Grouws (1979) identified as being associated with student achievement in experimental work, and Strong's findings are presented in a check-list format. Thus, Strong suggest at least implicitly that effective teaching is a series of independent behaviors. Thus, a teacher is defined as high or low depending upon the frequencies with which these behaviors are presented.

Hattie (2009), Farr (2010)

Two other new knowledge sources are provided by from Hattie (2009) and Farr (2010). We will touch briefly on these as we believe our point has already been established. Providing more information here simply reiterates that the "new" knowledge is not.

Hattie makes clear what his book is not about in four statements: "It is not a book about classroom life (it does not an nuances and details of what happens in classrooms but it describes research based upon what happens in classroom); it is not a book about what cannot be influenced in schools (poverty, inadequate nutrition); it is not a book that includes qualitative studies, and it is not a book about criticism of research" (p. VIII).

Hattie's work is a synthesis of roughly 800 meta-analysis studies relating teaching to achievement and is an extensive and valuable contribution. In reviewing this research, Hattie notes that his conclusions are based on over 50,000 studies which, included many millions of students of various ages and drawn from literature throughout the world, collected in various subjects. He noted "nearly all studies in the book are based on real students in front of real teachers and real schools—and that so many of the effects are powerful is a testament that excellence is happening" (p. ix). His findings appear in Appendix 3.3. As can be seen, these findings are similar to those presented by Strong (2011) and Good and Grouws (1979).

Farr (2010) studied Teach For America teachers and primarily those who had obtained large positive effects on student achievement over consecutive years and examined how they taught differently than Teach For America teachers who had considerably less impact on student achievement. These data also appear in Appendix 3.3. It is worth noting that Farr has provided an extensive discussion of how his results were obtained. However, technical information about observers training, reliability, and other issues that are normally expected in peer-reviewed published journals are not reported. Further, data from Ripley (2010) also appear in Appendix 3.3. Her article is a non-technical account of Farr's data, and there, as can be seen, the data reported by Good and Grouws (1979), Strong (2011), and Ripley (2010) overlap considerably. These four sources provide good consensus on general teacher behaviors that consistently relate to student achievement.

What Do We Know About the Relationship Between Instruction and Student Learning?

Obviously, this is a complex topic and, depending upon how one defines learning, there are multiple things that relate to the learning of particular content and particular contexts. Having said this, however, only a few general instructional strategies transcend subject matter, age of students, and so forth, and are consistently associated with better student achievement on standardized tests. General aspects of teaching have been reviewed, in one form or another, elsewhere (Brophy, 2006; Good, in press; Good & Brophy, 2008). In considering these dimensions, two points are important. First, these relationships have been known since at least the 1980s and, second, when investigators have subsequently looked for these relationships, they have found these same links between instruction and student achievement. An overview of these important variables is presented in Table 3.10 and then a more detailed explanation of these variables follow.

TABLE 3.10 General Instructional Variables Related to Students Achievement across Subject Areas

1.   **Opportunity to learn**—what content and at what cognitive level will students address the material? Student achievement is heavily influenced by opportunity to learn.

2.   **Appropriate expectations**—which students will receive a demanding curriculum? Will teachers primarily teach the whole class or groups of students (if groups, homogeneous or heterogeneous)?

3.   **Coherent curriculum and sequence**—given the content and expectations have been established for student performance, how will the curriculum be logically sequenced?

4.   **Effective use of time**—in delivering instructions teachers are prepared to start classes promptly, plan transitions well, and focus on key ideas.

5.   **Active teaching**—teachers are active presenters, model key ideas, actively supervise students' initial work, and then encourage students to build meaningfully on teacher's initial presentations.

6.   **Balance procedural and conceptual knowledge**—teachers allow students to understand knowledge as well as applying it. Students understand key concepts at both a procedural and conceptual levels.

7.   **Proactive management**—students know what to do, how to do it, and when confused how to access help appropriately. Teachers give careful thought to keeping students involved in all stages of the lesson.

8.   **Teacher clarity/teacher enthusiasm**—teachers focus students on the precise goals and intended procedures for the lesson. Teachers express that they care about the content being presented as well as the students who study it. Enthusiasm does not need to be dramatic or excessive, but needs to be expressed in a sincere fashion.

9.   **Instructional and curriculum pace**—teachers go through the curriculum briskly, but are attentive to students' concerns and reteach content if necessary.

10.   **Teaching to mastery**—teachers focus on students' learning all material presented. Tangential material is not presented to avoid confusion about what is essential to learn.

11.   **Supportive classrooms**—teachers encourage students and are supportive of them at all times, especially when they have difficulty. Teachers encourage students to support one another and work with them to establish a "we-ness" atmosphere.

12.   **Review and feedback**—effective teachers know that students learn from distributed practice and review; hence, key ideas are revisited on occasion. Teachers give frequent feedback to students, so that students know if they have made adequate progress and how to correct difficulties if they occur.

13.   **Adequate subject matter knowledge**—teachers need adequate knowledge of the subject(s) they teach. Of course, adequate or even exceptional knowledge of subject matter will not yield good learning if teachers cannot do most of the things listed above well (and, of course, without adequate subject matter knowledge the other twelve teaching behaviors listed above will have little value).

Opportunity to Learn.   Opportunity to learn content is critically important as it frames what students can learn. Opportunity to learn refers centrally to the content that is assigned and the level of conceptualization at which it is addressed. If students are not assigned material, they cannot learn it. Although this may seem self-evident to many readers, many policy makers (and educators) ignore this important consideration. The variation in how teachers frame instruction (whether they emphasize factual knowledge, conceptual knowledge, knowing versus applying) makes it clear that student learning opportunities will vary considerably from class to class. There is a vast literature illustrating the relationship between opportunity to learn and student achievement (Berliner & Biddle, 1995; Schmidt & Maier, 2009). Readers who have not read this literature might be thinking that the statement "If students are not assigned material, they cannot learn it" is woefully simplistic. Consider however, that there has been notable ado about American students' deficiencies in achievement in comparison to students in other countries. Policy makers have lamented that our eighth-grade students do much more poorly on algebra tests than those in other countries, such as Japan. However, opportunity to learn explains this deficiency (Berliner & Biddle, 1995; Good & Braden, 2000). The difference in algebra performance can partly be explained by the fact that algebra is taught considerably earlier in the curriculum in Japan than it is in the United States. Thus it is not surprising that American students do less well on algebra tests when they have had less opportunity to learn the material.

Appropriate Expectations.   As we noted in our review of the new research, there is consistent agreement that teachers should have high expectations for students' learning. However, this popular belief is not fully supported by extant research. A better way to state this relationship is that teachers should have appropriate expectations for student learning, and it is clear that both expectations that are too high or too low can have debilitating effects on student learning. The misunderstanding about high expectations occurs because much of the research on teacher expectations (e.g., Brophy & Good, 1970; Pidgeon, 1970) emphasized that teachers often reacted to students they believed to be less capable by providing them less stimulating learning environments. However, it is also the case that if teachers have expectations that are too high, these can also impact student achievement negatively. The silliness of holding excessively high expectations can be seen in the dismal results obtained following the creation of artificially high expectations for student performance in such reform movements as Goals 2000 and No Child Left Behind.

Coherent Curriculum Sequence.   After decisions are made about the expected material that will be addressed in the course and decisions are made about the opportunity for learning that will be provided to students, teachers need to develop a coherent and logical sequence of activities. Decisions need to be made about which topics are to appear initially and why this is the case. In some subjects the curriculum may be defined defacto by the textbook available, if teachers routinely follow the textbook. However, in most cases the textbook includes more information than can be meaningfully presented and understood in a given semester or year. Effective teachers carefully order the amount of material that students have the opportunity to learn in terms of the importance of particular subject-matter outcomes. Decisions have to be made about the sequencing of materials and when various student-learning activities and exams are to occur. More successful teachers are better able to organize a coherent curriculum and to present it in ways in which students understand the structure of what is to be learned.

Effective Use of Time.   For some time, we have known that how teachers use instructional time influences achievement (Berliner, Fisher, Filby, & Marliave, 1978) because the variation in time allocation varies notably from teacher to teacher. For example, some teachers spend but a small amount of time (15 to 20 minutes) in a period teaching mathematics where other teachers regularly spend 50 minutes in teaching mathematics. Differences in allocated time were also compounded by the fact that student engagement rates varied. For example, Berliner and colleagues found that in some classrooms students were engaged about 50% of the time and in other classrooms average engagement raters were about 90%. These are big differences. These data were collected in second- and fifth-grade classrooms, but they have been replicated, including more recently in high school settings (Smith, 2000). The use of time is complex because it is compounded by other variables, including setting (seatwork vs. whole class activity) and the difficulty and appropriateness of assigned work. For example, Burnstein (1980) found that higher student achievement was associated with moderately difficult assignments. Clearly, given the need to involve the whole class in seatwork, it appears that in-class assignments can be too difficult or too easy for maintaining student involvement and eventual success. Again, we see the importance of thinking about the combined effects of different variables.

Active Teaching.   Effective teachers are active instructors, and they regularly demonstrate and explain concepts thoroughly to students. And, after presenting guided practice, they then encourage students to generate their own examples and to apply content in ways that illustrate students' understanding of content and an ability to apply material. For older students or as self-regulation abilities increase, students are encouraged to assume more responsibility for managing their own learning.

Balance Procedural and Conceptual Knowledge.   Contentious debates in American education have revolved around the role of skill and understanding in promoting appropriate learning. We have had reading debates, featuring phonics versus reading for understanding. We have moved through cycles where phonics dominates and we have moved through cycles where whole language and/or other understanding approaches have dominated. These debates have been characterized as being so extreme and polarizing that Good (1996) described them as today's answer guaranteeing tomorrow's problem. That is, when phonics dominated and achievement was insufficient (as defined by policy makers and the media), advocates moved away from phonics, but the movement was so extreme as to create a new problem and, in time, the less than desired reading achievement scores led to the return of phonics. Similar debates have occurred in mathematics in the form of practice and conceptual emphasis. We have gone through cycles of understanding mathematics (as espoused by Brownell, 1947, and more recently by the National Council of Teachers of Mathematics, 1989), and cycles where practice, structure, skills, and drill ruled the day (Schoenfeld & Pearson, 2009).

These either/or debates have been tiresome and self-defeating. For example, as Good and his colleagues (in press) suggested, who would want students who understand the concepts embedded in math problems but who cannot use the ideas in practical ways or students who can do math but do not understand what they do? In short, these either/or debates are misleading, waste resources, and should no longer be tolerated. Fortunately, some are beginning to articulate this view forcefully, including the National Mathematics Advisory Panel (2008). If students are to learn, they need to be exposed to subject matter instruction that allows them the opportunity to master content at the skill, conceptual, and application levels.

The desirability of a combined focus on understanding and procedural knowledge has been illustrated empirically. Consider the Good and Grouws (1977, 1979) studies reviewed earlier in this chapter and the conclusions reached by Hiebert and Grouws (2007), who, after reviewing a large body of studies, convincingly argued that teaching requires both an emphasis upon understanding and skill efficiency. Elsewhere, Rakes, Valentine, McGatha, and Ronau (2010) reviewed 82 studies of strategies used to improve student learning in algebra. They found that the development of conceptual understanding was associated more highly with student achievement than those classrooms that focused mainly on procedural understanding. However, in reviewing their work, it is important to understand that their point is the relative importance of conceptual knowledge, not the absence of procedural information and practice.

Proactive Management.   Earlier we reviewed Kounin's (1970) seminal research illustrating that proactive management was much more important than reactive management—good managers were distinguished by how they prevented misbehavior, not how they dealt with it. These variables associated with good classroom management included alerting, accountability, "withitness," overlapping, lesson momentum, and variety and challenge in seatwork. These variables were highly associated with high student engagement and low frequency of serious misbehavior. As noted, these data were correlational, however they have been replicated extensively in correlational and experimental work (Evertson & Weinstein, 2006). In one powerful study, Freiberg, Huzinec, and Templeton (2009) illustrated that Kounin's management principles could be taught to teachers in ways so that teachers could implement them in their own teaching and these results were associated not only with better classroom management, but also with higher achievement. It is highly likely that the appropriate use of Kounin's variables like alerting and accountability lead not only to engaged students, but they also likely allow for teachers to move through the curriculum more quickly and thus provide more opportunity for students to learn content. Note, even within the Kounin management system, variables have no independent effect on student engagement. For example, teachers who alert frequently, but who do not follow with accountability are invariably poorer managers because students quickly learn that they do not have to pay attention to the teacher alerting. Teachers who say, "Work independently for 15 minutes and we will check how you are doing before assigning homework" and who fail to follow through on such statements consistently, will soon have some students who do not actively focus on learning the material during the 15-minute period.

Teacher Clarity/Teacher Enthusiasm.   Since the research by Rosenshine and Furst (1973), researchers have consistently found a relationship between teacher clarity and student achievement. As noted earlier, no teaching behavior has independent effects on student learning, and we suspect that teacher clarity is influential, not only because it helps to focus learners' attention on what is important, but also because it saves considerable time that can be spent on classroom instruction. Teachers who repeat assignments (especially if they do so inconsistently) generate many student questions and lost opportunity for learning. And, when students become confused, they not only disengage, but they also often attract other students to off-task activities.

Teachers need to be enthusiastic about the subject that they are presenting and its importance. After all, why should students be interested in the content if teachers are not? Teachers should model not only interest in the content, but also interest in students' responses and their learning. Considerable research has shown that models (like teachers) influence others not only by what they say but also through their actions.

Instructional and Curriculum Pace.   Teachers who are associated with better achievement gains go through the curriculum somewhat more quickly than do teachers who obtain less achievement from students. However, they do so in small steps that tend to minimize student frustration and allows for students to make continuous progress. Although this is a general finding across different subjects, its generality may still be limited to some degree depending upon the particular content that is being used. In subjects that tend to be hierarchal (like math), pace may be more likely to enhance achievement than in areas such as social studies where teachers have more freedom to move through the curriculum in a non-linear fashion. The reason that curriculum pacing is a fairly good predictor of student achievement in subjects that move in a linear fashion across the curriculum is that curricula often have a great deal of redundant material (Polikoff, 2012). Hence, knowledgeable teachers can move through review material more quickly than new material.

Teaching to Mastery. Effective teachers provide ample opportunities for students both to practice and apply the material. Using the material in application situations helps to demonstrate students' mastery (or the lack thereof) so that teachers may determine whether to provide new instruction or to supplement the course of study previously provided. In general, teaching to mastery helps to convey to students that material presented in class is not just for informational purposes, and that students need to be attentive as anything presented in the class is expected to be understood fully. This is not to suggest that enrichment materials should not be used as they can be important supplements to classroom learning. However, when supplementary learning materials are used, it should be very clear to students that they are for enrichment. In some classrooms there is so much clutter with the many asides being presented ("on the other hand, this reminds me of …"), it is difficult for students to separate central material from interesting qualifying "asides."

Supportive Classrooms. Supportive classrooms can be seen through various activities and attitudes. For example, supportive teachers (following student mistakes) are not critical of students, but rather encourage students to think about and to explore the reasons for their misunderstanding. Student errors are accepted as understandable, but they need to be corrected. As we have noted, effective teachers provide a strong academic focus. However, in addition, effective teachers also create and maintain pleasant, friendly classrooms in which teachers and students provide support for one another. These findings have been captured in various ways by different researchers. For example, Berliner et al. (1978) noted that effective teachers created convivial atmospheres; McCaslin (2009) and McCaslin and Burross (2008) refer to these supportive and effective classrooms as helping students to achieve an identity built upon participation and interpersonal validation; McCaslin and Good (2008) coded this concept as we-ness; and it has been termed "emotional support" by Pianta, Belsky, Houts, Morrison, and NICHD Early Child Care Research Network (2007).

Review/Feedback. It has long been known that much material is forgotten quickly after it has been initially learned. This is particularly the case when information is not learned in a meaningful way that has personal value to a learner. Many studies have shown that distributed practice is a better way to retain knowledge than is massed practice. For example, consider high-school students preparing for an exam in American History, who are prepared to devote 3 hours to prepare for the test. Research suggests that most students would retain much more information, if they studied for six 30-minute sessions (spread out over time) than if they spent 3 hours cramming the night before the exam. Similarly, teachers who obtained good student achievement often conduct brief daily, weekly, and monthly reviews especially over key concepts.

Teachers who provide feedback are much more likely to improve student learning as that feedback allows students to identify information and concepts that they have not fully mastered. As simple as this sounds, students often—perhaps typically—receive information from teachers on their homework or quizzes that simply provides a score and little if any information about the errors in their reasoning or memory. The evidence is clear—even simple efforts to provide students with information about their performance can lead to notable gains in student achievement.

Adequate Subject-Matter Knowledge.　A great deal of research exists to suggest that teacher knowledge (even advanced knowledge) correlates but weakly with student learning. To some this is counter-intuitive as it might seem that a teacher trained in advanced mathematics would be a wonderful asset for students who are trying to learn divisions with remainders in the third grade. However, this is likely to be the case only if well-trained mathematics teachers know how students think, the types of examples that students might understand and have an ability to break complex ideas down into smaller steps. Unfortunately, many teachers who have solid knowledge of their content area do not have sufficient understanding of students and teaching in order to be effective. Having said this, some lose sight of the important fact that teachers have to have at least adequate subject-matter knowledge, if they are to teach successfully. As we have noted often in this chapter, it is the blend of skills and knowledge that allows for effective communication and learning.

Conclusion

This chapter examined the history of research on teaching. In the 1950s the field mainly studied who teachers *were* (e.g., characteristics such as personality, years of experience, and so forth). The literature on teaching is voluminous. And, as Dunkin and Biddle (1974) noted, learning from this literature has been difficult not only because of its sheer size, but also because much research was not grounded in theory or observational study, and failed to use clear criteria for defining effectiveness (such as student achievement).

Still, despite this unproductive history, researchers continued to study the link between teaching and classroom learning. Some researchers also included observational measures of teaching, and this inclusion allowed the field to move forward. In time, such research enabled Rosenshine and Furst (1973) to identify several promising links between teaching and learning.

This research refuted the long-held belief that teachers' actions had but little impact on student achievement (Good et al., 1975). As noted, social scientists generally believed that heredity and social characteristics predicted student achievement. Research in the 1960s and 70s illustrated that teachers made a difference in student achievement, but researchers at that time still noted that the effects of SES on student learning were very influential (as they remain so today).

In the mid-1970s and early 1980s researchers (in part aided by government and foundational agencies' interest and resources) started to build upon earlier correlational research, and moved into classrooms to explore more fully student learning and actual classroom studies. This research produced a clear body of research that linked instruction to student achievement in experimental as well as correlational studies.

Information describing how teachers influenced student achievement was presented, and we emphasized that these behaviors should not be seen as individual behaviors but rather as a system of teaching. These instructional behaviors have a powerful impact on student achievement and potentially have considerable value for teacher education and classroom practice.

For various reasons this research moved on to new traditions and explored different research topics including subject matter differences in teaching, the importance of teacher cognition and beliefs, and other potentially important topics. For many the focus on instructional behavior was seen as inadequate for capturing the complexity of learning in social settings. After all, teachers and students held beliefs and cognitions that merited research attention. We agree with researchers of that era that classrooms are more than a set of instructional behaviors, and we also agree, that these issues merited attention. However, we believe that the study of new variables did not require ignoring or rejecting what had been learned through observational research.

As noted, research in the 1990s proceeded with little interest in studying teacher effects on student achievement, especially using purposeful samples (where teachers were known to vary in important ways). This omission (whether correct or incorrect) rendered this research as having little value for policymakers, who were primarily (and continue to be) interested in student achievement.

Ironically, the research relating instructional behavior and student achievement (Brophy & Good, 1986; Good & Brophy, 2008) has been rediscovered in the past few years. Although this "new" knowledge illustrated that information obtained years earlier still applies to current conditions of teaching and learning, it is unfortunate that we know little more about teacher effects than we did in the 1980s. It seems that efforts, including huge resources spent in replicating this research, could have been spent in more important ways to extend this knowledge by considering other ways—and perhaps even more important ways—in which teachers might influence students' learning. Unfortunately, we know little about teacher effects that impact other important outcomes of schooling, such as problem-solving or self-expression, to mention but a couple. Still, the information we do have is important and is valuable *if* applied appropriately. We will return to a consideration of this information in a later chapter and discuss its application value for use in high-stakes evaluation activities that are now in vogue.

Notes

1 Were teachers who had higher student involvement rates, whether math or social studies more likely to be clear, enthusiastic, and warm?

2 It is odd that no comment was made about Kounin variables generally because his 1970 work is discussed by the author in highly laudatory terms in her first chapter.

References

Alton-Lee, A. G., Nuthall, G. A., & Patrick, J. (1993). Reframing classroom research: A lesson from the private world of children. *Harvard Educational Review, 63*(1), 50–84.

American Educational Research Association, Committee on the Criteria on Teacher Effectiveness. (1953). Second report of the *Journal of Educational Research, 46,* 641–658.

Amidon, E. J., & Flanders, N. A. (1961). The effect of direct and indirect teacher influence on dependent prone students learning geometry. *Journal of Educational Psychology, 52,* 286–291.

Anderson, L. (1981). Short-term student responses to classroom instruction. *Elementary School Journal, 82,* 97–108.

Aspy, D. (1973, April). *A discussion of the relationship between selected student behavior and the teacher's use of interchangeable responses.* Paper presented at the annual meeting of the American Educational Research Association, New Orleans.

Barker, R. (1968). *Ecological psychology.* Stanford, CA: Stanford University.

Barr, R., & Dreeben, R. (1983). *How schools work.* Chicago, IL: University of Chicago Press.

Barth, R. S. (1972). *Open education and the American school.* New York, NY: Agathon.

Berliner, D. (1979). Tempus educate. In P. Peterson & H. Walberg (Eds.), *Research on teaching* (pp. 120–135). Berkeley, CA: McCutchan.

Berliner, D. (1992, February). *Educational reform in an era of disinformation.* Paper presented at the annual meeting of the American Association of College for Teacher Education. San Antonio, TX.

Berliner, D. (in press). Exogenous variables and value-added assessments: A fatal flaw if value-added assessments are linked to high-stakes decisions. *Teacher College Record.*

Berliner, D., & Biddle, B. (1995). *The manufactured crisis: Myths, fraud, and the attack on America's public schools.* New York, NY: Addison-Wesley.

Berliner, D., Fisher, C., Filby, N., & Marliave, R. (1978). *Executive summary of beginning teacher evaluation study.* San Francisco, CA: Far West Laboratory.

Bloom, D. (1980). *All our children learning.* Hightstown, NJ: McGraw-Hill.

Blumenfeld, P. (1992). The task and the teacher: Enhancing student thoughtfulness in science. In J. Brophy (Ed.), *Advances in research on teaching* (Vol. 2, pp. 81–114). Greenwich, CT: JAI Press.

Blumenfeld, P. & Marx, R. (in press). Teaching for understanding. In B. Biddle, T. Good, & I. Goodson (Eds.), *The international handbook of research on teaching.* Norwell, MA: Kluwer.

Blumenfeld, P. C., Hamilton, V. L., Bossert, S., Wessels, K., & Meece, J. (1983). Teacher talk and student thought: Socialization into the student role. In J. Levine & M. Wang (Eds.), *Teacher and student perceptions: Implications for learning* (pp. 143–192). Hillsdale, NJ: Erlbaum.

Borko, H., Cone, R., Russon, N. A., Shavelson, R. J. (1979). Teachers' decision making. In P. L. Peterson & H. J. Walberg (Eds.), *Research on teaching: Concepts, findings, and implications* (pp. 136–160). Berkeley, CA: McCutchan.

Borko, H., & Shavelson, R. J. (1983). Speculators on teacher education: Recommendations from research on teachers' cognitions. *Journal of Education for Teaching, 9,* 210–214.

Brophy, J. (2006). Observational research on generic aspects of classroom teaching. In P. Alexander & P. Winne (Eds.), *Handbook of educational psychology* (pp. 755–780). Mahwah, NJ: Erlbaum.

Brophy, J., & Good, T. (1970). Brophy-Good dyadic system (teacher-child dyadic interaction). In A. Simon & E. Boyer (Eds.), *Mirrors for behavior: An anthology of observation instruments continued, 1970 supplement (Vol. A).* Philadelphia, PA: Research for Better Schools.

Brophy, J., & Good, T. (1986). Teacher behavior and student achievement. In M. Wittrock (Ed.), *Handbook of research on teaching* (3rd ed., pp. 328–375). New York, NY: Macmillan.

Brownell, W.A. (1947). The place of meaning in the teaching of elementary school arithmetic. *Elementary School Journal, 47,* 256–265.

Burnstein, L. (1980). The analysis of multilevel data in educational research and evaluation. *Review of Research in Education, 8*(1), 158–233.

Carroll, J. (1963). A model of school learning. *Teachers College Record, 64,* 723–733.

Carroll, J. (1993). Educational psychology in the 21st century. *Educational Psychologist, 28,* 89–95.

Chang, S., & Raths, J. (1971). The school's contribution to the cumulating deficit. *Journal of Educational Research, 64,* 272–276.

Clark, C., Gage, N., Marx, R., Peterson, P., Stayrook, N., & Winne, P. (1979). A factorial experiment on teacher structuring, soliciting, and reacting. *Journal of Educational Psychology, 71,* 534–552.

Clark, C., & Peterson, P. (1986) Teachers thought processes. In M. Wittrock (Ed.), *Handbook of research on teaching* (3rd ed., pp. 255–296). New York NY: Macmillan.

Cohen, E. (1994). Restructuring the classroom: Conditions for productive small groups. *Review of Educational Research, 64,* 1–35.

Coleman, J., Campbell, E. Q., Hobson, C. J., McParland, J., Mood, A. M., Weinfeld, F. D., & York, R. L. (1966). *Equality of educational opportunity.* Washington, DC: Superintendent of Documents, U.S. Government Printing Office.

Cooper, H., & Good, T. (1983). *Pygmalion grows up: Studies in the expectation communication process.* New York, NY: Longman.

Corno, L. (1992). Encouraging students to take responsibility for learning and performance. *Elementary School Journal, 93,* 69–84.

Corno, L. (1993). The best-laid plans: Modern conceptions of volition in educational research. *Educational Researcher, 22,* 14–22.

Corno, L., & Mandinach, E. B. (1983). The role of cognitive engagement in classroom learning and motivation. *Educational Psychologist, 18,* 88–108.

Dembo, M., & Jennings, L. (1973, April). *Who is the "experienced" teacher?* Paper presented at the annual meeting of the American Educational Research Association.

Doyle, W. (1979). Classroom tasks and student abilities. In P. Peterson & H. Wahlberg (Eds.), *Research on teaching: Concepts, findings, and implications* (pp. 183–209). Berkeley, CA: McCutchan.

Doyle, W. (1983). Academic work. *Review of Educational Research, 53,* 155–199.

Dreeben, R. (1973). The school as a workplace. In R. Travers (Ed.), *Second handbook of research on teaching* (pp. 450–473). Chicago, IL: Rand McNally.

Dunkin, M., & Biddle, B. (1974). *The study of teaching.* New York, NY: Holt, Rinehart and Winston.

Ebmeier, H. (1978). *An investigation of the interactive effects among student types, teacher types, and treat-*

ment types in the mathematics achievement of fourth grade students (Unpublished doctoral dissertation). University of Missouri, Columbia.

Ebmeier, H., & Good, T. L. (1979). The effects of instructing teachers about good teaching on the mathematics achievement of fourth-grade students. *American Educational Research Journal, 16*(1), 1–16.

Emmer, E. (1973). *Classroom observation scales.* Austin, TX: Research and Development Center for Teacher Education.

Evertson, C., Anderson, C., Anderson, L., & Brophy, J. (1980). Relationship between classroom behavior and student outcomes in junior high math and English classes. *American Elementary Research Journal, 17,* 43–60.

Evertson, C. M., & Green, J. L. (1986). Observation as inquiry and method. In M. C. Wittrock (Ed.), *Handbook of research on teaching* (3rd ed., pp. 162–213). New York, NY: Macmillan.

Evertson, C., & Weinstein, C. (Eds.). (2006). *Handbook of classroom management: Research, practice, and contemporary issues.* Mahwah, NJ: Erlbaum.

Farr, S. (2010). *Teaching as leadership: The highly-effective teacher's guide to closing the achievement guide.* San Francisco, CA: Jossey-Bass.

Flanders, N. (1970). *Analyzing teacher behavior.* Reading, MA: Addison-Wesley.

Floden, R. (2001). Research on effects of teaching: A continuing model for research on teaching. In Richardson (Ed.), *Handbook of research on teaching* (4th ed., pp. 3–16). Washington, DC: American Education Research Association.

Freeman, D., & Porter, A. (1989). Do textbooks dictate the content of mathematics instruction in elementary schools? *American Educational Research Journal, 26*(3), 403–421.

Freiberg, H. J., Huzinec, C. A., & Templeton, S. M. (2009). Classroom management — A pathway to student achievement: A study of fourteen inner-city elementary schools. *Elementary School Journal, 110*(1), 63–80.

Gage, N. (1963). Paradigms of research on teaching. In N. Gage (Ed.), *Handbook of research on teaching* (pp. 94–141). Chicago, IL: Rand McNally.

Gallagher, J. (1970). Three studies of the classroom. In J. Gallagher, G. Nuthall, & B. Rosenshine (Eds.), *Classroom observation.* American Educational Research Association Monography Series on Curriculum Evaluation. Monograph No. 6. Chicago, IL: Rand McNally.

Getzels, J., & Jackson, P. (1963). The teacher's personality and characteristics. In N. Gage (Ed.), *Handbook of research on teaching* (pp. 506–582). Chicago, IL: Rand McNally.

Good, T. (1996). Teaching effects and teacher evaluation. In J. Sikula, T. Buttery, & E. Guyton (Eds.), *Handbook of research on education* (pp. 617–665). New York, NY: Macmillan.

Good, T. (2011). Reflections on editing *The Elementary School Journal* in an era of constant school reform. *The Elementary School Journal, 112*(1), 1–15.

Good, T. (in press). What do we know about how teachers influence student performance on standardized tests; and why do we know so little about other student outcomes? *Teacher College Record.*

Good, T., Biddle, B., & Brophy, J. (1975). *Teachers make a difference.* New York, NY: Holt, Rinehart, & Winston.

Good, T. L., & Braden, J. S. (2000). *The great school debate: Choice, vouchers, and charters.* Mahwah, NJ: Erlbaum.

Good, T. L., & Brophy, J. (2008). *Looking in classrooms* (10th ed.). New York, NY: Pearson.

Good, T., & Grouws, D. (1975). Teacher rapport: Some stability data. *Journal of Educational Psychology, 67*(2), 179–182.

Good, T., & Grouws, D. (1977). Teaching effects: A process-product study in fourth-grade mathematics classrooms. *Journal of Teacher Education, 28*(3), 49–54.

Good, T., & Grouws, D. (1979). The Missouri mathematics effectiveness project: an experimental study in fourth-grade classrooms. *Journal of Educational Psychology, 71*(3), 355–362.

Good, T., Grouws, D., & Ebmeier, H. (1983). *Active mathematics teaching.* New York, NY: Longman.

Good, T. L., Slavings, R. L., Harel, K. H., & Emerson, M. (1987). Students' passivity: A study of question asking in K-12 classrooms. *Sociology of Education, 60,* 181–199.

Good, T. L., Wood, M., Sabers, D., Olson, A. M., Lavigne, A., Sun, H., & Kalinec Craig, C. A. (in press). Strengthening grade 3–5 students' foundational knowledge of rational numbers. *Teachers College Record, 115*(9). Retrieved from http://www.tcrecord.org/content. asp?contentid=17021

Goodlad, J. (1984). *A place called school: Prospects for the future.* New York, NY: McGraw-Hill.

Graybeal, S. S., & Stodolsky, S. S. (1985). Peer work groups in elementary schools. *American Journal of Education, 93,* 409–428.

Gump, P. (1960). Intra-setting analysis: The third-grade classroom as a special but instructive case. In E. Willems & H. Rausch (Eds.), *Naturalistic viewpoints in psychological research* (pp. 200–220). New York, NY: Holt, Rinehart and Winston.

Harris, D. N. (2011). *Value-added measures in education.* Cambridge, MA: Harvard Education Press.

Hattie, J. (2009). *Visible learning: A synthesis of over 800 meta-analyses relating to achievement.* New York, NY: Routledge.

Hiebert, J., & Grouws, D.A. (2007). The effects of classroom mathematics teaching on students' learning. In F. K. Lester (Ed.), *Second handbook of research on mathematics teaching and learning* (pp. 371–404). Greenwich, CT: Information Age.

Jackson, P. (1968). *Life in classrooms.* New York, NY: Holt.

Jackson, P. W., Boostrom, R. E., & Hansen, D. T. (1993). *The moral life of schools.* San Francisco, CA: Jossey-Bass.

Jencks, C., Smith, M., Acland, H., Bane, M. J., Cohen, D., Gintis, H., … Michelson, S. (1972). *Inequality: A reassessment of the effect of family and schooling in America.* New York, NY: Basic Books.

Jensen, A. (1969). How much can we boost IQ and scholastic achievement? *Harvard Educational Review, 39,* 1–123.

Kleinfeld, J. (1972). *Instructional style and the intellectual performance of Indian and Eskimo students.* Final Report, Project No. 1-J-027, Washington, DC: Office of Education, U.S. Department of Health, Education, and Welfare.

Kounin, J. (1970). *Discipline and group management in classrooms.* New York, NY: Holt, Rinehart and Winston.

Leinhardt, G., & Putnam, R. T. (1987). The skill of learning from classroom lessons. *American Educational Research Journal, 24*(4), 557–587.

Lundgren, U. (1972). *Frame factors and the teaching process: A contribution to curriculum theory and theory on teaching.* Stockholm, Sweden: Almqvist and Wiksell.

Marx, R. (1983). Student perceptions in classrooms. *Educational Psychologist, 18,* 145–165.

McCaslin, M. (2009). Co-regulation of student motivation and emergent identity. *Educational Psychologist, 44*(2), 137–146.

McCaslin, M., & Good, T. (Eds.). (2008). Special Issue: School Reform Matters. *Teachers College Record, 110*(11).

McCaslin, M., & Good, T. (in press, a). *The handbook of educational psychology.* New York, NY: Macmillian.

McCaslin, M., & Good, T. (in press, b). *Listening in classrooms.* New York, NY: HarperCollins.

McCaslin, M., & Burross, H. L. (2008). Student motivational dynamics. In M. McCaslin & T. L. Good (Eds.), *Teachers College Record, Special Issue: School Reform Matters, 110*(11), 2452–2463.

Medley, D. M., & Mitzel, H. E. (1963). The scientific study of teacher behavior. In A. A. Bellack (Ed.), *Theory and research in teaching.* New York, NY: Bureau of Publications, Teachers College, Columbia University.

Mergendoller, J. R., Marchman, V. A., Mitman, A. L., & Packer, M. J. (1988). Task demands and accountability in middle-grade science classes. *Elementary School Journal, 88,* 251–265.

Moody, W., & Bausell, R. (1971, April). *The effect of teacher experience on student achievement, transfer and retention.* Paper presented at the annual meeting of the American Educational Research Association, New Orleans.

Moody, A., & Bausell, R. (1973, April). *The effect of relevant teaching practice on the elicitation of student achievement.* Paper presented at the annual meeting of the American Educational Research Association, New Orleans.

National Council of Teachers of Mathematics. (1989). *Curriculum and evaluation standards for school mathematics.* Reston, VA: NCTM.

National Mathematics Advisory Panel. (2008). *Foundations for success: The final report of the National Mathematics Advisory Panel.* Washington, DC: U.S. Department of Education.

Newmann, F. (Ed.). (1992). *Student engagement and achievement in American secondary schools.* New York, NY: Teachers College Press.

Newman, R. S., & Goldin, L. (1990). Children's reluctance to seek help with schoolwork. *Journal of Educational Psychology, 82,* 92–100.

Noddings, N. (1984). *Caring: A feminine approach to ethics and moral education.* Berkeley: University of California Press.

Nuthall, G. A. (1968). An experimental comparison of alternative strategies for teaching concepts. *American Educational Research Journal, 5*(4), 561–584.

Oser, F. (1994). Moral perspectives on teaching. In L. Darling-Hammond (Ed.), *Review of research in education* (Vol. 20, pp. 57–128). Washington, DC: American Educational Research Association.

Peterson, P., & Walberg, H. (Eds.). (1979). *Research on teaching: Concepts, findings, and implications.* Berkley, CA: McCutchan.

Philips, S. (1983). *The invisible culture: Communication in classroom and community on the Warm Springs Indian Reservation.* New York, NY: Longman.

Pianta, R. C., Belsky, J., Houts, R., Morrison, F., & NICHD Early Child Care Research Network. (2007). Opportunities to learn in America's elementary classrooms. *Science, 315*(5820), 1795–1796.

Pianta, R. C., La Paro, K., & Hamre, B. K. (2008). *Classroom Assessment Scoring System (CLASS).* Baltimore, MD: Paul H. Brookes.

Pidgeon, D. (1970). *Expectation and pupil performance.* Slough, England: NFER.

Polikoff, M. (2012). The redundancy of mathematics instruction in U.S. elementary and middle schools. *Elementary School Journal, 113*(2), 230–251.

Popham, W. (1971). Teaching skill under scrutiny. *Phi Delta Kappan, 52,* 599–602.

Pressley, M., & Levine, J. (Eds.). (1983). *Cognitive strategy research: Educational applications.* New York, NY: Springer-Verlag.

Rakes, C. R., Valentine, J. C., McGatha, M. B., & Ronau, R. N. (2010). Methods of instructional improvement in algebra: A systematic review and meta-analysis. *Review of Educational Research, 80*(3), 372–400.

Ripley, A. (2010, January). What makes a great teacher? *The Atlantic.* Retrieved from http://www.theatlantic.com/doc/print/201001/good-teaching

Rohrkemper, M., & Corno, L. (1988). Success and failure on classroom tasks: Adaptive learning and classroom teaching. *Elementary School Journal, 88,* 297–312.

Rosenshine, B., & Furst, N. (1973). The use of direct observation to study teaching. In R. Travers (Ed.), *Second handbook of research on teaching* (pp. 122-183). Chicago, IL: Rand McNally.

Rosenholtz, S., & Simpson, C. (1984). The formation of ability conceptions: Developmental trend or societal construction? *Review of Educational Research, 54,* 31–63.

Rosenthal, R., & Jacobson, L. (1968). *Pygmalion in the classroom: Teacher expectation and pupils' intellectual development.* New York, NY: Holt, Rinehart, & Winston.

Rowe, M. (1969). Science, silence, and sanctions. *Science and Children, 6,* 11–13.

Ryans, D. (1960). *Characteristics of teachers.* Washington, DC: American Council on Education.

Schmidt, W., & Maier, A. (2009). Opportunity to learn. In G. Sikes, B. Schneider, & D. Plank (Eds.), *The AERA handbook on educational policy research* (pp. 541–559). Washington, DC: American Educational Research Association.

Schoenfeld, A., & Pearson, P. (2009). The reading and math wars. In G. Sikes, B. Schneider, &

D. Plank (Eds.), *The AERA handbook on educational policy research* (pp. 560–580). Washington, DC: American Educational Research Association.

Shavelson, R. (1976). Teachers' decision making. In N. Gage (Ed.), *The psychology of teaching methods. 75th yearbook of the National Society for the Study of Education* (Part I). Chicago, IL: University of Chicago Press.

Shavelson, R. (1983). Review of research on teachers' pedagogical judgments, plans, and decisions. *Elementary School Journal, 83,* 392–413.

Shulman, L. (1986). Those who understand: Knowledge growth in teaching. *Educational Researcher, 15,* 4-14.

Shulman, L. S. (1987). Knowledge and teaching: Foundations of the new reform. *Harvard Educational Review, 57*(1), 1–23.

Shulman, L. (1992). Research on teaching: A historical and personal perspective. In F. Oser, A. Dick, & J. Patry (Eds.), *Effective and responsible teaching* (pp. 14–29). San Francisco, CA: Jossey-Bass.

Silberman, C. (1970). *Crisis in the classroom.* New York, NY: Random House.

Sizer, T. (1984). *Horace's compromise: The dilemma of the American high school.* Boston, MA: Houghton Mifflin.

Slavin, R. (1980). Cooperative learning. *Review of Educational Research, 50,* 315–342.

Smith, B. (2000). Quantity matters: Annual instructional time in an urban school system. *Educational Administration Quarterly, 365*(5), 652–682.

Smith, L. M., & Geoffrey, W. (1968). *The complexities of an urban classroom: An analysis toward a general theory of teaching.* New York, NY: Holt, Rinehart, & Winston.

Snow, R., Corno, L., & Jackson, D. (in press). Individual differences in cognitive and affective functioning in educational psychology. In D. Berliner & R. Calfee (Eds.), *The handbook of educational psychology.* New York, NY: Macmillian.

St. John, N. (1971). Thirty-six teachers: Their characteristics, and outcomes for black and white pupils. *American Educational Research Journal, 8,* 635–648.

Stodolsky, S. (1988). *The subject matters; classroom activity in math and social studies.* Chicago, IL: University of Chicago Press.

Strong, M. (2011). *The highly qualified teacher: What is teacher quality and how do we measure it?* New York, NY: Teachers College Press.

Taba, H., Levine, S., & Elzey, F. (1964). *Thinking in elementary school children.* Washington, DC: U.S. Department of Health, Education, and Welfare.

Tom, A. (1984). *Teaching as a moral craft.* White Plains, NY: Longman.

Waller, W. (1961). *The sociology of teaching.* New York, NY: Russell and Russell.

Webb, N. (1983). Predicting learning from student interaction: Defining the interaction variable. *Educational Psychologist, 18,* 33–41.

Weinstein, R. (1983). Student perceptions of schooling. *Elementary School Journal, 83,* 287–312.

Weinstein, R. (2002). *Reaching higher: the importance of expectations on schooling.* Cambridge, MA: Harvard University Press.

Winne, P. H., & Marx, R. W. (1982). Students' and teachers' views of thinking processes for classroom learning. *The Elementary School Journal, 82,* 493–518.

Withall, J. (1960). Research tools: Observing and recording behavior. *Review of Educational Research, 30,* 496–512.

Wright, C. J., & Nuthall, G. A. (1970). Relationships between teacher behaviors and pupil achievement in three experimental elementary science lessons. *American Educational Research Journal, 7*(4), 477–491.

Zimmerman, B. J., & Schunk, D. H. (Eds.). (1989). *Self-regulated learning and academic achievement: Theory, research and practice.* New York, NY: Springer-Verlag.

4

EVALUATION

Activities in Today's Schools

Setting the Stage

Policies in many of the Race to the Top (RttT) states were seamlessly orchestrated by a series of initiatives that gained momentum in the prior decade. For example, pay-for-performance programs experienced a significant rebirth in 2006. School turnaround gained renewed momentum during the No Child Left Behind Act of 2001. These programs address similar issues—quality; however, each initiative addresses this educational "problem" in different ways. In pay-for-performance, teachers deemed highly effective are rewarded. The underlying goals are to retain effective teachers and continue to support their employment (through pay incentives). In school turnaround, schools are punished for underperforming, and their autonomy and authority removed if they are unable to demonstrate improvement. Both of these ideas, rewarding high performance and punishing low performance, have been carried forward in Race to the Top.

Merit and Performance Pay: The Reincarnation

Merit and performance pay systems[1] are those that reward teachers for how well they teach. Teacher effectiveness can be measured in many ways, but popular methods include supervisor evaluations, student achievement, and portfolios. Hence, how well a teacher teaches can be measured by what the teacher does or the outcomes that he or she produces (e.g., student achievement). There are numerous purposes for performance pay, including: increasing teacher retention, particularly of highly performing teachers, and supporting teacher effort and improvement.

There are a number of assumptions inherit in performance pay systems. First is that teacher effectiveness, as measured by student achievement outcomes, varies between teachers/classrooms and varies widely and reliably enough to make merit decisions. A second assumption is that teachers make decisions about career persistence primarily on salary. A third assumption is that the measures used to determine pay incentives allow teachers to alter their instruction in ways that maintain or increase student performance outcomes. For example, if current performance of teachers is judged insufficient for a performance bonus on the basis of some measurement, this measurement should provide feedback about how teachers could improve their performance. We will address the accuracy of these assumptions later in this chapter.

History.　Pay-based systems and salary schedules date back to at least the 1920s. These systems were initially created to equalize salary differences that existed by race, gender, and teaching assignment (Tyack, 1974). Career ladder programs were created to provide teachers with opportunities for growth, to support longevity and professional development, and to encourage teachers to obtain further education. These programs primarily rewarded teachers for what they did with increased roles and responsibilities. According to Henson and Hall (1993), career ladders provided politicians with a way to support the use of objective performance evaluations, reward exemplary teaching, increase individual effort, and deliver public accountability. For educators, career ladders provided opportunities to tie promotion to professional development and support teachers' job satisfaction and commitment. It is also important to note that teachers were being rewarded for things they were doing outside of the classroom (e.g., mentoring, service on committees). As mentioned throughout this book, numerous educational reforms appear then disappear only to reappear again as a new and exciting plan. Merit pay is no different. Such programs emerged in the 1920s, the 1960s, and was advocated for again in *A Nation at Risk*. Early implementation was not successful and received significant opposition (Dee & Keys, 2004). Podgursky and Springer (2007) argue this was due to insignificant incentive (pay), competition from alternative compensation models, and lack of rigorous evaluation systems. Some argue that performance pay systems are not appropriate for education because the value that teachers produce is not easily measured and merit pay systems inhibit collaboration and teamwork (Murnane & Cohen, 1986). It appears that these challenges may have resulted in a decreased use of pay-for-performance systems, at least in the public sector. In 1993, 12.3% of public school districts reported using merit pay. In 2000, 5.5% reported using pay incentives (Ballou, 2001). So, despite these results, performance pay appears to have garnered renewed interest, particularly in Race to the Top.

Progression. In the last two decades, there has been a resurgence of performance pay, which has occurred simultaneously with two lines of research that support two of the underlying assumptions of merit pay programs. These lines of research also address some of the earlier limitations and failures of pay-for-performance. For example, one rationale for pay incentives is that such rewards will increase the retention of highly effective teachers. Research that emerged in the 2000s indicated that salary is related, in part, to a teacher's decision to remain in the profession (Imazeki, 2005; Ingersoll, 2001; Lankford, Loeb, & Wykcoff, 2002; Podgursky, Monroe, & Watson, 2004). Studies have shown a $1,000 dollar increase in salary increases retention 3%–6%, and this relationship varies by teacher ethnicity, experience, and level of education (Kirby, Berends, & Naftel, 1999). When considering teachers of all races, a $1,000 salary increases retention by 2.9%. This value is 5%–6% for Hispanics and Blacks (Kirby et al., 1999). These findings suggested that performance pay, as part of a teacher's salary, influence his or her intention to remain in the profession. Furthermore, it provided more concrete evidence about how small or large bonuses need to be in order to create change. These findings, however, do not indicate whether or not overall teacher effectiveness will improve.

In the 2000s, a large body of value-added research[2] emerged indicating that teachers varied significantly in their ability to acquire student achievement gains (Aaronson, Barrow, & Sanders, 2003; Ballou, Sanders, & Wright, 2004; Boyd, Grossman, Lankford, & Loeb, 2006; Kane, Rockoff, & Staiger, 2005; Rivkin, Hanushek, & Kain, 2005; Wright, Horn, & Sanders, 1997). Some of those same studies and others demonstrated that teacher characteristics (e.g., level of education, certification status, licensing exam score) had little relation to teacher effectiveness (Aaronson et al., 2003; Kane et al., 2005; Rivkin et al., 2005). This research has been challenged by others using different teacher characteristics (e.g., teacher experience: Clotfelter, Ladd, & Vigdor, 2006; Nye, Konstantopoulos, & Hedges, 2004; and content knowledge: Hill, Rowan, & Ball, 2005). Taken together, this body of research indicates that (a) teachers vary in their effectiveness, and (b) a considerable amount of variation (7%–21%) in student achievement can be explained by teacher effects (Gordon, Kane, & Staiger, 2006; Nye et al., 2004; Rivkin et al., 2005; Rockoff, 2004; Rowan, Correnti, & Miller, 2002; Sanders & Horn, 1998). Furthermore, given that teacher characteristics such as education and experience explain only a small proportion of variance in teacher effectiveness, many have concluded that it is what teachers do that is the critical factor in teacher effectiveness, not who teachers are (see Konstantopoulus, in press). Reasoning follows, then, that rewarding teachers for effectiveness (primarily measured by student achievement) will improve the quality of the teaching force and education as a whole. This undermined credential-based systems and paved the way for performance-based systems that were centered on a teacher's ability to demonstrate student achievement outcomes and gains. It also has challenged the variable of teacher experience, which has led to numerous changes across the country to teacher tenure legislation. These findings also support the underlying assumption that teachers differ substantially and that statistical programs can sufficiently detect such differences; a challenge that was not addressed successfully in earlier implementation of performance pay. These new statistical methods are also purported to be a more objective and rigorous measure of teacher effectiveness.

The implementation of No Child Left Behind (NCLB, 2001) brought significant experimentation with performance-based pay models. Simultaneously, funding for performance pay programs became available in 2006 through the $99 million dollar Teacher Incentive Fund (U.S. Department of Education [USDOE], 2012a). In 2006, Florida adopted E-comp, a compensation model that would reward the top 10% of teachers, as measured by student achievement (Florida Department of Education, 2006). Other notable pre-RttT performance pay systems were those in Denver, Houston, and Minnesota (Podgursky & Springer, 2007). Additional funding and programs came from the Milken Family Foundation and their Teacher Advancement Program (TAP). This program consisted of 347 schools and 80 districts for the 2011–2012 school year (National Institute for Excellence in Teaching, 2012).

Funding from the Teacher Incentive Fund continues and as of 2012 is at $299 million (USDOE, 2012a). In Race to the Top, many states include incentives for their top teachers. For example, in the District of Columbia Public Schools and in agreement with the Washington Teachers' Union, highly effective teachers can earn bonuses up to $25,000. In sum, support for performance pay is stronger than ever before with financial backing that makes wide adoption and even larger bonuses possible.

These two lines of research and substantial financial support have generated a rebirth of performance pay; however, some limitations still remain. First, it is still unclear how significant bonuses need to be in order to produce significant change. Although studies of teacher retention and salary indicate that fairly small increases can support retention, studies of bonuses as large as $15,000 have demonstrated insignificant results in terms of educational improvement (Ravitch, 2011). This may be because teachers are unclear as to what improvements in instruction need to be made to receive a bonus. Second, it is unclear if new statistical methods (value-added modeling) capture the impact of teachers on students while controlling for other confounding variables (Rothstein, 2010). It is also unclear if teachers' student achievement outcomes and teaching practices (e.g., observational data) are reliable and stable across time (Darling-Hammond, Amrein-Beardsley, Haertel, & Rothstein, 2012; Good, in press). If student achievement gains cannot be linked to consistent teaching practices, improvement from such programs is questionable. Furthermore, other and more recent evidence suggest that salary is a less powerful predictor of retention than teachers' perceptions of administration (Boyd et al., 2011), administrative support (Milanowski et al., 2009), student–teacher ratios, and institutional expenditure per pupil (Kirby et al., 1999); however given the correlational nature of these data, it is difficult to conclude that these variables cause teacher retention and satisfaction. Taken together, it is not surprising that merit pay programs have demonstrated minimal gains in terms of achievement and teacher retention.

Despite a history of limitations and challenges, performance pay continues to be implemented (Bowman, 2010; Perry, Enbergs, & Jun, 2009; Ravitch, 2011), and failure of such programs continues to occur (e.g., Marsh et al., 2011; Otterman, 2011). Given its renewed support and funding, it appears that this history has not informed current education reform. Unfortunately, even new methods of assessing a teacher's effect on student learning cannot eliminate the unintended consequences associated with merit pay (e.g., corruption, teaching to the test, narrowed curriculum: Ascher, 1996; Rothstein, 2010) that are expected to continue primarily because the context (e.g., high-stakes, emphasis on student test scores) remains the same.

School Turnaround

School turnaround is the second of many examples of reform efforts that have failed, been tried again, and is being carried forward. School turnaround is an educational initiative that identifies failing schools and requires that such schools adopt an improvement strategy. If progress is not made, schools risk potentially severe consequences.

History. Takeovers of low performing schools made appearances in the 1980s and 1990s in New Jersey when all 35 schools in the Jersey City district were taken over by the state in 1989, followed by the Newark school district in 1995 (MacFarquhar, 1995; Sullivan, 1987; Weischadle, 1979). Takeovers also occurred in both California and Ohio in the 1990s (Smarick, 2010). School turnaround reached its peak under the reauthorization of the Elementary and Secondary Act (1965) and the No Child Left Behind Act (NCLB; 2001). Under federal law, a greater emphasis was placed on school accountability. Schools were expected to meet adequate yearly progress (AYP) and standards set by the state. If such measures were not met, improvement timelines were put in place as were additional restructuring interventions. Schools that failed to meet AYP for 5 consecutive years were required to engage in restructuring, often termed "school turnaround." Restructuring under NCLB could occur in the following ways:

1. Reopen the school as a public charter school.
2. Replace the staff (which may include the principal) relevant to the failure to make adequate yearly progress.
3. Contract with an outside entity (e.g., private management company) with a demonstrated record of effectiveness to maintain school operation.

4. Turn the operation of the school over to the state.
5. Engage in significant changes in the school's staffing and governance, to improve student academic achievement in the school and that has substantial promise of enabling the school to make adequate yearly progress. (NCLB, 2001)

Progression. Since NCLB, these interventions in struggling schools have become equally if not more severe and more widespread. In 2006 to 2007 more than 740 schools under corrective action implemented new curriculum, and 700 used an outside expert (without providing any data that the experts had knowledge of what to do to improve the situation) to advise the school. In 400 of those schools, schools were restructured, and in 200, the school day extended. In 300 of the schools, staff members or the principal were replaced. The high stakes of failing became apparent in NCLB and continued under the Obama administration. In 2009, the School Improvement Grants (SIG) ramped up to $3.5 million to turnaround 5,000 of the worst performing schools. In Obama's Blueprint for Reform, failing schools were given four options:

1. turnaround: principal and teachers are fired; new principal may rehire up to 50% of former teachers;
2. restart: convert to a charter, or close and reopen under outside Management;
3. close; or
4. transform: principal is replaced if the principal has been at the school longer than 2 years (USDOE, 2009a).

Although the results of efforts to turn schools around were problematic, this theme continues to carry through in RttT with significantly more pressure on teachers and administrators. School turnaround allowed the nation to become accustomed to severe consequences for low performance and high-stakes interventions—improve or else. These initiatives assume that low performance is primarily due to staff and faculty. Such programs also assume that changes in leadership or faculty will solve low performance problems. The messages and underlying assumptions upheld by school turnaround and merit pay have been carried through in the form of accountability being practiced under RttT, but as with merit pay, school turnaround programs have shown limited success in both the business world where they originated (Hess & Gift, 2008) and in education (Malen, Croninger, Muncey, & Redmond-Jones, 2002).

Much reform has attempted to improve performance using the stick approach; seeking improvement through negative sanctions such as retaining students, public lists of low performing schools, and school turnaround. Other reform has attempted the carrot approach by using rewards and incentives for desired outcomes (e.g., merit pay). Carrot-and-stick approaches have proven to be unsuccessful in improving the complex problem of educational quality.

Accountability Gains Momentum

Both pay-for-performance and school turnaround initiatives were the building blocks leading up to high-stakes teacher evaluation. Merit pay programs illuminated the importance of having evaluation methods that would identify the best teachers, and that those teachers differ substantially from others. School turnaround programs emphasized accountability and consequences for not meeting designated goals. Ironically, in the latter there appears to be no acknowledgement that there might be teachers worth rewarding (excellent teachers) in low-performing schools.

Simultaneously, accountability at a more general level made gains. The Elementary and Secondary Education Act, passed in 1965, included funding for supplemental services and research (e.g., testing), which helped establish student achievement as one of the desired outcome variables in accountability. In 1971, Florida passed the Education Accountability Act in order to assess the effectiveness of current programs in meeting stated objectives. In 1973, 27 states had some form of accountability legislation, although many policies at the time were vague. Teacher evaluations were present in 12 states and varied from set standards of performance to mere recommendations. In only one state, South Dakota, was there a mention of tying teacher evaluation results to merit pay. In many cases, specific guidelines were not included in any accountability laws and districts were left on their own to implement the laws (Good, Biddle, & Brophy, 1975).

In 2009, only 15 states required annual teacher evaluations. Only four of those states used student test scores to measure, in part, effective teaching. This situation changed rapidly within 2 years. In 2011, 24 states and the District of Columbia required annual teacher evaluations. Twenty-three states included student test scores (as measured by growth and/or value-added measures) in teacher evaluations. The magnitude of this transformation is illuminated by the fact that 14 states, which include student test scores in teacher evaluations, utilize teacher evaluation results to fire teachers (National Council on Teacher Quality, 2011). Further, teacher tenure processes have come under significant fire in the past decade. Many states are responding to these criticisms by increasing the ease by which tenured teachers can be dismissed and this has happened with the ramping up of more rigorous and more frequent teacher evaluations for all.

The Fall of NCLB

All of these changes were occurring as NCLB was failing. Instead of closing the achievement gap, NCLB has resulted in a narrowed curriculum, teaching to the test, and lower standards for students (Nichols & Berliner, 2007; Payne, 2008; Ravitch, 2010). The flaws of NCLB led to a new reform effort that embraces the important contributions of NCLB but has sought to address NCLB's areas of weakness and unintended consequences. In March of 2010 President Obama submitted a *Blueprint for Reform*, a proposal that moved the focus from pass/fail to growth and progress by supporting and rewarding innovation and continuous improvement. Eligible subject matter was expanded, allowing subjects such as history and social studies to be recognized, although how these subject matters would be assessed was not addressed (USDOE, 2010a).

In September 2011, the Obama administration announced that states would have the option to waive aspects of NCLB.[3] In exchange for relief from federal mandates, states must provide alternative solutions that still meet the NCLB goals of accountability, college and career readiness, and measuring teacher and principal effectiveness. The waiver sought to improve educational outcomes and support locally based change and reform. The latter comes with caution. Waivers were granted initially on a 3-year period. States must prove their ability to successfully implement such efforts and achieve proposed results (USDOE, 2012b).

One waiver application requirement was the establishment of a state-developed evaluation and support system for teachers and principals to be developed with teacher and principal input which must include multiple valid measures (including student progress over time, and professional practice). The results must be provided to teachers for instructional improvement. As of February 2012, 37 states have been granted ESEA waivers (USDOE, 2012b).

Evaluation in Race to the Top Schools

Racing to the Top

In November 2009, the U.S. Department of Education announced Race to the Top, a $4 billion dollar program that awards states that propose coherent and rigorous plans to prepare students for success in college and the workplace and to compete in the global economy, build data systems that measure student growth and success and inform instruction, and recruit, develop, reward, and retain effective teachers and principals, and finally, turn around the lowest-achieving schools, despite having no knowledge base for turning around low achieving schools.

In the three application review phases since its release, a total of 18 states and the District of Columbia have been awarded RttT funds.[4] Due in part to the RttT initiative, many states are rushing to produce teacher evaluation systems that will, they hope, ultimately lead to a higher quality teacher workforce. According to RttT, states should:

(iv) use evaluations, at a minimum, to inform decisions regarding—
    (a) Developing teachers and principals, including by providing relevant coaching, induction support, and/or professional development;

   (b)   Compensating, promoting, and retaining teachers and principals, including by providing opportunities for highly effective teachers and principals … to obtain additional compensation and be given additional responsibilities;

   (c)   Whether to grant tenure and/or full certification (where applicable) to teachers and principals using rigorous standards and streamlined, transparent, and fair procedures; and

   (d)   Removing ineffective tenured and untenured teachers and principals after they have had ample opportunities to improve, and ensuring that such decisions are made using rigorous standards and stream- lined, transparent, and fair procedures. (USDOE, 2010d, p. 19504)

The Great Teachers and Leaders section of Race to the Top (USDOE, 2011a) touts the research demonstrating that teachers are the single most important school-level factor in student achievement (Hanushek & Rivkin, 2010; Sanders & Horn, 1994; Wenglinsky, 2000). Rewarding effective teachers and eliminat- ing ineffective teachers is one way in which RttT puts this research into action.

Data Collection: How Are Teachers Evaluated?

In RttT states, teacher evaluations are determined by a combination of factors. RttT requires that teachers are evaluated, in significant part, by student growth (USDOE, 2010d). Beyond that, states can use additional and multiple measures as they see fit. A number of states are using a combination of student achieve- ment data and observation scores.

Student Achievement. Although RttT clearly places an emphasis on growth, in most cases RttT grantees are using a combination of student achievement, student growth, and/or value-added scores to represent their student achievement portion of teacher evaluation. For student achievement, most states rely solely on state student achievement assessments and alternative assessments when such data are not available. In Delaware, for example, alternate assessments (internally and externally developed and approved) are included in the student achievement measure (Delaware Department of Education, 2012). Growth models measure students' progress on standardized test scores from one given point to another in relation to academically similar students. Value- added models estimate teachers' impacts on student growth over time (Collins & Amrein-Beardsley, in press). See Chapter 5 for details on the differences between these measures. Advocates of value-added indicate that these models can statistically control for a variety of variables (e.g., poverty, race), suggesting that these new statistical techniques can better capture the value teachers add to the students they serve. Some RttT grantees (e.g., Ohio, Tennessee, District of Columbia) use individual value-added scores to represent student growth data when available. Others substitute school-level value-added scores if individual ones are not available. Given the significant number of untested subjects, many teachers do not have the adequate amount of data to calculate individual value-added scores. Value-added scores have gained significant traction, with only minimal resistance. For example, the District of Columbia Public Schools initially proposed that value-added data represent 50% of a teacher's evaluation score, it has reduced this percentage now to 35% due to teachers' protests (District of Columbia Public Schools, 2011). This is a common percentage used in many RttT state plans.[5]

Observation Measures.   In all RttT grantee teacher evaluation models, teachers are observed. Observations are done, minimally, on an annual basis. Most states require 1–4 observations per teacher, per year. In some states (e.g., North Carolina), new teachers or probationary teachers are observed more frequently than more advanced teachers. Also, some states (e.g., Massachusetts, Delaware) reward highly effective teachers with fewer observations in subsequent years (Herlihy et al., in press).

In some RttT states (e.g., Arizona), the individual(s) eligible to be observers is not specified, but in most cases superintendents, principals, administrators, or instructional leaders are the designated individuals to be trained to and conduct observations. The training process is less consistent. In some states, training happens at the state level (e.g., Delaware), in others at the district level (e.g., Florida), and in other cases it is not specified (e.g., Colorado). Sometimes states (e.g., Georgia) require observers to be certified before conducting observations. In almost all cases only one observer is required (Herlihy et al., in press).

Data Use: High-Stakes Decision Making

States are using teacher evaluation data in numerous ways to both support effective teaching, but also to eliminate or improve ineffective teaching. In the former, teachers who receive effective or highly effective ratings may receive bonuses, become eligible for tenure, or receive fewer observations. In the latter, consequences for ineffective ratings include: remediation plans, frozen salaries, removal of tenure, dismissal, or termination (Herlihy et al., in press; Lavigne, in press).

A Detailed Illustration of Race to the Top: State Profiles

In order to better assess the complexity of accountability, we decided to examine how states are currently approaching the task. Race to the Top Phase 1 and Phase 2 winners provided a perfect opportunity for such an analysis, because many of these states are making significant progress in program implementation. Phase 1 (Tennessee and Delaware) and Phase 2 winners (District of

Columbia, Florida, Georgia, Hawaii, Maryland, Massachusetts, New York, North Carolina, Ohio, and Rhode Island) varied in the amount of information publicly available. In choosing states to include in the analysis below, we were limited by what information was provided. Further, at the time of our analysis states varied in the stage of implementation. We chose states that had begun implementation and/or provided teacher observation rubrics (given our interest in this area of research), and were a representative sample of the RttT states.

Tennessee, Massachusetts, and North Carolina were chosen. The three states differed in their initial appeal to the government. Tennessee was selected as one of two winners out of 40 in Phase 1 (score: 444.2); Massachusetts and North Carolina did not fare as well in Phase 1 (Massachusetts: 411.4; North Carolina: 414.0). By Phase 2, both states demonstrated improvement (Massachusetts: 471; North Carolina: 441.6) and were ranked, respectively, first and ninth (USDOE, 2010e). Some of these state analyses are noted elsewhere (Lavigne, in press).

Tennessee

Tennessee's proposed system to evaluate teachers, the Tennessee Educator Acceleration Model (TEAM), was implemented in 2011–2012 school year across the state (Tennessee Department of Education [TDOE], n.d.). Half of a teacher's evaluation consists of observations and conferences. The other half is composed of two other factors—student growth (35%) and achievement (15%). Based on the First to the Top Act (2010), these factors are combined to create a teacher effectiveness rating from 1 to 5, which will inform hiring, promotion, and firing decisions.

Teacher Observations.   Teachers are observed 4–6 times during the year.[6] Observations consist of announced, unannounced, full lesson, and 15-minute observations. Post-observation conferences are held with teachers to identify strengths and areas in need of improvement. The observation instrument is a 19-item, 5-point scale. Post-observation conferences presumably support continuous improvement of teaching practices.

Student Learning.   Achievement measures are used to assess student learning. The Tennessee Value-Added Assessment System (TVAAS) will measure a teacher's effectiveness by comparing a student's actual and projected growth. Student achievement, as measured on a standard scale, will also inform a teacher's effectiveness. Unfortunately, only 45% of Tennessee's teachers have TVAAS data. For teachers who do not have these data available, school-wide TVAAS or an alternative TDOE-approved measure will be utilized. Alternative assessments are currently being piloted for subject areas and grades that are not normally tested under NCLB.

Preliminary Findings. Mid-year data from 2011 to 2012 observations reflect discrepancies from initially predicted distributions. It was anticipated that districts would rate 3%–5% of teachers as 1s; 10%–25% as 2s; 40%–50% as 3s; 10%–25% as 4s; and 5%–10% as 5—variability that is necessary for differentiating highly effective teachers from those who are not. In Murfreesboro City Schools, almost half of teachers received a score of 5. In another county, 97% of teachers scored a rating of 3 or higher. Other teachers did not fare as well. In Fayette County schools only 1% of teachers received a 5 (Hubbard, 2012). It is unclear if the variation in scores across districts is due to inherent differences across principals or a true reflection of the unequal distribution of effective teachers across schools. Implementation has caused extensive distress across the state. In addition to providing solutions for the lack of TVAAS data, principals are spending extensive amount of time following the new guidelines. "For example, [a principal] is required to have a pre-observation conference with each teacher (which takes 20 minutes), observe the teacher for a period (50 minutes), conduct a post-observation conference (20 minutes), and fill out a rubric with 19 variables and give teachers a score from 1 to 5 (40 minutes)" (Winerip, 2011), which equates to just over 2 hours, for one teacher. In a school of 20 teachers, with 4–6 required observations per year, a principal could expect to spend 173–260 hours annually observing teachers. Given the time constraints, it is highly unlikely that these observations will be done well. Adjustments have already been made to reduce the required number of observations (TDOE, 2012).

Massachusetts

Massachusetts has devised a somewhat similar approach to teacher evaluation (Massachusetts Department of Elementary and Secondary Education, 2011). Under the Massachusetts Model System for Educator Evaluation, every educator engages in self-assessment at the start of the school year and proposes goals for their Educator Plan. In the second stage, educators engage in analysis, goal setting, and plan development (this may occur individually and/or in part with teams). Educators then implement the steps outlined in their plan. At mid-year, educators receive a formative review. Peer assessment and frequent, unannounced, brief observations are encouraged, but resources for doing so are not specified. At the end of the school year, educators receive a summative rating. Teachers are rated on four possible outcomes: unsatisfactory, needs improvement, proficient, and exemplary; teachers are expected to perform at the proficient level. Summative ratings will be created using multiple pieces of evidence (e.g., observations, student surveys, multiple measures of student learning).

Teachers also receive an impact on student learning rating (high, moderate, or low) based on growth and gain scores on state assessments and grade level and subject area district-determined measures of learning. Statewide, district, classroom-based assessments, in addition to growth percentile and gain scores on two measures (the Massachusetts Comprehensive Assessment System and the Massachusetts English Proficiency Assessment), are used.

As briefly mentioned above, teachers will include one self-determined student learning goal and one professional practice goal in their plans. Although choice seems desirable, it is not always the case. For example, in their classic book, *The Shopping Mall High School*, Arthur Powell, Eleanor Farrar, and David Cohen (1985) described the failure of another school reform that was largely based upon giving students wide choice in curriculum decisions. They found that given an abundance of choices, some students chose poorly and others more wisely. The measurement problem of self-selected goals is significant as some may pick ambitious and meaningful goals and others choose trivial ones. Clearly, some teachers would choose goals they can readily achieve while others may choose those less attainable. Each teacher's goal will be assessed as part of the summative evaluation. The Model System is currently being implemented in districts with underperforming (Level 4) schools. All districts participating in RttT started the Model System in the 2012–2013 school year.

North Carolina

The Teacher Evaluation Process in North Carolina (Public Schools of North Carolina, State Board of Education, n.d.) began in 13 districts in the 2008–2009 school year and in 39 districts in 2009–2010 school year. The remaining districts are currently implementing the Teacher Evaluation Process. Developed by the NC Professional Teaching Standards Commission, teachers are evaluated on five standards: demonstration of leadership, establishment of respectful environment for diverse students, content knowledge, facilitation of learning, and reflection on practice. Measures of student growth were added in the 2010–2011 school year. Teachers are rated on a 5-level scale: Not Demonstrated, Developing, Proficient, Accomplished, or Distinguished. Evaluations occur four times a year for probationary teachers. Career-status teachers receive an annual evaluation. In North Carolina's RttT implementation, teacher evaluation will be used for individual professional development, to inform remediation and dismissal decisions, and select highly effective teachers for Teacher Leaders. With nearly half of North Carolina teachers devoting more than half of classroom time to test preparation (Cavanagh, 2012), it is concerning how much more time will be spent on test preparation given that now a teacher's job will depend, in part, on those scores.

Expectations and Implications. As part of the evaluation system, North Carolina is identifying effective and highly effective teachers. Effective teachers are those whose students' growth (in the aggregate) meets expectations (*1 year* of expected growth) and whose ratings on the NC Educator Evaluation System are at the level of *proficient* or *higher*. Highly effective teachers are teachers whose students' growth (in the aggregate) significantly exceeds expectations (*more than 1 year* of expected growth) and whose ratings on the NC Educator Evaluation System are at the level of *accomplished* or *higher*. In addition to identifying effective teachers, North Carolina will remove ineffective teachers—those teachers who do not achieve proficiency (for beginning teachers, after their third year) may not continue to teach and will not be eligible for Continuing licenses. One wonders the number of teachers this will remove, and if the policy implications of this have been considered by decision makers in North Carolina. Tenure decisions will also be based on the new evaluation system. After 4 years of teaching, teachers can be considered for tenure. Tenure decisions will be based in part on meeting the definition of an effective teacher and possessing results from sixteen evaluations as required by the Teacher Evaluation. In sum, we see that the educational community is willing to implement radical and costly change without any evidence that the change is likely to succeed and will not result in harmful unintended consequences (see Lavigne, in press, for a more extensive discussion of unintended consequences of high-stakes teacher evaluation).

Teacher Recruitment.   In addition to keeping good teachers, North Carolina seeks to recruit the best possible teachers by utilizing information about traditional and alternative program graduate data. Citing a small number of studies indicating that TFA teachers are more effective, as measured by student exam performance, than graduates of traditional teacher programs, particularly in high school math, English, and science, and middle school math, North Carolina will be seeking to increase the number of Teach for America (TFA) teachers in high-need schools. Again, the feasibility of this policy decision begs for analysis. Teach for America is incredibly successful at attracting high-achieving college graduates to hard-to-staff schools (Maier, 2012). Teach for America teachers impact student learning, but for a short time. Recent research indicates that a mere 14.8% remain after five years (Donaldson & Johnson, 2011). Furthermore, a wider review of the research on TFA indicates that these teachers are no more effective than colleagues prepared through other routes (Heilig & Jez, 2010). Veltri (2010) argues that a compressed model of preparation that offers limited lesson demonstrations, observation of expert modeling, reflection on practice, and collaboration with seasoned professionals leaves TFA teachers remarkably unprepared.

A Three-State Comparison: Summary

In comparing the Massachusetts, North Carolina, and Tennessee approaches, a few differences emerge. The Massachusetts model appears to allow for more flexibility in implementation. For example, when warranted, rubrics may be combined to create hybrid rubrics to capture individuals who hold multiple roles within a school district. Further, multiple artifacts are stressed in the Massachusetts model, including, but not limited to peer observations, observations outside of the classroom, and parent feedback. In Tennessee, the Department of Education pilots and determines any and all rubrics to be utilized across the state. Further, Tennessee has a more prescribed formula by which teacher ratings will be calculated (how much each component, e.g., student test scores, will contribute to a teacher's final evaluation). This is less clear in the Massachusetts and North Carolina models. In all models, who does the observations is problematic. In North Carolina, the stakes are clearly defined for teachers who do well or fail to perform.

Similarly, all states are using more than just value-added scores to assess their teachers. Classroom observations represent a significant component of teacher ratings in all three states. Furthermore, some states have made distinct improvements in the number of observations that will be conducted. For example, previously Tennessee only required one or two annual observations.[7] Further, recent research suggests it may be more valuable to train numerous individuals to do observations rather than have a single observer rate a teacher multiple times (Bill & Melinda Gates Foundation, 2013). Who is doing the observation may undermine any benefits gained by increasing the number of observations. In Tennessee, principals are primarily responsible for observing their teachers, whereas in Massachusetts peer observation is encouraged. Unfortunately, the use of principals or peers is inherently flawed. Principals are not impartial, particularly if their own evaluations will be penalized if observation scores of their teachers do not align with value-added scores as seen in one state (Hubbard, 2012). The accuracy by which principals are able to evaluate teachers is questionable (Strong, 2011). If states were willing to invest in better training, better results might be obtained. One may question the ability of an ineffective teacher to recognize effective teaching. Furthermore, as states struggle with budgets, it is unclear how it will be possible to employ unbiased, independent observers. It is also vital to question the wisdom of a policy that takes excellent teachers out of the classroom and involves them in peer observation especially since there is no reason to believe that good teachers are necessarily good observers. We return to these issues in Chapter 5.

The Role of Teacher Evaluation

Public Outcry of Teachers

As briefly illustrated above, states are moving forward to make modifications that will allow for decisions to be made on a teacher's career trajectory. In some cases, this information has been made public. These two issues in addition to doubts about new statistical methods to assess a teacher's impact on student learning, have caused a stir in the teacher, teacher educator, and educational community.

A Media-Based Illustration of Protest.   Heated protests have emerged across the nation. The most prominent being the 7-day protest by the Chicago Teachers Union. Although teacher evaluation was only one part of the protest for a better teacher contract, the protest made national news and dominated headlines all of September 2012. It also brought the spotlight back to how teachers should be evaluated, what measures are fair, and to what extent should such measures be used in teacher evaluation.

Other notable protests occurred across the nation and in cities like Los Angeles (*Los Angeles Times*, n.d.) and New York City (NYC Department of Education, n.d.) over the public release of teacher evaluation data. Although these data were subsequently released, again, it brought into question who should have access to these data, and why? In at least 18 states and the District of Columbia, public access to teacher evaluation data is permissible under open-records laws (Sawchuk, 2013). Public figures have made significant stances for (e.g., New York Mayor Michael Bloomberg) or against (e.g., Bill Gates), wide, public dissemination of such data (Gates, 2012; Kaplan, 2012). Some argue that it is a parent's and student's right to have access to such knowledge, whereas others argue it is important to protect the privacy of teachers. Other possible concerns include the implications of releasing such information before significant understanding of the accuracy of newly developed teacher evaluation methods, and the impact on teacher-student relationships if students become privy to this knowledge. Other than the potential right to have access to knowledge, it is unclear how making teacher evaluation data public will benefit teachers and their students. Absent from this conversation is the unintended consequences of disseminating this information widely, particularly for teacher morale, collaboration, and collective efficacy (Lavigne, in press).

Much of the media has documented the implementation of teacher evaluation and related protests, but it hasn't been until recently that the validity and reliability of such measures have been brought into question. Furthermore, only limited attention in the media has been devoted to unintended consequences. These have been primarily anecdotal (for example, see Strauss, 2012).

Organizations and Citizens Take a Position

Since the beginning, statewide teachers' unions have been involved in the protests and local educational changes around teacher evaluations. However, it wasn't until recently that larger, national union organizations made evident their stances on these controversial changes in teacher evaluation and the role, they believe, teacher evaluation should play in education reform.

National Education Association. In 2011, the National Education Association (NEA) approved and released a statement on teacher evaluation. Their belief in high-quality teacher evaluations includes the belief that evaluations should be based on multiple indicators, including, but not limited to teacher practice, teacher growth, and teachers' contribution to student learning and growth (NEA, 2011). Interestingly, few Race to the Top evaluations place a significant or explicit emphasis on *teacher* growth. The District of Columbia Public Schools IMPACT system does include community and collaboration—the extent to which teachers engage with colleagues and their community in meaningful ways—as one variable in a teacher's evaluation (District of Columbia Public Schools, 2011). The statement put forth by the NEA also illustrates their support of evaluation systems that provide support for struggling teachers; however, they argue that teachers should not be given more than a year to demonstrate improvement in deficiencies. It is their belief that teachers, after due process, should be dismissed if they fail to meet appropriate expectations or fail to improve after being placed on an improvement plan. With this statement, NEA aligns itself with some of the more severe uses of teacher evaluation data.

The NEA released a statement in 2012 in support of reducing high-stakes standardized testing mandates. Whether or not the high-stakes of teacher evaluation will create similar unintended consequence of high-stakes testing is yet to be seen (Lavigne, in press), but could shape NEA's future position on teacher evaluation, particularly in its evaluative uses. It appears, however, that although NEA believes in high-quality teacher evaluation, it does not believe that high-stakes standardized testing should be a significant measure (Otterman, 2011). The NEA is also one of the first organizations to formally address the concerns of the ability of schools and districts to observe teachers and observe teachers well.

American Federation of Teachers. Rather than opposing new changes, in 2012, the American Federation of Teachers (AFT) released a report echoing the importance of higher standards for teachers and calling for a professional exam that has similar rigor to the bar exam used to determine if a candidate is qualified to practice law:

> Just as in professions widely recognized for having a set of rigorous professional standards, such as law or medicine, teaching must raise standards for entry into the profession through a process similar to the bar process in law or the board process in medicine. The process must require candidates to demonstrate competence in essential dimensions of successful teaching before being allowed to take responsibility for a classroom and become a teacher of record. Such an assessment system would entail several components aligned with clearly articulated essential dimensions of professional teaching that together would constitute a threshold for entrance into the profession.
>
> *(2012, p. 3)*

Using survey results from first-year teachers, the report targets how teachers are prepared and the standards up to certification and entry into the classroom. To that end, the report includes a call for higher standards of quality in teacher preparation programs including higher GPA standards for those in the teacher preparation pipeline. Unfortunately, a greater focus on who teachers *are* instead of what teachers *do* is likely a maladaptive response.

Public Opinion—Gallup Poll Data.   Some of these same sentiments have been expressed by the public. A review of the 1990 Gallup poll (Elam, 1990) indicated that 87% of Americans believed that the quality of the teaching staff is a very important factor in choosing schools (the only direct question posed about teacher quality). When asked about the biggest problems facing schools, the most commonly listed issue was drugs in schools (39%) followed by discipline (19%) and lack of funding (13%). Teacher quality failed to make the list. The limited emphasis placed on teacher and school quality is not ironic given that 73% of respondents blamed societal problems for the challenges facing public education, not the schools.

Twenty years later, however, the 2010 Gallup poll (Bushaw & Lopez, 2010) illuminated quality of teaching as the *most* important component of education, according to respondents. It is possible that the increased emphasis on teachers and schools emerged from concern over the widening achievement gap between the rich and the poor (Reardon, 2011). School funding, lack of discipline, and overcrowded schools were identified as the biggest problems, respectively, facing public schools. Results indicated limited support for the No Child Left Behind Act; 28% of respondents indicated NCLB was hurting school performance, whereas 45% felt it was making no difference, although the important contributions of NCLB, a greater focus on measuring student learning has "stuck" with American policy makers. Accountability was absent from the 1990 poll, but standardized tests were gaining momentum as documented by the presence of grade exit examinations and core courses (Elam, 1990). Twenty years later (Bushaw & Lopez, 2010), almost three fourths of respondents indicated that student achievement data should be tied very or somewhat closely to teacher pay; substantial support for the rebirth of merit pay. A majority (71%) indicated that quality of work rather than a standard scale (27%) should determine teacher pay. However, teacher evaluation, in the public's opinion, should be used to improve teaching (60%) first, and second, as a way to determine ineffectiveness and potentially firing decisions (26%). Ironically, the ways in which states will use teacher evaluation to improve teaching is less clear.

Respondents to the 2011 Gallup poll (Bushaw & Lopez, 2011) were also asked about how four factors (academic degree, student test scores, experience, and principal evaluations) should contribute to a teacher's salary. Americans indicated that all four factors were very important almost equally (academic degree: 38%; experience: 38%; student achievement: 29%; principal evaluations: 38%).

In prior polls, Americans endorsed different ideas about how to raise educational quality; however in the 2011 poll 72%–80% of respondents believed that larger classes with more effective teachers would raise educational quality more than smaller classes with less effective teachers. Lack of funding (44%) was the most frequently cited problem facing public schools. The public has endorsed the fact that teachers make a difference and that some teachers are much more effective than are others.

In the 2012 Gallup poll, although 71% of respondents have trust in teachers, 57% agreed that entrance requirements to teacher education programs should be more rigorous, and 67% believed that this would enhance the quality of the teacher workforce. In the 2012 poll, respondents were asked about their feelings on including test scores in a teacher's evaluation. According to the results, the nation is split: 52% favoring and 47% opposing the inclusion of students' performance on test scores in teacher evaluation (Bushaw & Lopez, 2012).

However, the negative media attention towards teaching appears to be tainting the public's opinion. Respondents often rate the schools they know the best, but rate the overall perception of public education lower. And although the public indicates a trust in teachers, they simultaneously believe that entrance standards to teacher education programs need to be raised. Many have commented on the damaging effects media has had on citizens' global beliefs about American education (Good, in press; Marx, in press).

In examining the *Phi Delta Kappan*/Gallup polls, some interesting trends emerge. First, issues that were raised in 1970 such as student achievement growth and accountability disappear (Elam, 1973), but then reemerge in 2010 in more detail and elaboration (Bushaw & Lopez, 2010). What does seem to hold stable is citizen's critique of funding for public education. Examining additional polls illustrates that concern over funding dipped in the mid-1980s, and has shown enormous growth and consensus in the last 15 years (20% in 2005, 36% in 2010, and a peak of 44% in 2011 (see Bushaw & Lopez, 2010)). Finally, who should be responsible for school quality and how school quality can be improved again returns to earlier perceptions documented in 1970: teachers (Elam, 1973). The underlying message of school turnaround (improve or else) has trickled down to teachers. Based on these findings, it appears that policy makers and citizens sometimes differ sharply in their opinion about education, leaving open the question as to what audience policy makers respond to. However, at present there is a convergence that individual teachers are the important lever for enhancing student achievement and this leads to substantial support for high-stakes teacher evaluation.

Conclusion

The current evaluation that is occurring today in Race to the Top states has been driven by numerous changes that have emphasized the importance and need for teacher evaluation methods that differentiate between levels of teacher effectiveness, increase the perception that accountability is important in education, that teachers matter in student learning and, hence, their impact on students should be documented, evaluated, responded to, and used in ways to advance education. These changes, however, have been met with a number of challenges in regards to implementation (see Chapter 5).

Education reform continues to use ineffective programs and to implement others with little evidence of success. Pay-for-performance and school turn around are just two examples of how inefficiency is maintained and carried forward. No one would argue against placing highly effective teachers in every classroom. It is less clear, however, that evidence has been used to guide current teacher evaluation models that seek to ultimately identify effectiveness. For example, why are certain measures given more weight than others in a composite score? What is the evidence that this combination of measures will result in the most reliable and valid measure of teacher effectiveness? What rationale was used to decide the number of observations and who would be best qualified to do the observations? These are questions that must be answered in order for modern day teacher evaluation to have the potential to be effective.

Protests may have driven some changes (e.g., percentage of a teacher's evaluation that is determined by value-added) but have not had a significant impact on the direction of teacher evaluation; a process primarily driven by student test scores with a growing emphasis on value-added. This may be because protests have primarily focused on the use of student test scores rather than possible methodological limitations in teacher evaluation. Despite the caution, warning, and concern in particular research circles (Baker et al., 2010; Darling-Hammond et al., 2012), value-added is continuing to be of top priority for newly granted RttT states. It is unlikely that protests by teachers and citizens will be productive because (a) current trends are being supported by major teacher organizations, (b) there is a greater concern about how to adopt and implement these new evaluations rather than concern about the quality and accuracy of such evaluations, and (c) even if protesters emphasize research-based evidence, there is no indication that policy makers use research-based evidence to make decisions. It is unlikely that protests will sidetrack the blind support given for new methods of teacher evaluation that is driven by significant political and financial power. Given this unfortunate forecast, there are ways that teachers, schools, and districts can cope to ensure that they are maintaining high quality instruction and maintaining an emphasis on student learning despite the continued constraints and challenges. We present more on this in Chapter 6.

Now that we have presented a snapshot of modern day teacher evaluation, we return in Chapter 5 to these common (and not so common) methods used to assess teacher effectiveness. Given the limited rationale presented by RttT states about why certain methods were chosen, the method of implementation, and the emphasis placed on each measure, we fill in these information gaps by paying particularly close attention to the strengths and limitations of each method.

Notes

1 For a broader discussion of merit pay see Jacobson, Hickox, and Stevenson (1996).
2 According to Darling-Hammond, Amrein-Beardsley, Haertel, & Rothstein (2012), "value-added models enable researchers to use statistical methods to measure changes in student scores over time while considering student characteristics and other factors often found to influence achievement" (p. 8).
3 As of November 2012, 37 states and the District of Columbia have submitted requests for waivers (USDOE, 2012b). In February 2012, ten states were approved for flexibility: Colorado, Florida, Georgia, Indiana, Kentucky, Massachusetts, Minnesota, New Jersey, Oklahoma, and Tennessee.
4 Phase 1 winners include Delaware and Tennessee (USDOE, 2010b). The following were awarded funds in Phase 2: District of Columbia, Florida, Georgia, Hawaii, Maryland, Massachusetts, New York, North Carolina, Ohio, and Rhode Island (USDOE, 2010c). Phase 3 winners include Arizona, Colorado, Illinois, Kentucky, Louisiana, New Jersey, and Pennsylvania.
5 For a comprehensive review of how all states and the District of Columbia use student growth and value-added models see Collins & Amrein-Beardsley, in press.
6 In Year 2, the number of observations was based on licensure states and evaluation scores from Year 1 (TDOE, 2012).
7 In Chapter 5 we provide a more comprehensive discussion on reliability of observation instruments and strategies to improve reliability.

References

Aaronson, D., Barrow, L., & Sanders, W. (2003). *Teachers and student achievement in Chicago public high schools.* Chicago, IL: Federal Research Bank of Chicago.

American Federation of Teachers. (2012). *Raising the bar: Aligning and elevating teacher preparation and the teaching profession.* Retrieved from http://www.aft.org/pdfs/highered/raisingthebar2012.pdf

Ascher, C. (1996). Performance contracting: A forgotten experiment in school privatization. *Phi Delta Kappan,* 77(9), 615–629.

Baker, E. L., Barton, P. E., Darling-Hammond, L., Haertel, E., Ladd, H. F., Linn, R. L., ... F Shepard, L. A. (2010). *Problems with the use of student test scores to evaluate teachers.* Retrieved from http://www.epi.org/publications/entry/bp278

Ballou, D. (2001). Pay for performance in public and private schools. *Economics of Education Review,* 20(1), 51–61.

Ballou, D., Sanders, W., & Wright, P. (2004). Controlling for student background in Value added assessment of teachers. *Journal of Educational and Behavioral Statistics,* 29(1), 37–66.

Bill & Melinda Gates Foundation. (2012). *Gathering feedback for teaching: Combining high-quality observations with student surveys and achievement gains.* Retrieved from http://www.metproject.org/downloads/MET_Gathering_Feedback_Research_Paper.pdf

Bill & Melinda Gates Foundation. (2013). *Ensuring fair and reliable measures of effective teaching: Culminating findings from the MET Project's three year study.* Retrieved from www.metproject.org/downloads/MET_EnsuringFair_and_Reliable_Measures_Practitioner_Brief_.pdf

Bowman, J. S. (2010). The success of failure: The paradox of performance pay. *Review of Public Personnel Administration,* 30(1), 70–78. doi:10.1177/0734371X09351824

Boyd, D., Grossman, P., Ing, M., Lankford, H., Loeb, S., & Wyckoff, J. (2011). The influence of school administrators on teacher retention decisions. *American Educational Research Journal, 48*(2), 303–333.

Boyd, D., Grossman, P., Lankford, H., & Loeb, S. (2006). How changes in entry requirements alter the teacher workforce and affect student achievement. *Education Finance and Policy, 1,* 176–216.

Bushaw, W. J., & Lopez, S. J. (2010). A time for change: The 42nd annual Phi Delta Kappa/Gallup poll of the public's attitudes toward the public schools. *Phi Delta Kappan, 92,* 9–26.

Bushaw, W. J., & Lopez, S. J. (2011). *The 43rd annual Phi Delta Kappa/Gallup poll of the public's attitudes toward the public schools.* Retrieved from http://www.pdkintl.org/poll/index.htm

Bushaw, W. J., & Lopez, S. J. (2012). Public education in the United States: A nation divided. *Phi Delta Kappan, 94*(1), 8–25.

Cavanagh, S. (2012, March 8). Survey: N.C. teachers say that high-stakes tests dominate classes. *Education Week.* Retrieved from http://blogs.edweek.org/edweek/state_edwatch/2012/03/survey_nc_teachers_dissatisfied_with_high-stakes_tests.html?qs=North+Carolina

Clotfelter, C. T., Ladd, H. F., & Vigdor, J. L. (2006). Teacher-student matching and the assessment of teacher effectiveness. *Journal of Human Resources, 41*(4), 778–820.

Collins, C., & Amrein-Beardsley, A. (in press). Putting growth and value-added models on the map: A national overview. *Teachers College Record.*

Darling-Hammond, L., Amrein-Beardsley, A., Haertel, E., & Rothstein, J. (2012). Evaluating teacher evaluation. *Phi Delta Kappan, 93*(6), 8–15.

Dee, T., & Keys, B. J. (2004). Does merit pay reward good teachers? Evidence from a randomized experiment. *Journal of Policy Analysis and Management, 23,* 471–488.

Delaware Department of Education. (2012, August). *DPAS II guide revised for teachers.* Retrieved from http://www.doe.k12.de.us/csa/dpasii/files/DPASTeachFullGuide.pdf

District of Columbia Public Schools. (2011). *An overview of IMPACT.* Retrieved from http://www.dc.gov/DCPS/In+the+Classroom+Ensuring+Teacher+Success/IMPACT+(Performance+Assessment)/An+Overview+of+IMPACT

Donaldson, M. L., & Johnson, S. M. (2011). Teach for America teachers: How long do they teach? When do they leave? *Phi Delta Kappan, 93*(2), 47–51.

Elam, S. M. (1973). *The Gallup polls of attitudes toward education 1969–1973.* Bloomington, IN: Phi Delta Kappa, Inc.

Elam, S. M. (1990). The 22nd annual Gallup poll of the public's attitudes toward the public schools. *Phi Delta Kappan, 72*(1), 41–55.

Elementary and Secondary Education Act (ESEA). (1965). (Pub.L. 89–10, 79 Stat. 27, 20 U.S.C. ch. 70)

First to the Top Act. (2010). Senate Bill No. 5. Retrieved from http://www.tn.gov/firsttothetop/docs/First%20to%20the%20Top%20Act%20of%202010.pdf

Florida Department of Education. (2006, February 10). Florida department of education unveils "effectiveness compensation" plan for teachers. Retrieved from http://www.fldoe.org/news/2006/2006_02_10.asp

Gates, B. (2012). Shame is not the solution. *New York Times.* Retrieved from http://www.nytimes.com/2012/02/23/opinion/for-teachers-shame-is-no-solution.html

Good, T. (in press). What do we know about how teachers influence student performance on standardized tests, and why do we know so little about other outcomes? *Teachers College Record.*

Good, T. L., Biddle, B. J., & Brophy, J. E. (1975). *Teachers make a difference.* New York, NY: Holt, Rinehart & Winston.

Gordon, R., Kane, T. J., & Staiger, D. O. (2006, March). *Identifying effective teachers using performance on the job.* Hamilton Project discussion paper. The Brookings Institution. Retrieved from http://www.brookings.edu/views/Papers/200604hamilton_1.pdf

Hanushek, E. A., & Rivkin, S. G. (2010). Generalizations about using value-added measures of teacher quality. *American Economic Review, 100*(2), 267–71.

Heilig, J. V., & Jez, S. J. (2010). *Teach for America: A review of the evidence.* East Lansing, MI: Great Lakes Center for Educational Research and Practice.

Henson, B. E., & Hall, P. M. (1993). Linking performance evaluation and career ladder programs: Reactions of teachers and principals in one district. *Elementary School Journal, 93*(4), 323.

Herlihy, C., Karger, E., Pollard, C., Hill, H. C., Kraft, M. A., Williams, M., & Howard, S. (in press). State and local efforts to investigate the validity and reliability of scores from teacher evaluation systems. *Teachers College Record.*

Hess, F. M., & Gift, T. (2008). The turnaround. *American School Board Journal, 195*(11), 31–32.

Hill, H. C., Rowan, B., & Ball, D. L. (2005). Effects of teachers' mathematical knowledge for teaching on student achievement. *American Educational Research Journal, 42*, 371–406. Retrieved from http://sitemaker.umich.edu/lmt/files/hillrowanball.pdf

Hubbard, J. (2012, January 4). Principals' teacher ratings vary widely by district. *The Tennessean.* Retrieved from http://www.tennessean.com/article/20120104/NEWS04/301040090/Principals-teacher-ratings-vary-widely-by-district

Imazeki, J. (2005). Teacher salaries and teacher attrition. *Economics of Education Review, 24*, 431–449.

Ingersoll, R. (2001). Teacher turnover and teacher shortages: An organizational analysis. *American Educational Research Journal, 38*(3), 499–534.

Jacobson, S. L., Hickox, E. S., & Stevenson, R.B. (1996). *School administration: Persistent dilemas in preparation and practice.* Westport, CT: Greenwood.

Kane, T. J., Rockoff, J. E., & Staiger, D. O. (2005, July). *Identifying effective teachers in New York City.* Paper presented at NBER Summer Institute.

Kaplan, T. (2012). Albany to Limit the Disclosure of Teacher Evaluations. *New York Times.* Retrieved from http://www.nytimes.com/2012/06/22/nyregion/albany-to-limit-disclosure-of-teacher-evaluations.html?_r=0

Kirby, S., Berends, M., & Naftel, S. (1999). Supply and demand of minority teachers in Texas: Problems and prospects. *Educational Evaluation and Policy Analysis, 21*(1), 47–66.

Konstantopoulos, S. (in press). Teacher effects, value-added models, and accountability. *Teachers College Record.*

Lankford, H., Loeb, S., & Wyckoff, J. (2002). Teacher sorting and the plight of urban schools: A descriptive analysis. *Educational Evaluation and Policy Analysis, 24*(1), 37–62.

Lavigne, A. L. (in press). Exploring the intended and unintended consequences of high-stakes teacher evaluation on schools, teachers, and students. *Teachers College Record.*

Los Angeles Times (n.d.). Retrieved from http://www.latimes.com/news/local/teachers-investigation

MacFarquhar, N. (1995, April 14). Judge orders a state takeover of the Newark school district. *New York Times.* Retrieved from http://www.nytimes.com/1995/04/14/nyregion/judge-orders-a-state-takeover-of-the-newark-school-district.html?pagewanted=all&src=pm

Maier, A. (2012). Doing good and doing well: Credentialism and teach for America. *Journal of Teacher Education, 63*(1), 10–22. doi:10.1177/0022487111422071

Malen, B., Croninger, R., Muncey, D., & Redmond-Jones, D. (2002). Reconstituting schools: "Testing" the "theory of action." *Educational Evaluation and Policy Analysis, 24*(2), 113–132.

Marsh, J. A., Springer, M. G., McCaffrey, D. F., Yuan, K., Epstein, S., Koppich, J., ... Peng, A. (2011). *A big apple for educators: New York City's experiment with schoolwide performance bonuses: final evaluation report.* Retrieved from http://www.rand.org/pubs/monographs/MG1114.html

Marx, R. W. (in press). Reforming again: Now teachers. *Teachers College Record.*

Massachusetts Department of Elementary and Secondary Education. (2011). *Educator evaluation FAQ.* Retrieved from http://www.doe.mass.edu/edeval/faq.html?section=R

Milanowski, A. T., Longwell-Grice, H., Saffold, F., Jones, J., Schomisch, K., & Odden, A. (2009). Recruiting new teachers to urban school districts: What incentives will work? *International Journal of Education Policy & Leadership, 4*(8), 1–13.

Murnane, R., & Cohen, D. (1986). Merit pay and the evaluation problem: Why most merit pay plans fail and few survive. *Harvard Education Review, 56*, 1–17.

National Council on Teacher Quality. (2011). *State of the states: Trends and early lessons on teacher evaluation and effectiveness policies.* Retrieved from http://www.nctq.org/p/publications/docs/nctq_stateOfTheStates.pdf

National Education Association. (2011). *New policy statement on teacher evaluation and accountability-adopted as amended.* Retrieved from http://www.nea.org/grants/46326.htm

National Education Association. (2012). NEA supports resolution to roll back high-stakes testing. Retrieved from http://www.nea.org/home/51693.htm

National Institute for Excellence in Teaching. (2012). *TAP research summary.* Retrieved from http://www.tapsystem.org/publications/tap_research_summary_0210.pdf

Nichols, S. L., & Berliner, D. C. (2007). *Collateral damage: How high-stakes testing corrupts America's schools.* Cambridge, MA: Harvard Education Press.

NYC Department of Education. (n.d.). Retrieved from http://schools.nyc.gov/Teachers/Teacher Development/TeacherDataToolkit/default.htm

No Child Left Behind Act of 2001, Pub. L. 107-110, 20 U.S.C. § 6301 et. seq.

Nye, B., Konstantopoulos, S., & Hedges, L.V. (2004). How large are teacher effects?. *Educational Evaluation and Policy Analysis, 26,* 237–257.

Otterman, S. (2011, July 17). New York City abandons teacher bonus program. *New York Times.* Retrieved from http://www.nytimes.com/2011/07/18/education/18rand.html

Payne, C. M. (2008). *So much reform, so little change: The persistence of failure in urban schools.* Boston, MA: Harvard Education Press.

Perry, J. L., Engbergs, T. A., & Jun, S. Y. (2009). Back to the future? Performance-related pay, empirical research, and the perils of persistence. *Public Administration Review, 69*(1), 39–51. doi:10.1111/j.1540-6210.2008.01939_2.x

Podgursky, M., Monroe, R., & Watson, D. (2004). The academic quality of public school teachers: An analysis of entry and exit behavior. *Economics of Education Review, 23,* 507–518.

Podgursky, M., & Springer, M. G. (2007). Credentials versus performance: Review of the teacher performance pay research. *Peabody Journal of Education, 82*(4), 551–573. doi:10.1080/01619560701602934

Powell, A. G., Farrar, E., & Cohen, D. K. (1985). *The shopping mall high school: Winners and losers in the educational marketplace.* Boston, MA: Houghton Mifflin.

Public Schools of North Carolina, State Board of Education. (n.d.). *Professional development.* Retrieved from http://www.ncpublicschools.org/profdev/training/teacher/

Ravitch, D. (2010). *The death and life of the great American school system: How testing and choice are undermining education.* New York, NY: Basic Books.

Ravitch, D. (2011, March 29). Thoughts on the failure of merit pay. *Education Week.* Retrieved from http://blogs.edweek.org/edweek/Bridging-Differences/2011/03/thoughts_on_the_failure _of.html

Reardon, S. F. (2011). The widening academic achievement gap between the rich and the poor: New evidence and possible explanations. In G. J. Duncan & R. J. Murnane (Eds.), *Whither opportunity? Rising inequality and the uncertain life chances of low-income children* (pp. 91–116). New York, NY: Russell Sage Foundation Press.

Rivkin, S., Hanushek, E. A., & Kain, J. F. (2005). Teachers, schools, and academic achievement. *Econometrica, 73,* 417–458.

Rockoff, J. (2004). The impact of individual teachers on student achievement: Evidence from panel data. *American Economic Review, 94*(2), 247–252.

Rothstein, J. (2010). Teacher quality in educational production: tracking, decay, and student achievement. *Quarterly Journal of Economics, 125*(1), 175–214.

Rowan, B., Correnti, R., & Miller, R. J. (2002). What large scale, survey research tells us about teacher effects on student achievement: Insights from the Prospects study of elementary schools. *Teachers College Record, 104,* 1525–1567.

Sanders, W. L., & Horn, S. P. (1994). The Tennessee value-added assessment system (TVAAS) mixed model methodology in educational assessment. *Journal of Personnel Evaluation in Education, 8*(1), 299–311.

Sanders, W., & Horn, S. P. (1998). Research findings from the Tennessee value-added assessment system (TVAAS) database: Implications for educational evaluation and research. *Journal of Personnel Evaluation in Education, 12*(3), 247–256.

Sawchuk, S. (2013, January 3). Access to teacher evaluations divides advocates. *Education Week.* Retrieved from http://www.edweek.org/ew/articles/2012/03/28/26evaluation_ep.h31. html

Smarick, A. (2010). The turnaround fallacy. *Education Next, 10*(1), 20–26. Retrieved from http:// educationnext.org/files/ednext_20101_20.pdf

Strauss, V. (2012). An unintended consequence of value-added teacher evaluation. *Washington Post.* Retrieved from http://www.washingtonpost.com/blogs/answer-sheet/post/an-unintended-consequence-of-value-added-teacher-evaluation/2012/04/29/gIQA1R5mpT_blog. html

Strong, M. (2011). *The highly qualified teacher: What is teacher quality and how do we measure it?.* New York, NY: Teachers College Press.

Sullivan, J. F. (1987, December 22). School takeover bill gains in Jersey. *New York Times.* Retrieved from http://www.nytimes.com/1987/12/22/nyregion/school-takeover-bill-gains-in-jersey.html

Tennessee Department of Education. (2012). *Number of observations.* Retrieved from http://team-tn.org/assets/misc/A_numberofobservations_12_13_Updated.pdf

Tennessee Department of Education. (n.d.). *Tennessee first to the top: How TEAM works.* Retrieved from http://team-tn.org/how-team-works.

Tyack, D. (1974). *The one best system: A history of American education.* Cambridge, MA: Harvard University Press.

U.S. Department of Education. (2009a, August 26). *Obama administration announces historic opportunity to turn around nation's lowest-achieving public schools* [Press release]. Retrieved from U.S. Department of Education at http://www2.ed.gov/news/pressreleases/2009/08/08262009. html

U.S. Department of Education. (2009b). *Race to the Top Fund.* Retrieved from http://www2. ed.gov/programs/racetothetop/index.html

U.S. Department of Education. (2010a). *ESEA reauthorization: A blueprint for reform.* Retrieved from http://www2.ed.gov/policy/elsec/leg/blueprint/index.html

U.S. Department of Education. (2010b). *Delaware and Tennessee win first race to the top grants.* Retrieved from http://www.ed.gov/news/press-releases/delaware-and-tennessee-win-first-race-top-grants

U.S. Department of Education. (2010c). *Nine states and the District of Columbia win second round race to the top grants.* Retrieved from http://www.ed.gov/news/press-releases/nine-states-and-district-columbia-win-second-round-race-top-grants

U.S. Department of Education. (2010d). *Race to the Top: Phase 2 application guidelines.* Retrieved from http://www2.ed.gov/programs/racetothetop/applicant.html

U.S. Department of Education. (2010e). *States' applications for phase 2.* Retrieved from http:// www2.ed.gov/programs/racetothetop/phase2-applications/index.html

U.S. Department of Education. (2011a). *Great teachers and leaders: State considerations on building systems of educator effectiveness.* Retrieved from http://www.ed.gov/programs/racetothetop/great-teachers.doc

U.S. Department of Education. (2011b). *Department of Education awards $200 million to seven states to advance K-12 reform.* Retrieved from http://www.ed.gov/news/press-releases/department-education-awards-200-million-seven-states-advance-k-12-reform

U.S. Department of Education. (2012a). *Teacher incentive fund.* Retrieved from http://www2. ed.gov/programs/teacherincentive/funding.html

U.S. Department of Education. (2012b). *26 more states and D.C. seek flexibility from NCLB to drive education reforms in second round of requests.* Retrieved from http://www.ed.gov/news/press-releases/26-more-states-and-dc-seek-flexibility-nclb-drive-education-reforms-second-round

Veltri, B. T. (2010). *Learning on other people's kids: Becoming a Teach for America teacher.* Charlotte, NC: Information Age.

Weischadle, D. E. (1979, December 9). The Trenton school takeover. *New York Times*. Retrieved from http://select.nytimes.com/gst/abstract.html?res=F70D17F63D5F12728DDDA00894D A415B898BF1D3

Wenglinsky, H. (2000). *How teaching matters: Bringing the classroom back into discussions of teacher quality*. Princeton, NJ: The Milken Family Foundation and Educational Testing Service.

Winerip, M. (2011, November 6). In Tennessee, following the rules for evaluation off a cliff. *New York Times*. Retrieved from http://www.nytimes.com/2011/11/07/education/tennessees-rules-on-teacher-evaluations-bring-frustration.html?pagewanted=all.

Wright, S. P., Horn, S. P., & Sanders, W. L. (1997). Teacher and classroom context effects on student achievement. *Journal of Personnel Evaluation in Education, 11*, 57–67.

5

ASSESSING THE ASSESSMENTS

Promises and Pitfalls of Teacher Evaluation Methods

Introduction

In Chapter 4 we illustrated that Race to the Top (RttT) states are primarily using value-added assessment and classroom observations to assess effective teaching. We illuminated some initial problems with RttT teacher evaluation design and methodology, particularly in implementation. Some of these problems have arisen because limited attention has been given to the research-based evidence on how to use these methods and use them well. Furthermore, there is significant oversight as to what these methods can and, more importantly, cannot tell us. Hence, this chapter is devoted to evaluating the methods for teacher evaluation. We will briefly describe each method, its forms, and its most popular and frequent uses. For each method we will discuss strengths and limitations with a specific focus on what information each method can provide about effective teaching.

Classroom Observations

As noted in Chapter 3, the development of classroom observation methods and actual research mushroomed in the 1970s and 80s. During this period, many observational systems were developed and used in studies for describing and improving teaching. Much has been written about observation research and methods. Here we document that there is a rich and complex literature on the purposes and uses of observational systems.

A seminal chapter entitled "Observation as Inquiry and Method" was written by Carolyn Evertson and Judith Green and appeared in the 1986 *Handbook of Research on Teaching*. Evertson and Green noted that there were four phases in the history in classroom observational research:

Phase I. Exploratory (ca. 1939–1963)
Phase II. Instrument development (ca. 1958–1973)
Phase III. Use of instruments to link teaching and achievement (ca. 1973–1986)
Phase IV. Expansion and new directions (ca. 1980–1986)

Readers can find detailed discussion of these phases and representative studies in Evertson and Green, however, for our purposes, the recognition of these phases is sufficient for providing a brief introduction to the history of classroom research as a focused method of inquiry. During the exploratory phase, researchers were beginning to explore the many aspects of what occurs in classrooms. In the instrument development phase, they attempted to develop ways of codifying classroom events. In Phase III (as discussed in Chapter 3), researchers began to use observational instruments to link teaching and student achievement. The fourth phase, co-occurring at the time Evertson and Green were writing, was the discussion of new emerging directions in observational research including the use of narrative records and ethnographic methods.

Here, we will focus mainly on quantitative observation measures as these are presently very popular; however, as noted in Chapter 3, qualitative methods in the 1990s were very popular and became the dominant form of classroom research. More recently there has been the return to quantitative measures. We turn our attention to describing these methods and guidelines considering their appropriate use. We will focus upon observational methods using category systems, checklist, and sign/rating systems. Evertson and Green (1986) provide extensive discussion of various points including observation as a research and decision-making process, observation as a measure of recording and documenting, and as a way of adjusting observation to a particular context.

As in many areas of education, interest in observation gained attention, suddenly subsided, only to resurface in the past few years. As early as the 1980s, teacher evaluation was criticized for a system primarily based on principals' ratings during a single observation, and that sometimes ratings were a result of teacher characteristics (e.g., experience, credentials), not what teachers actually were doing in the classroom (Cramer, 1983; Johnson, 1984; Natriello & Dornbusch, 1981; Stodolsky, 1984). Today there appears to be less concern about principals conducting observations, although criticisms of limited observations are starting to be addressed in various research circles.

Types of Classroom Observation Systems.   Classroom observations typically fall into one of two categories: high inference or low inference. Low-inference observation instruments allow for the exploration of distinct, descriptive,

TABLE 5.1 Example Classroom Management and Organization Item from a Low-Inference Checklist: The Classroom Observation and Assessment Scale for Teaching Candidates*

Indicator		2.1 Management of Instructional Time
Yes	No	
____	____	Begins class promptly
____	____	Engages students in learning activities for a majority of the available class time
____	____	Routines are established for recurring activities
____	____	Provides sufficient time for students to complete instructional activities
____	____	Makes smooth transition between activities

* Table adapted from Cloud-Silva and Denton (1989)

targeted, and fairly objective teaching practices. Low-inference observations also include time sampling in which a rater may be asked to report on the presence of a particular practice at set time intervals. In other cases, a rater may be asked to note every time a particular behavior occurs (e.g., number of times a teacher asks an academically-related question). The checklist is another example of a low-inference system; the presence or absence of a particular behavior (e.g., teacher identifies lesson objectives) is noted typically at the conclusion of an observation period (see Table 5.1).

It is worthy to note that some of these low-inference observation instruments have been referred to as category systems (Rosenshine, 1970) or sign systems[1] (Medley, 1982; Rosenshine & Furst, 1973), but for the remainder of this book we will refer to the overarching terms (e.g., low inference, high inference) to describe observation instruments.

The more subjective types of classroom observation systems are high-inference instruments, which include rating scales that require the observer to make judgments about more global teaching practices (e.g., teacher clarity) (Rosenshine, 1970). In these types of systems, variables are usually rated on a 5- or 7-point scale that seeks to assess and determine the quality to which a variable occurs (e.g., poor, satisfactory, exemplary). In 1970, Rosenshine noted that low-inference instruments:

> ... have become very popular in descriptive educational research and in teacher training because they offer greater ... specificity and because an "objective" count of a teacher's encouraging statements to students appears easier for a teacher to accept than a "subjective" rating of his warmth.
>
> *(p. 281)*

Interestingly, this trend has shifted to a strong preference for high-inference observation instruments. Rosenshine and Furst (1973) make the point that in their work high-inference variables were more highly associated with effects on students. A shift towards these more global codes that are created as measures of effective teaching also are a shift *back* towards the idea of single coding—one teaching practice equals one code—a common conceptualization of classroom observation prior to 1970. The 1970s were defined by the work of Flanders and Stallings. Flanders (1970) demonstrated the potential for multiple coding. Stallings (1977) work was an extension of this. As part of the Stallings Classroom Observation, raters are asked to code interactions in a 5-minute segment by identifying who, to whom, how, and what. It appears, however, that this research is no longer represented in popular classroom instruments of today. For more information on observational system design see Rosenshine and Furst (1973) and Evertson and Green (1986).

Observers.   A number of different individuals can be involved in the process of observing and evaluating teachers, including: administrators, peers, master teachers, and outside evaluators. Typically, administrators have done observations; however, research on principals' ratings of teachers in relationship to teachers' student achievement gains is relatively weak with correlations between .10 and .23 (Medley & Coker, 1987). Research using a variety of different observers (e.g., administrators, teacher education students, citizens with no background in education) indicates that the ability for administrators to correctly identify highly effective and ineffective teachers (as measured by value-added) is no better than by chance. As illustrated in Chapter 3, administrators tend to rate fairly low in their ability to correctly classify teachers among a number of possible observers—elementary students are the most accurate judges (correct 50% of the time), whereas administrators and teacher educators are the worst (correct 31% of the time) (Strong, Gargani, & Hacifazlioglu, 2011).[2]

These concerning findings about the value of principals' judgments are not entirely at the fault of the principal. There are a number of factors that alter judgment accuracy. Some teachers are easier to classify than others (Strong et al., 2011). For example, principals are able to detect teachers in the extremes, the most and least effective teachers as measured by student achievement gains, but have more difficulty distinguishing between teachers in the middle (Jacob & Lefgren, 2008). It is interesting to note that this is a problem with both observation and value-added measures. This is incredibly concerning given that this represents 80% of teachers (with each tail of the distribution representing 10%). It is equally distressing that policy makers are unaware of this condition or do not care. It also raises the question about how much transformation can occur if change is primarily based on being able to accurately identify the

10% worst and 10% best of the teacher workforce. We expand on this issue below and in Chapter 6.

Other biases can arise because exposure to a teacher, or what we refer to as opportunity to assess, has an important impact on accuracy. The longer a principal has known a teacher, the better able a principal is to correctly identify a teacher's effectiveness (Harris & Sass, 2010). Clearly, then, principals are biased observers because of their existing relationship with teachers. This also puts new teachers at risk of being incorrectly evaluated and is a potentially fatal flaw if evaluations are being used in high-stakes settings. This potential flaw takes on even more meaning given that in the next few years principals in most schools will be dealing with high numbers of new teachers (see Chapter 6). Further, research has demonstrated that principals' ratings are influenced by situational factors such as additional work that a teacher does beyond classroom instruction (Epstein, 1985), although it is not known to what extent principals use this information when evaluating teachers. Recent research has, however, illustrated that administrators tend to rate their own teachers higher (.10 of a point) than administrators from other schools (Bill & Melinda Gates Foundation, 2013).

There has been significant research conducted to examine administrators' ability to rate teachers, but it is less clear why some teachers and content areas are easier to rate than others, particularly the cognitive processes that occur that result in more or less accurate decisions. Further, there is limited research on other types of observers. In the 1980s there was support for peer evaluations (Darling-Hammond, Wise, & Pease, 1983; Natriello & Dornbusch, 1981), and this interest reemerges again in some Race to the Top states (e.g., Massachusetts). Peer review has been shown to be beneficial beyond its main purpose of evaluation. For example, research has shown that teachers believe peer observation builds collegiality (Munson, 1998), supports reflection (Wilkins & Shin, 2010), and has been found to support new teacher retention (Odell & Ferraro, 1992). One limitation of this research is that a majority of it has been conducted in non-evaluative, low-stakes settings. Research on colleagues and peers as evaluators has demonstrated that teachers generally demonstrate high levels of agreement when rating other teachers (83%); however, their accuracy, as a group, is fairly low (37%), suggesting that they may be reliable, but not accurate judges of a teacher's effectiveness as measured by value-added scores (Strong et al., 2011). Peers, in general, whether from a different or the same grade range rate teachers .10-.20 points lower than administrators from the same school or a different one and are less likely to use extreme values of a rating scale (Bill & Melinda Gates Foundation, 2013). It is also unclear if feedback from peers is more well received than from administrators, and if this feedback from observations is implemented in any meaningful kind of way that has an impact on student outcomes. Regardless, *reported positive experiences* from peer evaluation or coaching does not necessarily correlate with significant changes in student achievement outcomes (Murry, Ma, & Mazur, 2009).

Nature of Observations. For some time, researchers have commented on the appropriate number and time of observations in order to best capture a teacher's practices. A single 30-minute observation has been deemed an ineffective sample of teaching time in order to assess teaching effectiveness (Emmer & Peck, 1973). Early research indicated that increasing observation time from 10 to 50 minutes long increased reliability as much as .37 (Rowley, 1978). Interestingly, more recent research using observation has used a wide variation in length of observation from approximately 2 minutes (Strong et al., 2011) to 45 (Good et al., 2006). In the former, coding happens after the conclusion of watching a continuous two-minute clip, in the latter, observers watched for 10-minute segments during a live observation, separated by 5-minute coding periods. More recent research has indicated that 15-minute observations are indeed less reliable than 50-minute observations, but limited changes in scoring occur beyond 15 minutes and this additional observation time makes a difference in scores for some domains (e.g., instruction) and not others (e.g., classroom environment; Bill & Melinda Gates Foundation, 2013). Further, increasing the number of observation periods from one to five has been shown to increase reliability from .15 to .50 (Rowley, 1978). Others have emphasized the importance of multiple raters (Epstein, 1985). More recently, reliability estimates as large as .67 have been achieved when four different observers have observed a teacher on four different occasions (Bill & Melinda Gates Foundation, 2012); however, later findings indicated that reliability could be increased more by having multiple observers rather than multiple observations (Bill & Melinda Gates Foundation, 2013). Hence, findings from the Measures of Effective Teaching (MET) project indicate that *at least* two different individuals should rate a teacher (Bill & Melinda Gates Foundation, 2013); but it is unclear who that second person should be when it comes to districts applying this knowledge to their own practices.

Furthermore, in a study of 17 states, only 1 state, North Carolina, requires more than one observer in their teacher evaluation and that is only the case with a certain subset of teachers—probationary teachers. Of the 17 states, none require multiple raters as part of their standard teacher evaluation and observation protocol (Herlihy et al., in press). Given what is known about the reliability of single and multiple raters, state plans to *not* endorse the use of multiple raters could have important and detrimental legal implications (Pullin, 2013). It is important to note, however, that reliability estimates can only be increased with multiple observations and observers if, at a minimum, the assumptions that teaching is stable and that teachers are observed in conditions that require similar teaching practices are met (Stodolsky, 1984). Furthermore, although the MET Project has extended upon existing knowledge about classroom observations, in the MET Project and in the work described by Strong and colleagues (2011) observations were done by video, not live. It is unclear if these high levels of reliability were achieved because of format. At this point in time, most states practice live, not video observation, making such findings less generalizable.

Popular and Modern Uses.   When used in classrooms for professional development or evaluation purposes, classroom observations typically consist of a pre-conference, an observation, followed by a post-conference, a long recommended practice with little data to support it. Race to the Top teacher observation plans usually include an announced, unannounced, and a walk through visit. The walk through is derived from the concept that individuals in social and clinical psychological settings can be assessed in small increments of time. In most cases, observers draw upon non-verbal cues such as facial expressions and body language. A meta-analysis of 38 studies found that accuracy between 30 second and 4- to 5-minute observations do not differ significantly. The overall effect size of the accuracy of these "thin slices" studies is .39 (Ambady & Rosenthal, 1992). This research indicates that observers can detect effective teaching by assessing non-verbal cues and body language; however, the large knowledge base on teacher expectations is just one example of why a great amount of attention needs to also be placed on verbal cues.

One of the more commonly used and general observation instruments is The Framework for Teaching. The Framework for Teaching is a high-inference observation instrument consisting of 76 indicators grouped into 22 observation items (Danielson Group, 2011). The CLASS instrument (Pianta, LaParo, & Hamre, 2008) is another popular high-inference PK-12 instrument that includes 11 dimensions that organize across three domains: emotional support, classroom organization, and instructional support scored in 15-minute cycles on a 1–7 scale. Both measures were included in the Measures of Effective Teaching (MET) Project. Other popular subject-specific instruments highlighted in the MET project and used elsewhere are: Mathematics Quality of Instruction (Hill et al., 2008), Protocol for Language Arts Teaching Observations, Quality Science Teaching, and the UTeach Teacher Observation Protocol (see Appendix 5.1).

Strengths.   Observations are the most direct way to observe what a teacher does in the classroom. Observations can be used in both formative and summative ways. Some studies have shown significant changes in teachers' behaviors once teachers are made aware of their teaching practices and interactions with students (Good & Brophy, 1974). Others have documented change in intent but not behavior when teachers are made aware of student learning outcomes (Doyle & Redwine, 1974). It is unclear, then, to what extent providing a teacher with knowledge has in a teacher's ability to change teaching practices. It may very well be that the way in which teachers are provided with information and subsequent support are the key. And, although many feel that information about one's teaching behavior is sufficient to allow a teacher to change their classroom interaction patterns if they choose to do so, but it is not so simple. Withall (1956) collected 12 weeks of classroom data in one eighth-grade art class in the laboratory school of the University of Chicago. The data indicated that some students enjoyed considerably more teacher contact than did other students in the classroom. Withall provided this information to the instructor who indicated that he wanted to change his interaction patterns with these students and others. Even though the teacher was motivated to change his behavior, the data collected after the intervention indicated that the instructor did not find it easy to change his interaction patterns and much of the imbalance that had been observed before the intervention continued. Classrooms, and the interactions that occur within them, are complex. Furthermore, although there is a widely held belief that feedback improves performance, this has not been the case and is much more complex—feedback has highly variable effects on performance (Kluger & DeNisi, 1996).

Another strength of observation as a measure is that observation instruments have shown moderate but consistent relationships to student achievement gains (Bill & Melinda Gates Foundation, 2012; Gallagher, 2004; Kimball, White, Milanowski, & Borman, 2004; Milanowski, 2004), suggesting that these instruments do capture teaching practices that are indeed linked to student learning. There is limited research on the extent to which it should be expected these two measures correlate given a number of exogenous variables that are inadvertently captured in these measures (Berliner, in press).

Checklist or rating scales are often used in descriptive ways and can be less time consuming and costly. These instruments can be developed in ways that correlate with high-inference observational measures (Emmer & Peck, 1973). The use of multiple instruments that require different levels of inference is beneficial in providing a more comprehensive picture of effective teaching because in combination conclusions can be made about both how teachers teach and how well.

Limitations. Classroom observation instruments and research have been criticized for their lack of theoretical and conceptual frameworks (Fenstermacher, 1978; Ornstein, 1995a, 1995b). Furthermore, as more and more research emerges about the requirements of conducting observations and conducting them well, there are practical limitations in the ability for schools and districts to adhere to such guidelines, which could seriously compromise any teacher evaluation system. Thus, without major investments in training, the benefits of improving teaching are likely more illusionary than real. Below we provide additional challenges and limitations to classroom observations.

Simplicity. In many scientific arenas, and particularly when it comes to theory, simplicity is preferred over complexity, particularly if the same information or predictions can be made using a simple explanation rather than a complex one. We argue, however, that simplicity is often a limitation rather than a strength of classroom observation instruments because observation variables, when simplified, do not fully capture the intended teaching practice nor important nuances in the complexity of classrooms (Ing & Webb, 2012).

For example, policy makers and educational researchers who do not specialize in observational research may fail to recognize that variables often assume different meaning in relationship to other variables. Consider these variables that are considered aspects of good teaching: alerting (this can be done in many ways, such as keeping students in suspense about who will be called on next by selecting randomly), throwing out challenges (suggesting that the next question is difficult or tricky), or by informing students that their seatwork will be checked (before the class ends), and accountability (e.g., asking students to show their answers, asking students to respond in unison, asking listeners to comment on peers' responses, checking seatwork for correctness). Further, the nuanced relationships between variables are important; use of alerting with accountability is vastly different than alerting not followed by accountability.

Some may see these comments as excessive nit picking as surely the absence or presence of alerting and accountability (AA) are "obvious," and much of the time that may be the case. However, these obvious variables can be inordinately difficult to interpret. We use two examples to make the point. First, if the teacher alerts too frequently, and alerts only low ability students, the teacher, in fact, is communicating low expectations. Second, if the teacher alerts without subsequent accountability, it is a serious management mistake (as students will quickly learn to ignore teacher directions if no accountability follows). We could go on, but our point is, hopefully, clear—the quality, timing, and distribution of management variables are often important, and it is likely that the subtle differences in quality is what separates average from very good managers. These important nuances will not be captured in most observation instruments nor in overall teacher evaluation scores and ranks (as most states have proposed), limiting the ability of such systems to correctly identify good, average, and poor teachers. Some would even take this point to the extreme. As McNeil and Popham (1973) noted, "… observations are most beneficial for recording and analyzing the teaching act—not judging it. Effective teaching cannot be proven by the presence or absence of any instruction variable" (p. 233). To this end, it is unclear how Race to the Top states will systematically use observational data to improve instructional practices.

Validity.   Technical reliability does not assure validity. For example, we have long known that teachers' appropriate use of management principles like AA strongly correlate with appropriate student behavior (Kounin, 1970), and these AA principles have been demonstrated by experimental research that directly relates these variables to student achievement (Good & Grouws, 1979; Evertson, Emmer, & Brophy, 1980; Freiberg, Huzinec, & Templeton, 2009) as noted in Chapter 3. However, if state X develops reliable coders, it does not mean that their AA agreements are a valid measure of AA. It only means that state X coders agree on their measurement. It does not mean that the original researchers would have agreed with the coding of these variables. Reliability does not equate to validity.

Reliability.   Reliability estimates do not always ensure a methodologically sound instrument. High interrater reliability fails to address a variety of issues related to reliability and variation such as interactions between raters, teachers, and lessons, points on a scale, the frequency of instrument target behaviors, and chance agreement, to name a few (Hill, Charalambos, & Kraft, 2012). As noted by Hill and colleagues (2012), there is limited information about how the number of items on an observation rubric alters reliability. Further, many states are moving forward with instruments containing a particular number of items or indicators and with a particular number of observations with limited research-based evidence as to why these number of observations or indicators were chosen. Table 5.2 offers a number of questions related to the assessment of reliability in observation instruments.

Error.   Error can come in a number of forms. For example, some researchers have found that training on observation instruments generally raises administrators' ratings of teachers. Furthermore, elementary school teachers are rated .25 higher than secondary teachers (Ligon & Ellis, 1986). This latter finding is interesting because elementary and secondary *principals* tend to hold different criteria for effective teaching. Elementary principals tend to favor warmth, creativity, and organization, whereas secondary principals show a preference for systematic, task-oriented, and structured teaching (Tuckman & Hyman, 1977). If a particular instrument places a greater emphasis on some of these practices than others, systematic bias will occur. The questions and issues outlined in Table 5.2 are important to consider to determine if systematic bias exists and to what extent such bias compromises the use of observations, particularly in high-stakes settings. Other issues include low reliability across raters, inconsistencies between written narratives and observation system scores (Brauchle, McLarty, & Parker, 1989), and skewed and inflated observation scores (Ellett & Garland, 1987). Others have found that contextual variables such as the number of students in the classroom, if additional teachers are present, and instructional method (e.g., group work) can result in systematic differences in classroom quality (Curby et al., 2011). Also, some content areas may be easier to assess than others. For example, correlations between principals' ratings of teachers and student achievement are stronger in math than language arts (Riner, 1991). This is, in part, because math is more linear but also because most of the teacher effect research using student achievement outcomes has been collected in math classrooms. This could significantly alter how teachers are subsequently rated on observation instruments. Unknowingly, some observation instruments may be biased towards a particular instructional method. A number of these errors are described in Table 5.3.

TABLE 5.2 Reliability Issues Associated with Classroom Observation*

Questions	Related Issues
When should observer agreement be measured?	1. Prior to data collection 2. Training does not guarantee against observer skill deterioration as data collection proceeds.
On what kinds of data should observer agreement be calculated?	1. Agreement should be computed on the same unit(s) of behavior that will be used in the data analysis. 2. Agreement should be computed on subcategories of behavior as well as the larger, subsuming categories.
With whom should agreement be obtained?	1. High interobserver agreement may not mean agreement with the original categories, because systematic misinterpretation can exist even with high agreement. 2. Observers' scores should also be compared with a criterion. This is known as criterion-related agreement.
Under what conditions should agreement be calculated?	1. Coding in the setting may differ from coding of unambiguous samples in a laboratory or training session. 2. Ways to heighten observer vigilance and maintain accountability should be considered.
How can agreement be measured?	1. *Intraclass correlation coefficients*: Useful after a study is completed, but impractical during or before. Highly effected by the variance between subjects. 2. *Simple percentage agreement*: Drawbacks are that low frequencies in some categories and high frequencies in others may make interpretations ambiguous. Does not account for false inflation due to chance agreement.
Which agreement coefficient is appropriate?	1. Dependent upon the type of observation system, number of categories, type of data, unit(s) of analysis, and purpose. 2. If nominal comparisons cannot be obtained, then marginal agreement methods should be used. 3. If there are only a few categories and/or frequency distributions are unequal, then correction for chance agreement should be made.

* This table was adapted from Evertson, C., & Green, J. (1986). Observation as inquiry and method. In M. Whitrock (Ed.), *Handbook of research on teaching* (3rd ed., pp. 162–213). New York, NY: Macmillian.

Stability. We have known for some time that teacher effects on student achievement vary widely from year to year. This is due, in part, to the fact that most teachers have new students each year made up of different student characteristics (Good, in press). Additionally, within a given day there is significant variation in teaching quality. Using observational data from Grades 3 and 5, Curby and colleagues (2011) found that emotional support was the most stable across a given day. Instructional support was the least stable. Results

TABLE 5.3 Common Errors Associated with Using Classroom Observation Systems*

Type of Error	Definition
1. Central tendency	When using rating scales, observers tend toward the subjective midpoint when judging a series of stimuli.
2. Leniency	When using rating scales for which a "yes," "sometimes," "rarely," or "no" is required, observers tend to be lenient.
3. Primacy effects	Observers' initial impressions have a distorting effect on later judgments.
4. Logical errors	Observers make judgment errors based on theoretical, experiential, or commitment-based assumptions (e.g., the assumption that because a teacher shows warmth to a class, she/he is also instructionally effective).
5. Failure to acknowledge self	The influence of the observer on the setting is often overlooked. The investigator's role may lead to the establishment of particular teaching behaviors that are not typical.
6. Generalization of unique behavior	Judgments may be based on evidence from an unrepresentative sample.
7. Unrepresentative sampling	Errors may occur based on samples which do not represent the general group of behaviors that do not occur frequently enough to be observed reliably.
8. Reactions of the observed	Reactions of participants being observed can distort the process or phenomena being observed (e.g., teachers who are anxious about being observed may behave differently than they would at a calmer time).
9. Failure to account for situation or context	Leads to incorrect conclusions from assumptions of functional equivalents (e.g., reading time 1 = reading time 2). Can lead to overlooking what is being taught, changes in activities, variations in rights and obligations for participation, hence can distort conclusions.
10. Lack of consideration for the speed of relevant action	Errors may occur based on the omission of crucial features because of the rapidity of actions in the classroom.
11. Lack of consideration for the simultaneity of events	Errors may occur based on failure to account for more than one activity occurring at a time; more than one message being sent at a time (e.g., use of different channels – verbal and nonverbal).
12. Failure to insure against observer drift	Errors caused by changes in the way the observer uses a system as time goes on. Can lead to obtaining descriptions that do not match the original categories or that vary from each other (Kugle, 1978).

* This table was adapted from Evertson C., & Green J. (1986). Observation as inquiry and method. In M.. Whitrock (Ed.), *Handbook of research on teaching* (3rd ed., 162–213). New York, NY: Macmillian.

also indicated that the beginning of the day and transitions are related to lower-quality classroom interactions. This type of within-day variability is important to note and recognize. Of course, all observations cannot be conducted at the same time; however, there should be some sort of standards and guidelines to ensure to the best of one's ability similar observation conditions.

Interestingly, Berliner (1976) noted that "Usually people think of 'good' teachers as flexible. Such teachers are expected to change methods, techniques, and styles to suit particular students, curriculum areas, time of day or year, etc. That is, the standard of excellence in teaching commonly held implies a teacher whose behavior is inherently unstable" (p. 8). This provides a unique and perplexing problem for teachers, administrators, policy makers, and those establishing the psychometric properties of observation instruments.

Given a number of assumptions that need to be met before conducting and making conclusions about classroom observation data, some have argued for a more flexible approach to the issue of stable teaching practices. Stodolsky (1984) argued that

> … elementary school teachers who are essentially generalists can and do create a rather broad repertoire of organizational and pedagogical arrangements. Rather than presume that teachers exhibit consistent patterns of behavior, a flexibility of approach, tied to subject matter and curriculum, seems a more accurate characterization of teaching at the elementary level. The important of context, as assayed through subject matter and activity segment properties, cannot be underestimated.
>
> *(p. 16)*

Adequate Variation. Observers rarely endorse ratings on the extremes (Bill & Melinda Gates Foundation, 2013), however, when they do, they tend to be more generous (see leniency effect, Table 5.3). Unfortunately, normal distributions and variation are important especially in correlational studies that seek to link teaching practices to student achievement outcomes. This is also concerning if one purpose of the observations is to differentiate between teachers. If differentiation is important, administrators appear to do a better job of differentiating between teachers than peer raters do (Bill & Melinda Gates Foundation, 2013).

Of course, these limitations are even more important if observational data are used to make high-stakes decisions. Many of these already established challenges will only be exacerbated due to the natural corruption of measures under high-stakes conditions. According to Campbell's Law, the greater emphasis on any given quantitative variable to make high-stakes decisions, the greater probability of corruption and distortion of the processes in question (see Nichols & Berliner, 2007, for a discussion of Campbell's Law). There is limited information about how observers' ratings are altered under high-stakes conditions.

Student Achievement

Today, student achievement is a primary concern in educational policy and continues to garner importance in Race to the Top. As noted in Chapter 4, it is expected that states will use teachers' impact on student achievement outcomes as a significant measure in the evaluation of teachers. Furthermore, recently funded and widely publicized work (the MET Project) advocates that 33% to 50% of a composite teacher evaluation score be composed of student achievement gains on state achievement tests (Bill & Melinda Gates Foundation, 2013). In the context of accountability, these standardized tests have an interesting and evolving history. For many Americans, the ACT and SAT are the most notable standardized tests as they serve as gatekeepers to higher education. Standardized tests grew in popularity as education became more government controlled and funded. The need to assess students at a mass level served as a response to growing concerns about the state of American education and advocacy for efficiency. In the last 50 years, standardized testing has ballooned. By 1982, 36 states had some type of testing program in place. Some of these states (e.g., Arizona, Nebraska, New Mexico, South Carolina, Wisconsin) focused entirely on testing as a means of school improvement (Odden & Doughtery, 1982). Some raised concerns about "curricular reductionism" (Popham, 1983) and teaching to the test (Darling-Hammond & Wise, 1985). We will return to this in Chapter 6.

Measures of Student Achievement.   Student achievement can be measured using norm-referenced or criterion-referenced tests. Norm-referenced test results are often reported in terms of percentiles; the percentage of students that scored above or below a particular point. Criterion-referenced tests measure what content and skills are mastered and, because they illustrate what students know, are generally more useful. Results from these tests are often reported in raw scores, scale scores, or the percentile of students who passed a particular standard. Under previous educational reforms (e.g., NCLB), schools were expected to attain a particular achievement level. Student achievement was often characterized by scale or raw scores, i.e., overall performance on a given test, otherwise termed "Annual Yearly Progress" (AYP). These scores, however, do not take into account where schools or students started or how much growth was achieved. Hence, there has been a significant shift towards measuring the *progress* students make in a particular school or with a given teacher. Simple gain scores are one way to capture progress from pre- to post-test. Growth models also measure progress, but in a more complex way. Growth models can measure change in scores across more than one time point and can account for differences between tests across grades. These models can also provide information about both expected and actual growth. Since growth models are the most relevant to today's education reform, we focus on two of the mostly commonly used growth models below (Harris, 2011).

Student Growth Percentiles.   There were significant concerns regarding the ways in which achievement was measured under NCLB. In 2005, the Growth Model Pilot Program (GMPP) was launched allowing states to use growth models to demonstrate achievement as mandated under NCLB (Spellings, 2005). Student percentile growth statistically measures test score growth across groups of peers, accounting for students with similar prior achievement, grades, and subjects. At an individual student level, a student's achievement at the *end* of the year is compared with that of students who started at a similar achievement level at the *start* of the year.

Value-Added.   Value-added modeling is used to determine the teacher's (or school, district) contributions to students' test score gains. It is purported to be a better measure of a teacher's effect on students. Recent value-added research has made noticeable waves and many states are or are considering using these scores to evaluate teachers (Collins & Amrein-Beardsley, in press). Value-added models can potentially control for covariates such as student characteristics; however, there is debate about to what extent such controls should be used, and if used, actually do as intended (Amrein-Beardsley, 2008; Kupermintz, 2003). For more information about specific value-added models see Sanders, Saxton, and Horn (1997).

Strengths.   Advocates of using student test scores as one or a significant measure in teacher evaluations claim that although it is not a perfect measure, it is better than many of the existing teacher evaluation methods. Studies examining the validity of value-added scores have generally been positive, but with great variation. For example, studies that compare administrators' ratings of teachers to value-added outcomes return correlations of between .20 and .50 (Jacob & Lefgren, 2005; Kimball et al., 2004; Medley & Coker, 1987; Milanowski, 2004). In a study by Schacter and Thum (2004), correlations between value-added and observational scores ranged from .55 to .70. Moderate relationships have been found with observations done using the Classroom Assessment Scoring System (CLASS; Pianta et al., 2008), however, in studies in which students were randomly assigned to classrooms for part of the study correlations between ratings on the Danielson Framework (2007) and value-added scores ranged from .012 to .34. These correlations were stronger for student surveys (Bill & Melinda Gates Foundation, 2012). Given this huge amount of variation, it is hard to make any sound conclusion about validity, but all studies show some positive relationship between value-added scores and other measures of teacher effectiveness. Harris (2012) reasoned that although these correlations are weak, they may be as good as it gets given the inherit issues of reliability and validity in all measures. Hill (2009) argued that these correlations are not strong enough to use in high-stakes settings.

Limitations.   In the last decade, and particularly in the last 5 years, significant concern has been raised in academic circles and elsewhere about the use and benefit of value-added as a measure of effective teaching.

Reliability.   Value-added measures have generally demonstrated fairly low reliability. In a Koedel and Betts (2007), reliability was .57 in mathematics, and even lower in reading, .46. Low reliability may be due, in part, to evidence indicating that teachers' value-added scores are composed of similar amounts of "error" and "true score" variance (Kane, Rockoff, & Staiger, 2006; McCaffrey, Sass, Lockwood, & Mihaly, 2009). These findings continue to be confirmed. A study examining value-added teacher rankings in five school districts found that for teachers who scored in the bottom 20% of rankings in one year, only 20%–30% had similar rankings the following year. Further, often these fluctuations from year to year are large—74%–93% of teachers fluctuate one or more deciles across years, depending on the statistical model used (Darling-Hammond, Amrein-Beardsley, Haertel, & Rothstein, 2012). One concerning fluctuation would be teachers who move from the bottom to the top of the distribution across years. Assuming VAM scores are accurate and are indicative of improvement over time; these eventual high-performing teachers may be fired before they reach their peak. Recent research indicates that only 1% of the teacher sample changed from one end of the distribution to another (Kersting, Chen, & Stigler, 2013) as compared to 10% to 30% in other studies (Goldhaber & Hansen, 2010; McCaffrey et al., 2009). Other findings indicate that teachers at the top of the value-added distribution are more stable than those at the bottom (Kersting et al., 2013; Golhaber & Hansen, 2010; McCaffrey et al., 2009). Further, teachers' performance, as measured by value-added tend to improve during the first 4 years, and then begins to stabilize (Kersting et al., 2013). Findings similar to this have been noted elsewhere (Darling-Hammond, 1999; Henry, Fortner, & Bastian, 2012; Johnson, Berg, & Donaldson, 2005).

In sum, these findings illustrate a great deal of concern about the use of value-added scores in making high-stakes decisions. Value-added scores may be fair and reliable for some teachers (e.g., those at the top of the distribution) but not for others (e.g., beginning teachers). Inconsistent findings regarding the consistency of value-added scores needs much more research. The damaging and legal implications of firing highly effective teachers or giving bonuses to ineffective teachers are huge.

Limited Control.   Value-added models have come under significant criticism for not providing enough control for variables such as socioeconomic status and other demographic differences (Linn, 2001; Kupermintz, 2003). Not all variables can be controlled for in statistically sound ways and may result in a great deal of fluctuation of value-added scores across time. For example, life events may have either positive or negative effects including death of a family member, a divorce, or a pending marriage. Changes in the school environment including the loss of teachers that teach in adjoining grade levels, changes in principal or supervisors, or changes in state tests or standards may affect value-added scores. Finally, changes in student composition in ways that are either difficult to control for statistically or those that are impossible to control for such as a large increase in the number of special education students taught may have a significant impact on teachers' value-added scores. Essentially, exogenous variables make it nearly impossible to control for all variables that may affect a teacher's effect on student achievement outcomes (Berliner, in press) and this is one explanation for the overall conclusion that value added has low reliability but moderate convergent validity (Hill, Kapitula, & Umland, 2011). These fluctuations in teacher value-added scores are notable, and this has been known for a long time (Good & Grouws, 1975). For a more extended discussion of this point and on teacher effects, in general, see Good (in press) and Konstantopoulos (in press).

Ability to Improve Instruction.   It is unclear how information about student achievement, particularly as used in current models, can be used to help improve instruction. E. F. Lindquist who wrote in 1938 "all of this improvement in the technique of measurement, however, is of very little consequence unless it is accompanied by a corresponding progress in the application of the tests results for the improvement of instruction in the individual schools" (as cited in Peterson, 1987, p. 39). This point is reiterated nearly 50 years later (Popham, 1983) and resurfaced again recently (Mandinach & Honey, 2008). This concern is exacerbated in the use of value-added because it seeks to illustrate a teacher's effect on students, rather than what students have or have not learned. Two additional problems fuel this concern. First, there is wide variation in the correlations between observational measures and value-added scores. Further, large variation in value-added scores from year to year may not coincide with large and similar changes in teachers' practices. For example, in a study of the Houston Independent School District (HISD) teachers subject to high-stakes consequences based on value-added scores, one teacher noted the following:

> I do what I do every year. I teach the way I teach every year. [My] first year got me pats on the back. [My] second year got me kicked in the backside. And for year three my scores were off the charts. I got a huge bonus, and now I am in the top quartile of all the English teachers. What did I do differently? I have no clue.
>
> *(Collins, in progress, as cited in Amrein-Beardsley & Collins, 2012, p. 12)*

These issues make it difficult for administrators and teachers to conclude what practices were systematically related to higher or lower value-added scores. In particular, if teachers and statisticians are unable to parse out differences due to changes in student characteristics from changes in teaching practices, any potential of instructional improvement from using VA scores is lost.

In sum, although it is possible to conceive of value added as an absolute measure, it is exceedingly difficult to do and for this reason models in use involve the making of relative comparisons. Teachers' rankings are based on a mean score of a comparison group. Most commonly this comparison group is teachers within the same district (Kupermintz, 2003). What this means is that within any given district, including teachers in public and private schools, approximately half of the teachers will be ineffective! This is sad news and especially so for parents spending the money to send their children to private school. If same parents pull their children out of a particular school in the district and place them in another school, the same finding will hold true. Part of the argument about making value-added rankings public is that it is the right of the parent to know, but unfortunately, it is unclear if parents will be better informed with this new knowledge.

Harris (2011) has written a very comprehensive book (favorable toward the use of value added) dealing with technical issues and popular misconceptions about value added. But even here, in an extended examination of value added, there is no discussion of the policy implications of its widespread use implied in firing teachers and other high-stakes consequences. Even those who effectively warn of the many potential problems in using of value added do not address important policy implications (Darling-Hammond et al., 2012).

Student Ratings

Student ratings provide information about students' perceptions, beliefs, and judgments about a particular teacher and his or her practice. Students are essentially the outcome of an education system and a teacher's practices, in part, it would seem logical that their opinions may be included in one way or another. Many teachers likely gather a great deal of informal feedback. In K-12 education, however, formal anonymous student surveys have not been used in a consistent way.

Brief History.   Student evaluations of teachers have existed for some time and are still a staple in higher education. Subsequently, a significant body of research exists on student ratings of college instructors, but fewer studies exist on the student ratings' of teachers in K-12 settings. Interest in elementary and secondary school students' perceptions of teachers emerged simultaneously with the growing interest in classroom observation research. The relationships teachers form with students and vice versa are an important part of teacher behavior. Hence, it was only appropriate that part of measuring teacher-student relationships was gathering students' perspectives. An example of early interest in this included the exploration of how cognitive needs work in alignment with or apart from affective needs (Della Piana & Gage, 1955). Interest in student-teacher relationships has endured (see Brophy & Good, 1974) and continues today (see Sabol & Pianta, 2012, for a review) and often assesses teachers' emotional and social support for students. Research on the ability for students to identify effective teaching is limited despite renewed interest (Bill & Melinda Gates Foundation, 2012). Many cities have used student surveys as part of a teacher's evaluation (e.g., Memphis, for which the information represents 5% of a teacher's evaluation), and others are starting to collect data (e.g., Pittsburgh, Georgia) or have plans to use student surveys for evaluations in the near future (e.g., Chicago) (Cuban, 2012).

Strengths. Proponents of the inclusion of students' ratings in teacher evaluation argue that (a) students are the primary recipients of what a teacher does in the classroom, they are the client, and therefore an important stakeholder, and (b) they have the greatest amount of interaction with the teacher and, hence, have the greatest opportunity to observe and evaluate a teacher.

Reliability. Follman (1992) reviewed nearly 60 studies on early childhood, elementary, and secondary students' ratings of teachers. He concluded that elementary students, including pre-schoolers as young as 4 years of age, can rate reliably and are no more or less reliable or susceptible to bias than other potential raters. Measures of students' ratings of teachers tend to have high reliability in elementary settings (.64-.90; Della Piana & Gage, 1955), with split-half reliability estimates ranging from .72 to .96. Immediate test-retest reliabilities across in Grades 3, 5, and 7, range from .56 to .67. Delayed re-test reliability ranges from .33 to .55 (see Follman, 1992, for a review). More recent studies have found within year reliability to range from .70 to .85 (Bill & Melinda Gates Foundation, 2010). The high reliability of student perception data puts this measure at an advantage, and even more so because it is more reliable than most of the popular and tried measures of teacher evaluation.

Validity. Evidence suggests that students' scores on a test of lesson comprehension correlate well with their evaluations of teachers (Gage et al., 1971), which suggests that students can gauge their own learning. Regardless of age group, student perception data shows strong correlations with teachers' value-added scores ($r = .66$), thereby making such data a preferred measure (Bill & Melinda Gates Foundation, 2010). Further, research has found that students are more accurate judges of teachers than are principals, as measured by the correlations between their ratings and teachers' student achievement outcomes (Bill & Melinda Gates Foundation, 2012; Strong, 2011).

There is also evidence that student ratings can be used to improve ratings of teacher effectiveness (Gage, Runkle, & Chatterjee, 1963; Tuckman & Oliver, 1968) suggesting that this measure has the potential to improve teaching. Teachers make more positive adjustments to negative ratings from students rather than to those from administrators (Tuckman & Oliver, 1968).

Limitations.   There is some concern that elementary and secondary school students assess and note different aspects of teachers and teaching, which raises concerns about student surveys as a valid measure of a single overarching concept. For example, younger students place a greater emphasis on teacher-student relationships whereas older students place a greater emphasis on student learning (Peterson, Wahlquist, & Bone, 2000). Other research suggests that students, particularly elementary students, are not good raters of teacher effectiveness because their ratings vary substantially from that of college supervisors and teaching supervisors of student teachers. However, it is not clear what these systematic low correlations reveal about the nature of students or others as raters of teacher effectiveness (Payne, 1984). More research is needed to determine why these ratings differ systematically, and to better understand how good teaching is conceptualized across the lifespan using developmental approaches. Furthermore, some research has shown that students are biased raters of teacher. In particular, they are biased to the sex, age, and attractiveness of the teacher, and this bias varies by age of student. For example, when given black and white photos to rate, attractiveness was the most significant factor in second graders' ratings; attractive teachers were rated less likely to give students too much work to do, more likely to be friendly, more likely to encourage student interaction, be more organized, and in general, be better teachers. Appearance or attractiveness was found to be a consistently important factor, regardless of age of the student, followed by age. Less attractive and older teachers were rated lower than their more attractive and younger counterparts (Goebel & Cashen, 1979). Given the increased interest in including student perception data and that some of this work, taken together, provides contradicting conclusions, it is pertinent that more research is done to illustrate the ways in which age and development ultimately affect the type of information students can provide about a teacher's effectiveness.

Other Measures

A variety of different measures can be used to help evaluate teacher effectiveness. Some of these include instructional artifacts such as: portfolios, lesson plans, student assessments, student work, rubrics, and assignments. Parent ratings and teacher self-reports are additional measures. Portfolios are a common practice in teacher education and are present in K-12 settings. Without going into great detail, we briefly discuss a number of these additional measures that have or could be used to assess a teacher's effectiveness. Our discussion is limited given that these measures haven't received great attention in state Race to the Top plans for teacher evaluation.

Parent Ratings

Parent ratings allow another way to assess teacher effectiveness, albeit, indirectly. Parents, one part of the taxpaying population and with children receiving the services of schools, are important stakeholders. Parents may also work in partnership, especially in the early grades, with teachers to reinforce learned concepts or ensure continuity in learning practices in both home and school settings. Parents are also members of the school community.

Schools have not, to this date, systematically included parents' perceptions of their child's teacher (Loup, Garland, Ellett, & Rugutt, 1996). The most substantial knowledge base that does exist about teachers' perceptions is from the annual Gallup polls. The Gallup polls offer the most widely available and publicized views parents' hold towards schools and teachers at a local and more global level. These data, however, are not specific enough to be used in an informative way to improve teaching practices.

In Epstein's (1985) study of parents' ratings of elementary teachers, parents' ratings were not related to teachers' experience or credentials but to teacher leadership, teachers' use of parent involvement, and teachers' reported discipline problems. Greater teacher leadership and parent involvement and fewer discipline problems were related to higher ratings by parents. More specifically, parents' ratings of teachers were highly associated with whether the teacher frequently involved parents (at the classroom level) in learning activities at home ($r = .466$), provided many ideas for parents ($r = .517$), sent parents communications ($r = .529$), improved more parents' understanding of the school program ($r = .495$), and sent the message that parents should help at home ($r = .332$). Parents were also found to give higher ratings to teachers of younger grades, in part perhaps because young children often identify most favorably with their teachers.

Although parental reports and principal reports of teacher effectiveness have demonstrated a weak to moderately positive correlation ($r = .27$, Epstein, 1985; $r = .09$, Petersen, 1987), parents' perspectives may provide a unique data source rather than a source of confirmation or alignment.

Teacher Self-Reports

Although not a significant variable in teacher evaluation, historically, teachers have been asked to report on their teaching as a main part of reflection and growth. Teacher self-reports are generally in the form of annual surveys in which include questions on their practices and other variables. A review of related literature by Hook and Rosenshine (1979) found that teacher self-reports were not good indicators of actual teaching practices. The self-reports, however, may be useful for self-identification under a particular philosophy or approach or used as a way to organize teachers on a continuum. This may be more helpful for teacher and school-level reflection or for research purposes, but not to make high-stakes decisions. Accuracy of self-reports, retrospectively, tend to be very low for behaviors that occur either rarely and very frequently (Sudman & Bradburn, 1982). Regardless, several large-scale studies include teacher surveys in their data collection protocol.[3]

Given the number of limitations of the historically dominant measure of teacher effectiveness, classroom observations, researchers have been seeking other measures that capture similar variables. Brian Rowan and colleagues (Rowan & Correnti, 2009; Rowan, Jacob, & Correnti, 2009) have done significant work on instructional logs as one form of teacher self-report data. Instructional logs are time diaries in which teachers are asked to report on specific teaching practices frequently. The researchers suggested 20 logs for a single teacher during a given year in order to accurately and reliably capture a teacher's practices.

One strength of instructional logs is that they have significantly high rates of reliability. Researchers have noted 73%–90% agreement in teacher-observer matches (Camburn & Barnes, 2004). Rowan and colleagues (2009) estimate that a single teacher log costs $27.50 including all the materials and training. If schools were to abide by the recommendation of 20 logs per year, the cost to schools for a single teacher would be $550.00 annually. It is important to note that instructional logs are better at measuring instruction rather than classroom management or organization (Rowan et al., 2009). These measures would best be used as an additional source of information of teacher effectiveness (for extended information about content coverage and opportunity to learn) rather than as a substitute for a more comprehensive measure such as classroom observations.

Conclusion

There are a great number of ways effective teaching can be measured, and with each, different information is acquired about what a teacher does in the classroom and the types of related outcomes. Information about various measures is varied and research is infrequently conducted in the context of high-stakes evaluation. It is possible to measure some types of good teaching for specific outcomes (we have more to say about this later), but we wonder about the extent to which this will be done reliably. Here we address a few problematic issues. First, consider the distribution of scores issue using observation instruments. How do we score a rubric item like "teacher communicates well with students"—Outstanding? Good? Average? Needs improvement? Consider this hypothetical example. We carefully define what separates outstanding from good and so forth. We train 10 coders to a high level, we randomly select 150 teachers in the state, and the coders code four different lessons with 90% reliability. We find that on this random set of teachers 20% are outstanding, 25% good, 40% average, and 15% poor. What then happens when principals grade teachers? Will they apply these absolute standards to their teachers or will they rank their teachers in relative ways? If teachers are evaluated in using an absolute rating method, a significant number could be rated high or low, limited variation and making it difficult to differentiate employee effectiveness. On the contrary, if teachers are ranked, score inflation is controlled. A teacher's ranking will be relative to the other teachers located in the same school, which may increase a number of unintended consequences such as competition, and reduce collaboration (Lavigne, in press).

Defining good teaching is difficult because there are many things that we hope students develop/learn in school, however, even if we limit our definition of good teaching to the ability to achieve higher student achievement than do other teachers teaching similar students under similar conditions, utilizing a statewide instrument is an ambitious if not daunting task. For example, is it possible to use the same rubric for judging the teaching of seventh-grade Algebra and a discussion of a classic book in Grade 11 English? The answer is yes and no. There are some elements of teaching/communication that transcend context, but there are also context effects that are likely to be huge in some instances. So the appropriate use of any rubric varies with the desired learning outcome. In our judgment, the forms of rubric that are in use will more likely be more accurate in assessing lessons that focus upon skills and concepts than those that address problem solving. Why is this? Basically because we know much more about the teaching of skills and concepts than we do about teaching problem solving (Hiebert & Grouws, 2007). And, the rubrics in use are partly based upon this literature addressing conceptual teaching.

So our reaction to the use of observational measures of teaching is differentiated. We have no problem with their use to measure basic skills of teaching. Good communication skills, good management, and building a warm classroom climate are fine, but they cannot be equated with good teaching. In some contexts they may be sufficient for good learning, but in others they are not. We advocate for the work of others that has sought to identify common characteristics that emerge across a number of observation instruments and systems (Emmer & Peck, 1973). For example, as noted in Appendix 5.1[4] the in MET project five instruments are being used to observe teaching. These instruments include the Danielson Framework for Teaching, the CLASS Assessment System, the Framework for Teaching (FFT), the Mathematical Quality of Instruction (MQI), the Protocol for Language Arts Teaching Observation (PLATO), and the Quality of Science Teaching (QST). Using these instruments involves a great deal of time and expense and it might be possible to develop an instrument that integrates measures across these five instruments. Clearly, if subject specific information is needed, it may be necessary to use a single instrument, but for general purposes it might be good to come up with an integrative instrument that reduces time and cost.

As we read the accounts of classroom observation that states the plan to use, we reached the unfortunate judgment that their observation plans were glib and shallow. This is not because their efforts are not sincere or because their goals are not good ones. Today's policy makers would be well served by studying the historical literature on classroom observational research. Policy makers (or staffers) who are diligent students might come to understand the difficulty of mastering the observational method. Establishing coder agreement to the high reliability needed to make accurate and fair judgments cannot be done easily or sufficiently and almost always is quite costly.

Although individuals and some agencies have actively pointed out the dangers of using standardized achievement measures, it is noteworthy that teacher educators and educational researchers have never provided any organized, comprehensive, sustained response to the misuse of standardized measures (comments on policy considerations are especially sparse). As we will see in this book, passive resistance (at best) continues to surface in current debates around teacher education and more generally in higher education (Gift & Gift, 2012; Pianta, 2012). And, both sadly and ironically, we conclude that many of the achievement measures that we use were developed because there was little faith in teachers' ability to evaluate their students fairly or accurately. As we will reiterate, it is often ignored that teacher grades remain a better predictor for success in college than do standardized tests (D'Agostino & Powers, 2009), and this is true for both American and foreign students who attend American universities (Fu, 2012; Soares, 2011).

Notes

1   For an example of a sign system, see the Classroom Observation Keys for Effectiveness Research developed by Coker and Coker (1979).
2   See a critique of this work in Chapter 3.
3   Some of the most prominent large-scale studies that include teacher surveys are those developed by National Center for Education Statistics, and the Trends in International Mathematics and Science Study.
4   Note that the appendix has only four instruments because one of the instruments does not have a protocol provided in the MET project.

References

Ambady, N., & Rosenthal, R. (1992). Thin slices of expressive behavior as predictors of interpersonal consequences: A meta-analysis. *Psychological Bulletin, 111*(2), 256–274.

Amrein-Beardsley, A. (2008). Methodological concerns about the education value-added assessment system. *Educational Researcher, 37*(2), 65–75.

Amrein-Beardsley, A., & Collins, C. (2012). The SAS Education Value-Added Assessment System (SAS® EVAAS®) in the Houston Independent School District (HISD): Intended and unintended consequences. *Education Policy Analysis Archives, 20*(12). Retrieved from http://epaa.asu.edu/ojs/article/view/1096

Berliner, D. (in press). Exogenous variables and value-added assessments: A fatal flaw. *Teachers College Record.*

Berliner, D. C. (1976). Impediments to the study of teacher effectiveness. *Journal of Teacher Education, 27*(5), 5–13.

Bill & Melinda Gates Foundation. (2010). *Learning about teaching: Research report.* Retrieved from http://www.metproject.org/downloads/Preliminary_Findings-Research_Paper.pdf

Bill & Melinda Gates Foundation. (2012). *Gathering feedback for teaching: Combining high-quality observations with student surveys and achievement gains, Research report.* Retrieved from http://www.metproject.org/downloads/MET_Gathering_Feedback_Research_Paper.pdf

Bill & Melinda Gates Foundation. (2013). *The reliability of classroom observations by school personnel: Research paper.* Retrieved from http://www.metproject.org/downloads/MET_Reliability%20of%20Classroom%20Observations_Research%20Paper.pdf

Brauchle, P., Mclarty, J. & Parker, J. (1989). A portfolio approach to using student performance data to measure teacher effectiveness. *Journal of Personnel Evaluation in Education, 3,* 17–30.

Brophy, J., & Good, T. (1974). *Teacher–student relationships: Causes and consequences.* New York, NY: Holt, Rinehart, & Winston.

Camburn, E., & Barnes, C. A. (2004). Assessing the validity of a language arts instruction log through triangulation. *Elementary School Journal, 105*(1), 49–74.

Cloud-Silva, C., & Denton, J. (1989). The development and validation of a low-inference observation instrument to assess instructional performance of teaching candidates. *Journal of Classroom Interaction, 24*(2), 7–14.

Coker, J. G., & Coker, H. (1979). *Classroom observations keyed for effectiveness research: Observer training manual.* Carrollton, GA: National Institute for Effectiveness-Directed Education.

Collins, C., & Amrein-Beardsley, A. (in press). Putting growth and value-added models on the map: A national overview. *Teachers College Record.*

Cuban, L. (2012, December 11). Students evaluating teachers. [Web log comment]. Retrieved from http://larrycuban.wordpress.com/2012/12/11/students-evaluating-teachers/

Curby, T. W., Stuhlman, M., Grimm, K., Mashburn, A., Chomat-Mooney, L., Downer, J. ... Pianta, R. C. (2011). Within-day variability in the quality of classroom interaction during third and fifth grade. *Elementary School Journal, 112*(1), 16–37.

Cramer, J. (1983) Yes–Merit pay can be a horror, but a few school systems have done it right. *American School Board Journal, 170*(9), 33–34.

D'Agostino, J. V., & Powers, S. J. (2009). Predicting teacher performance with test scores and grade point average: A meta-analysis. *American Educational Research Journal, 46*(1), 146–182.

Danielson, C. (2007). *Enhancing professional practice: A framework for teaching* (2nd ed.). Alexandria, VA: ASCD.

Danielson Group. (2011). *Framework for teaching: Components of professional practice.* Retrieved from http://charlottedanielson.com/theframeteach.htm

Darling-Hammond, L. (1999). *Teacher quality and student achievement: A review of state policy evidence.* Seattle: University of Washington, Center for the Study of Teaching and Policy.

Darling-Hammond, L., Amrein-Beardsley, A., Haertel, E., & Rothstein, J. (2012). Evaluating teacher evaluation. *Phi Delta Kappan, 93*(6), 8–15.

Darling-Hammond, L., & Wise, A. E. (1985). Beyond standardization: State standards and school improvement. *The Elementary School Journal, 85*(3), 315–336.

Darling-Hammond, L., Wise, A. E., & Pease, S. R. (1983). Teacher evaluation in the organizational context: A review of the literature. *Review of Educational Research, 53,* 285–328.

Della Piana, G. M., & Gage, N. L. (1955). Pupils' values and the validity of the Minnesota Teacher Attitude Inventory. *Journal of Educational Psychology, 46*(3), 167–178.

Doyle, W., & Redwine, J. M. (1974). Effect of intent-action discrepancy and student performance feedback on behavior change. *Journal of Educational Psychology, 66*(5), 750–755.

Ellett, C. D., & Garland, J. (1987). Teacher evaluation practices in our largest school districts: Are they measuring up to the "state-of-the-art" systems? *Journal of Personnel Evaluation in Education, 1*(1), 69–92.

Emmer, E. T., & Peck, R. F. (1973). Dimensions of classroom behavior. *Journal of Educational Psychology, 64*(2), 223–240.

Epstein, J. L. (1985). A question of merit: Principals' and parents' evaluations of teachers. *Educational Researcher, 14*(7), 3–8.

Evertson, C., & Green, J. (1986). Observation as inquiry and method. In M. C. Wittrock (Ed.), *Handbook of research on teaching* (3rd ed., pp. 162–213). New York, NY: Macmillian.

Everston, C. M., Emmer, E. T., & Brophy, J. E. (1980). Predictors of effective teaching in junior high mathematics classrooms. *Journal of Research in Mathematics Education, 11*(3), 167–178.

Fenstermacher, G. D. (1978). A philosophical consideration of recent research on teacher effectiveness. In L. S. Shulman (Ed.), *Review of research in education* (Vol. 6, pp. 157–185). Istaca, IL: F. E. Peacock.

Flanders, N. A. (1970). *Analyzing teaching behavior*. New York, NY: Addison-Wesley.

Follman, J. (1992). Secondary school students' ratings of teacher effectiveness. *High School Journal, 75*(3), 168–178.

Freiberg, H. J., Huzinec, C. A., & Templeton, S. M. (2009). Classroom management—a pathway to student achievement: A study of fourteen inner-city elementary schools. *Elementary School Journal, 110*(1), 63–80.

Fu, Y. (2012). *The effectiveness of traditional admissions criteria in predicting college and graduate success for American and international students* (Unpublished doctoral dissertation). University of Aruzibam Tucson.

Gage, N. L., Belgard, M., Rosenshine, B., Unruh, W. R., Dell, D., & Hiller, J. H. (1971). Explorations of the teacher's effectiveness in lecturing. In I. Westbury & A. A. Bellack (Eds.), *Research into classroom processes: Recent developments and next steps* (pp. 175–217). New York, NY: Teachers College Press.

Gage, N. L., Runkel, P. J., & Chatterjee, B. B. (1963). Changing teacher behavior through feedback from pupils: An application of equilibrium theory. In W. W. Charters & N. L. Gage (Eds.), *The social psychology of education* (pp. 173–181). Boston, MA: Allyn & Bacon.

Gallagher, H. A. (2004). Vaughn Elementary's innovative teacher evaluation system: Are teacher evaluation scores related to growth in student achievement? *Peabody Journal of Education, 79*(4), 79–107.

Gift, K., & Gift, T. (2012, April 13). Colleges: Making the grade? *Teachers College Record*. Retrieved from http://www.tcrecord.org/Content.asp?ContentID=16758

Goebel, B. L., & Cashen, V. M. (1979). Age, sex, and attractiveness as factors in student ratings of teachers: A developmental study. *Journal of Educational Psychology, 71*(5), 646–653.

Goldhaber, D., & Hansen, M. (2010). *Is it just a bad class? Assessing the stability of measured teacher performance*. CEDR Working Paper 2010-3. University of Washington, Seattle. Retrieved from http://www.cedr.us/publications.html

Good, T. (in press). What do we know about how teachers influence student performance on standardized tests, and why do we know so little about other outcomes? *Teachers College Record*.

Good, T. L., & Brophy, J. E. (1974). Changing teacher and student behavior: An empirical investigation. *Journal of Educational Psychology, 66*(3), 390–405.

Good, T. L., & Grouws, D. A. (1975). Teacher rapport: Some stability data. *Journal of Educational Psychology, 67*(2), 179–182. doi:10.1037/h0076995

Good, T. L., & Grouws, D. (1979). The Missouri mathematics effectiveness project: An experimental study in fourth-grade classrooms. *Journal of Educational Psychology, 71*(3), 355–362. doi:10.1037//0022-0663.71.3.355

Good, T. L., McCaslin, M., Tsang, H. Y., Zhang, J., Wiley, C. R. H., & Bozack, A. R. (2006). How well do first-year teachers teach: Does type of preparation make a difference? *Journal of Teacher Education, 57*(4), 410–430. doi:10.1177/0022487106291566

Harris, D. N. (2011). *Value-added measures in education: What every educator needs to know*. Cambridge, MA: Harvard Education Press.

Harris, D. N. (2012, October 15). *How do value-added indicators compare to other measures of teacher effectiveness?* Retrieved from http://www.carnegieknowledgenetwork.org/briefs/value-added/value-added-other-measures/

Harris, D. N., & Sass, T. R. (2010). *What makes for a good teacher and who can tell?* Retrieved from http://myweb.fsu.edu/tsass/Papers/IES%20Harris%20Sass%20Principal%20Eval%2034.pdf

Henry, G. T., Fortner, C. K., & Bastian, K. C. (2012). The effects of experience and attrition for novice high-school science and mathematics teachers. *Science, 335*(6072), 1118–1121. doi:10.1126/science.1215343

Herlihy, C., Karger, E., Pollard, C., Hill, H. C., Kraft, M. A., Williams, M., & Howard, S. (in press). State and local efforts to investigate the validity and reliability of scores form teacher evaluation systems. *Teachers College Record.*

Hiebert, J., & Grouws, D. A. (2007). The effects of classroom mathematics teaching on students' learning. In F. K. Lester (Ed.), *Second handbook of research on mathematics teaching and learning* (pp. 371–404). Greenwich, CT: Information Age.

Hill, H. (2009). Evaluating value-added models: A validity argument approach. *Journal of Policy Analysis and Management, 28*(4), 700–709.

Hill, H. C., Blunk, M. L., Charalambous, C. Y., Lewis, J. M., Phelps, G. C., Sleep, L., & Ball, D. L. (2008). Mathematical knowledge for teaching and the mathematical quality of instruction: An exploratory study. *Cognition and Instruction, 26*(4), 430–511.

Hill, H. C., Charalambosus, C. Y., & Kraft, M. A. (2012). When rater reliability is not enough: Teacher observation systems and a case for the generalizability study. *Educational Researcher, 41*(2), 56–64.

Hill, H. C., Kapitula, L., & Umland, K. A. (2011). Validity argument approach to evaluating teacher value-added scores. *American Educational Research Journal, 48*(3), 794–831.

Hook, C. M., & Rosenshine, B. V. (1979). Accuracy of teacher reports of their classroom behavior. *Review of Educational Research, 49*(1), 1–11.

Ing, M., & Webb, N. M. (2012). Characterizing mathematics classroom practice: Impact of observation and coding choices. *Educational Measurement Issues and Practice, 31*(1), 14–26.

Jacob, B., & Lefgren, L. (2008). Can principals identify effective teachers? Evidence on subjective performance evaluation in education. *Journal of Labor Economics, 26*(1), 101–136.

Johnson, S., Berg, J., & Donaldson, M. (2005). *Who stays in teaching and why: A review of literature on teacher retention.* The Project on the Next Generation of Teachers. Cambridge, MA: Harvard Graduate School of Education.

Johnson, S. M. (1984). Merit pay plans for teachers: A poor prescription for reform. *Harvard Educational Review, 54,* 175–185.

Kane, T. J., Rockoff, J. E., & Staiger, D. O. (2006). *What does certification tell us about teacher effectiveness? Evidence from New York City.* Working Paper #12155. Retrieved from http://www.nber.org/papers/w12155

Kersting, N. B., Chen, M., & Stigler, J. W. (2012). Value-added teacher estimates as part of teacher evaluations: Exploring the effects of data and model specifications on the stability of teacher value-added scores. *Education Policy Analysis Archives, 21*(7). Retrieved from http://epaa.asu.edu/ojs/article/view/1167

Kimball, S. M., White, B., Milanowski, A. T., & Borman, G. (2004). Examining the relationship between teacher evaluations and student assessment results in Washoe County. *Peabody Journal of Education, 79*(4), 54–78.

Kluger, A. N., & DiNisi, A. (1996). The effects of feedback interventions on performance: A historical review, a meta-analysis, and a preliminary feedback intervention theory. *Psychological Bulletin, 119*(2), 254–284.

Koedel, C., & Betts, J. R. (2007). *Re-examining the role of teacher quality in the educational production function* (Working Papers 708). Retrieved from http:// econpapers.repec.org/paper/umcw-paper/0708.htm

Konstantopoulos, S. (in press). Teacher effects, value-added models, and accountability. *Teachers College Record.*

Kounin, J. (1970). *Discipline and group management in classrooms.* New York, NY: Holt, Reinhart, and Winston.

Kupermintz, H. (2003). Teacher effects and teacher effectiveness: A validity investigation of the Tennessee value added assessment system. *Educational Evaluation and Policy Analysis, 25,* 287–298.

Lavigne, A. L. (in press). Exploring the intended and unintended consequences of high-stakes teacher evaluation on schools, teachers, and students. *Teachers College Record.*

Ligon, G., & Ellis, J. (1986). Adjusting for rater bias in teacher evaluations: Political and technical realities. *Journal of Personnel Evaluation in Education, 8*(4), 377–400.

Linn, R. L. (2001). A century of standardized testing: Controversies and pendulum swings. *Educational Assessment, 7*(1), 29–38. doi:10.1207/S15326977EA0701_4

Loup, K., Garland, J., Ellett, C., & Rugutt, J. (1996). Ten years later: Findings from a replication of a study of teacher evaluation practices in our 100 largest school districts. *Journal of Personnel Evaluation in Education, 10*(3), 203–226.

Mandinach, E. B., & Honey, M. (2008). *Data-driven school improvement: Linking data and learning.* New York, NY: Teachers College Press.

McCaffrey, D. F., Sass, T. R., Lockwood, J. R., & Mihaly, K. (2009). The Inter-temporal variability of teacher effect estimates. *Education Finance and Policy, 4*(4), 572–606.

McNeil, J. D., & Popham, W. J. (1973). The assessment of teacher competence. In R. M. W. Travers (Ed.). *Second handbook of research on teaching* (pp. 218–244). Skokie, IL: Rand McNally.

Medley, D. M. (1982). Systemic observation. In H. E. Mitzel, J. H. Best, & W. Rabinowitz (Eds.), *Encyclopedia of educational research* (5th ed., Vol. 4, pp. 1841–1851). New York, NY: The Free Press.

Medley, D. M., & Coker, H. (1987). How valid are principals' judgments of teacher effectiveness? *Phi Delta Kappan, 69,* 138–140.

Milanowski, A. (2004). The relation between teacher performance evaluation scores and student achievement: Evidence from Cincinnati. *Peabody Journal of Education, 79*(4), 33–53.

Munson, B. R. (1998). Peers observing peers: The better way to observe teachers. *Contemporary Education, 69*(2), 108–110.

Murry, S., Ma, X., & Mazur, J. (2009). Effects of peer coaching on teachers' collaborative interactions and students' mathematics achievement. *Journal of Educational Research, 102*(3), 203–212.

Natriello, G., & Dornbusch, S. M. (1981). Pitfalls in the evaluation of teachers by principals. *Administrator's Notebook, 29,* 1–4.

Nichols, S. L., & Berliner, D. C. (2007). *Collateral damage: How high-stakes testing corrupts America's schools.* Cambridge, MA: Harvard Education Press.

Odden, A., & Dougherty, V. (1982). *State programs of school improvement: A 50 state survey.* Denver, CO: Education Commission of the States.

Odell, S. J., Ferraro, D. P. (1992). Teacher mentoring and teacher retention. *Journal of Teacher Education, 43*(3), 200–204.

Ornstein, A. C. (1995a). Beyond effective teaching. *Peabody Journal of Education, 70*(2), 2–33.

Ornstein, A. C. (1995b). The new paradigm in research on teaching. *Educational Forum, 59,* 124–129.

Peterson, K. D., (1987). Teacher evaluation with multiple and variable lines of evidence. *American Educational Research Journal, 24,* 311–317.

Peterson, K. D., Wahlquist, C., & Bone, K. (2000). Student surveys for school teacher evaluation. *Journal of Personnel Evaluation in Education, 14*(2), 135–153.

Pianta, R. C. (2012, May 6). Stop complaining about teacher assessments; find alternatives. *The Chronicle of Higher Education.* Retrieved from http://chronicle.com/article/Tired-of-Debating-Teacher/131803/

Pianta, R. C., LaParo, K., & Hamre, B. K. (2008). *Classroom Assessment Scoring System* (CLASS). Baltimore, MD: Paul H. Brookes.

Popham, W. J. (1983). Measurement as an instructional catalyst. In R. B. Ekstrom (Ed.), *Measurement, technology, and individuality in education* (pp. 19–30). San Francisco, CA: Jossey-Bass.

Pullin, D. (2013). Legal issues in the use of student test scores and value-added models (VAM) to determine educational quality. *Education Policy Analysis Archives, 21*(6). Retrieved from http://epaa.asu.edu/ojs/article/view/1160

Riner, P. S. (1991). Are principals valid judges of teacher effectiveness? A study of the criterion-related validity of a high inference teacher rating instrument. *Journal of Research and Development in Education, 24*(3), 20–29.

Rosenshine, B. (1970). Evaluation of classroom instruction. *Review of Educational Research, 40*(2), 279–300.

Rosenshine, B., & Furst, N. (1973). The use of direct observation to study teaching. In R. M. W. Travers (Ed.), *Second handbook of research on teaching* (pp. 122–183). Chicago, IL: Rand McNally College Publishing.

Rowan, B., & Correnti, R. (2009). Studying reading instruction with teacher logs: Lessons from the study of instructional improvement. *Educational Researcher, 38*(2), 120–131.

Rowan, B., Jacob, R., & Correnti, R. (2009). Using instructional logs to identify quality in educational settings. *New Directions for Youth Development, 121,* 13–21.

Rowley, G. (1978). The relationship of reliability in classroom research to the amount of observation: An extension on the Spearman-Brown formula. *Journal of Educational Measurement, 15,* 165–180.

Sabol, T. J., & Pianta, R. C. (2012). Recent trends in research on teacher-child relationships. *Attachment and Human Development, 14*(3), 213–231. doi:10.1080/14616734.2012.672262

Sanders, W. L., Saxton, A. M., & Horn, S. P. (1997). The Tennessee Value-Added Assessment System: A quantitative, outcomes-based approach to educational assessment. In J. Millman, (Ed.), *Grading teachers, grading schools. Is student achievement a valid evaluation measure?* (pp. 137–162). Thousand Oaks, CA: Corwin.

Schacter, J., & Thum, Y. M. (2004). Paying for high- and low-quality teaching. *Economics of Education Review, 23*(3), 411–430.

Soares, J. A. (2011). *SAT wars: The case for test-optional college admissions.* New York, NY: Teachers College Press.

Spellings, M. (2005, November). *Secretary Spellings announces growth model pilot* [Press Release]. U.S. Department of Education. Retrieved from http://www.ed.gov/news/pressreleases/2005/11/1182005.html

Stallings, J. A. (1977). *Learning to look: A handbook on classroom observation and teaching models.* Belmont, CA: Wadsworth.

Stodolsky, S. (1984). Teacher evaluation: the limits of looking. *Educational Researcher, 13*(9), 11–18.

Strong, M. (2011). *The highly qualified teacher: What is teacher quality and how do we measure it?* New York, NY: Teachers College Press.

Strong, M., Gargani, J., & Hacifazlioglu, Ö. (2011). Do we know a successful teacher when we see one? Experiments in the identification of effective teachers. *Journal of Teacher Education, 62*(4), 367–382.

Sudman, S., & Bradburn, N. M. (1982). *Asking questions: A practical guide to questionnaire design.* San Francisco, CA: Jossey-Bass.

Tuckman, B. W., & Hyman, R. T. (1977). *Teacher behavior is in the eye of the beholder: The perception of principals.* New York, NY: American Educational Research Association.

Tuckman, B. W., & Oliver, W. F. (1968). Effectiveness of feedback to teachers as a function of source. *Journal of Educational Psychology, 59,* 297–301.

Wilkins, E. A., & Shin, E. (2010). Peer feedback: Who, what, when, why, and how. *Kappa Delta Pi Record, 46,* 112–117.

Withall, J. (1956). An objective measurement of a teacher's classroom interactions. *Journal of Educational Psychology, 47*(4), 203–212.

6

THE CURRENT MESS

Can We Improve Teacher Evaluation?

Introduction

It is clear that accountability has "stuck" with American education and will push forward despite protests and limitations of teacher evaluation plans. In contemporary accountability, there are a number of stakeholders (e.g., policy makers, teachers, parents, teacher educators) that face different challenges and possess different needs and agendas. For example, policy makers need to demonstrate that taxpayer money is being well spent—financial resources that go directly or indirectly to teachers need to result in the desired outcome (currently defined as student achievement).

In this chapter, we provide an overview of what has been learned thus far. We then turn to address stakeholders' roles in current accountability, with a particular focus on teacher education. After illustrating the "mess" that encapsulates teacher evaluation, we turn to the future and provide a number of strategies (both general and specific) that various stakeholders can use to manage during this challenging time. We place a heavy emphasis on teacher education because teacher education is both at risk of extinction, a belief held by most critics and some teacher educators, and fuels the next generation of teachers. We also believe that teacher education possesses what we believe to be one of the greatest opportunities for enhancing teaching and learning in public schools.

A Brief Summary

Throughout this book we have suggested that the history of student and teacher evaluation has been an issue for some time. In general, assessments of teachers and students have moved from low-stake and informative assessments to increasingly more serious evaluations that have consequences for students and teachers that are significant including great retention for students and dismissal for teachers. There have been some exceptions as high-stakes tests, especially for students, have emerged at different times.

For the most part, teacher educators and educational researchers have been passive (and at times even active supporters) as policy makers have increased evaluative criteria and their consequences. We will argue that the situation must change and that educators and teacher education programs must, at a minimum, be at the table, and be active and articulate speakers. We believe, however, that this will not be enough and teacher education must be more active, even forceful in their debates with policy makers about what constitutes good practice and begin to show how it can be measured.

We have consistently illustrated that reform movements in the United States have mobilized quickly and without any real data to support the reform. Reformers have generated sweeping policies for practice that involve considerable time and resources even to the point of completely replacing existing curriculums with new ones. Not only have these reforms been expensive, they have also been notably and consistently ineffective. Our review has touched upon many reform efforts that have stemmed from a crisis—a perceived problem that has major and negative consequences for our economy and equality of life if not responded to quickly.

The amazing thing about these reforms is that they quickly disappear and new ones quickly reemerge. Given the failure rates of passed reforms, it is remarkable that new reforms can gain traction. As we have noted, there are many possible explanations as to why reforms come and go with considerable support from policy makers and educators. Among these reasons are the perceived crises (something has to be done now), the belief that teaching is easy (some simple solutions can solve this problem), and newness sells; publishers like to publish something that is forward looking, and also clearly writing new curriculum materials or tests involves a considerable amount of money for some.

At one time teachers were believed to be relatively unimportant in the achievement of school students, that is school achievement was largely due to issues of heredity, class, and social status. In the 1970s and throughout the 1980s, researchers built a knowledge base that showed the importance of teachers and actually linked instructional process to student achievement. Thus, for some time it has been known that teachers impact achievement in important ways. Research of over 40 years has consistently documented the importance of appropriate teacher expectations, good proactive management skills, opportunity to learn, active teaching, and a balance of conceptual and procedural information.

Despite these gains, educational researchers for various reasons forgot these gains in knowledge and pursued other important questions about classrooms, teachers, and learning. These new questions were legitimate and potentially important, but they were not integrative; and information on teacher effects linking instructional behavior and achievement was not advanced such that what is known about teaching effects on achievement today is little more than what was known in 1986.

Recent efforts, spurred by Race to the Top, mandates teacher evaluation on the teachers' ability to "add value"—that is to increase the achievement of their students more than other teachers do in similar circumstances. This research has largely replicated what was known years earlier. This is valuable in one sense as it illustrates that despite the various changes in American classrooms (e.g., increased diversity) that this knowledge still obtains in today's classrooms.

Chapters 4 and 5 have illustrated the responses of states and educators to the increased demand for evaluating teachers through classroom observation and student achievement. Already apparent are the wide differences in states' approaches and that it seems reasonable to predict that the consequences of teacher evaluation following Race to the Top will have uneven effects and in some instances even undesirable outcomes.

It is clear that accountability has moved beyond its focus on students, teachers, and schools and now is demanding increased accountability from teacher education programs that prepare today's teachers and administrators. Just as we noted inappropriate evaluation of teachers in today's schools (see Chapters 4 and 5), below we will note the inadequate and poorly conceived efforts for evaluating teacher education programs that have manifested. We have referred to the present situation unkindly as a mess. But we can think of no other way to describe it. In the remainder of this chapter we share some ideas for addressing and improving the current situation. We do not have answers. Problems that were created over 50 years cannot be solved in 1 year or 2. However, we do believe that we have some important considerations that may stimulate thoughtful and useful practice and that over time we can do better than we did in the past.

In sum, throughout this book we have made numerous arguments to explain how we have come to be where we are today in regards to demands for holding teachers and students accountable. Those arguments include (a) the circular nature of education reform, (b) the ahistorical nature of education reform, (c) the rise in popularity, accessibility, and funding of testing, and (d) a renewed emphasis on teachers matter. We offer one additional illustration that helps describe how accountability in today's schools has emerged and the role of teacher education in that evolution.

Arriving at Accountability: Yet Another Illustration

The Role of Teacher Education

Criticism of teacher education has a long history. A number of books have addressed the adequacy or the inadequacy of teacher education so we limit the discussion of this topic here and offer a few hypotheses as to why teacher education has struggled to be successful. First, teacher education tries to improve normative practice and to this end it often prepares teachers for schools that could or should be rather than what schools are. New visions of classroom life offer promise, but they need eventually to be based upon research to show that the "new" is better. More pragmatically, teachers must be able to function in schools that exist even if new teachers want to alter normative practice in time. In some ways teacher education programs are like federal reforms, attempting to do too much too quickly with limited time, and *no* data. We believe teacher education programs need to allocate their resources strategically.

Second, teacher education programs tend to focus too much on theory in the absence of practical experience. More time should be spent on the basic building blocks of instructional teaching for meaning, good management, and building supportive classrooms that demand performance, while providing a safe climate for learning. Others have expressed this concern in the past. Consider this criticism of teacher education by B.O. Smith (1980):

> When the faculty of pedagogy does not know what it is about, it grabs any and every newfangled idea and purpose that any organization or agency offers, suggests, or insists upon. It will take on the task of providing courses, workshops, or any device for meeting such demands as the call for urban education, sex education, drug education, or human relations education, even though the faculty is already falling far short of performing the task it was created to do: to train teachers in the knowledge of skills of classroom work.
>
> *(p. 87)*

We do not suggest that teacher education programs have not evolved since 1980, as there has been increased attention to field experiences. Still, we wonder if teacher education programs try to do too much with limited resources (see Good, in press). Other criticisms of the past include the attraction and recruitment of low academic students to teacher preparation and lack of new knowledge (see Ginsberg & Kingston, in press, for a review).

Today, criticism of teacher education programs includes mediocre preparation, limited focus on knowledge and clinical training, and, again, that teacher education does not attract the most academically accomplished students. Ironically, Teach for America (TFA) recruits some of the top students in the nation; however, in a review of the literature, TFA graduates' impact on student learning is no greater than that of teachers prepared through other routes. Moreover, they leave the profession at high rates—80% leave by the fourth year of teaching (Heilig & Jez, 2010). At one point, higher levels of education and professional development were valued and this was apparent in merit pay and pay schedules that placed valued on these achievements. Furthermore, research has supported other teacher characteristics, such as teacher experience matters up to a point for student achievement (Clotfelter, Ladd, & Vidgor, 2007; Murnane & Philips, 1981; Nye, Konstantopoulos, & Hedges, 2004; Rowan, Correnti, & Miller, 2002). In general, however, most research on teacher characteristics has been overshadowed by substantial evidence that education and other teacher characteristics such as test scores, experience, and salary are not important factors in student achievement (Bill & Melinda Gates Foundation, 2010; Greenwald, Hedges, & Laine, 1996; Hanushek, 1986, 2003). Teacher education, then, is in the difficult position now of proving its worth—that teacher education matters. Just as teachers and schools have been ranked on value-added measures, teacher education is not far behind. The stakes are equally high—loss of or increase in funding or the worst possible outcome, program closure.

Teacher Education Caught in a Vise.   High-stakes teacher evaluation has a clearly defined trickle-down effect on teacher education. Just as teachers may lose their jobs, teacher education faculty may find themselves in a similar spot if they are unable to demonstrate the effect their graduates have on student learning outcomes. As Ginsberg and Kingston (in press) illustrate, teacher education has primarily proven its worth by documenting the types of students that are attracted to their programs and the test scores achieved on certification exams. Further, teacher education has historically not been interested in measuring and documenting their graduates' performance once they have left the program. This, unfortunately, has left teacher education susceptible to a number of parties interested in doing this *for* teacher education, primarily using value-added data. For example, the National Council for Teaching Quality (NCTQ) will soon release its own rating of all teacher preparation programs in the country. Findings will be published by *U.S. News and World Report*. Everyone is subject to review.

Policy makers want to know if teacher graduates improve the achievement of the students they teach in schools. Just as public schools have been challenged in the last 30 to 40 years by alternative education (charter schools and voucher programs), in the past few years teacher education has come under pressure from alternative teacher education programs because of the perceived inadequacy of traditional teacher education programs. It is not our intent to enter this debate (relative comparison of traditional and non-traditional education programs), but simply to note that now *all* teacher education programs are under some pressure to illustrate that they have value. Alternative teacher education has not proved to be an inexpensive magic bullet.

How Is Teacher Education Responding?   As shown above, up to this point teacher education has not engaged proactively to prevent this progression. So, in part, teacher education has been part of the problem. Wineburg (2006) noted that answering the increased calls demanding that university-based teacher education programs illustrate their effectiveness, is a "tall order" as the research illustrating a relationship between teacher education programs and classroom teaching, as others have reported, is sparse (Cochran-Smith & Zeichner, 2005; Rice, 2003). Given this situation, Wineburg conducted a survey to see how teacher education programs were collecting evidence about program effectiveness. She received responses from 240 institutions—about 65% of all American Association of State Colleges and Universities (AASCU). These results might provide an interesting point of departure for AASCU teacher education programs that want to begin to assess or to improve the assessments of its graduates. Wineburg did not call for any particular assessment plan, but does advocate the need for teacher education programs to develop ways of studying their graduates. She argued, "We would urge universities to work to develop evidence-based cultures that will demonstrate quality of teacher education program graduates and be valuable to institutions as well as to the public at large" (p. 63). However, it may well be that what is useful to the institution and what is useful to the policy makers are notably different. For example, policy makers are likely to be concerned only with ability to increase achievement, whereas institutions may want evidence pertaining to the professional collegiality that a teacher projects, teachers' dispositions, as well as a teacher's professional growth over time, and the ability to provide students with convivial and warm classrooms.

Others have also recognized the need for teacher education programs to provide evidence of value and some have even called for strong and immediate action in the face of uncertainty. For example, Pianta (2012) succinctly, but clearly, identified many deficiencies associated with the use of value-added measures to evaluate teachers and teacher education programs. Despite these limitations, he suggested that for political reasons, as well as for those related to institutional responsibility, that teacher educators should begin to collect data about their programs and its effects. He argued the case this way:

> We in teacher preparation need to know the learning gains of the students taught by our graduates, and we should know how well they teach. Even if the tests are lousy, narrow, and imperfect, they are important to employers and provide one form of information that could be useful for program-driven planning, quality control, and evaluation."
>
> *(para. 8)*

We agree with this general sentiment that teacher educators need to know how graduates perform in the classroom, but we are not persuaded that value-added measures will be of value in doing this. Ginsberg and Kingston (in press) although recognizing the need for evidence about the efficacy of teacher education programs, also note several obstacles. They make the point that teacher candidates are not randomly assigned to teacher education programs. In some cases, programs seek to develop teachers for particular settings or roles (e.g., urban schools, mathematics, social justice leaders). Furthermore, teachers often hold degrees from multiple institutions making it difficult to parse out the effects of a teacher education program from other forms of education. This issue becomes even more complex when considering that some teachers have multiple degrees or certificates in teaching from a number of institutions.

Ginsberg and Kingston (in press) provided a thorough and thoughtful review of the state of teacher education and addressed the challenge of current accountability pressures on teacher education and how teacher education is responding to calls for evidence of their value. One powerful aspect of their work is a clear demonstration of how teacher education's quality controls compare favorably to other professional preparation programs including medical, engineering, journalism, psychology, and athletic training, among many others. We found their general discussion valuable, especially the new information about some of the quality control issues that have been developed in teacher education programs. For example, Ginsberg and Kingston provide evidence that refutes one long-standing criticism of teacher education programs—that programs are long on theory, but short on practical experience. They provide evidence that teacher education students are involved in a considerable amount of clinical activity in schools and with students. However, whether or not this clinical experience actually improves the performance of pre-service teachers when they enter the classroom has not been established, and this, above all, has been the biggest threat to teacher education to date. If teacher education is to remain viable, they must collect evidence to show that they matter.

Evaluating the Effectiveness of Teacher Education Programs. At present there is considerable discussion and controversy about using value-added models for assessing the quality of teacher education programs by examining the effectiveness of their graduates when they begin to teach (Ginsberg & Kingston, in press). As we discussed earlier in Chapter 5, evaluating teachers in a single school or in a single school district is an arduous task. Clearly, attempting to study the effects of teacher education programs is inordinately difficult for many reasons, including the fact that program graduates will enter teaching in diverse school districts across many states. Nonetheless, some educators are beginning to contemplate dealing with these complexities. Henry, Kershaw, Zulli, and Smith (2012) noted the various accountability reforms that have followed Race to the Top and its insistence upon the need for states to assess the effectiveness of their teachers. They stated, "In response, states are scrambling to create sophisticated databases that are able to link practicing teachers to their preparation programs as well as to the achievement data of the students they teach." (p. 335). These authors discussed many of the same technical issues in using value-added procedures that we and others have noted in using student achievement to gauge teacher effectiveness (Amrein-Beardsley & Collins, 2012; Gabriel & Lester, 2013; Konstantopoulos, in press). However, they also illustrated that the issue is considerably broader than choice of the statistical model that will be used (even though this is a major task as well). Their paper provided a thorough discussion of other issues involved in evaluating teacher preparation programs (TPP) including selection decisions, students to be included or excluded, teachers (including the issue of how to use students that have multiple teachers and teachers who have multiple students), reporting decisions (how should scores be reported—teacher ranks, actual scores), and transparency (use of simple models that the media and citizens can interpret or of more complex models). However, Henry et al. were calmly positive despite their review of the difficult and multiple decisions that have to be made in linking teacher education graduates to their effects on students and reciprocally making inferences about the performance of individual graduates (teachers) who are teaching disparate students in diverse locations.

> The empirical work to date has established "proof of concept" for incorporating student test scores into the evaluation of TPP. It shows that a sufficient signal can be found in student test scores to reliably attribute effects to individual TPP even with the "noise" of confounding variables and nonrandom sorting of teachers and students into schools and classrooms.
>
> *(pp. 351–352)*

Floden (2012) broadened the scope of outcomes when he suggested that teacher preparation programs might be considered as exhibiting high quality in at least four ways: (a) high-quality faculty and/or state-of-the-art technology equipment; (b) high-quality coursework that includes appropriate content, skills, supervision, and research knowledge; (c) high-quality learning (evidence that teacher preparation students make clear gains in the knowledge and skills that are important for teaching); and (d) high-quality teaching (evidence that graduates have high levels of knowledge skills important for teaching that will lead to high VAM scores when they begin teaching). These are important distinctions as the current policy debate focuses primarily on the link between teacher education programs and their graduates' ability to increase student achievement. Floden provided various caveats and considerations (one exceedingly well done consideration is his description of labor market effects on a program's VAM scores), and yet his conclusion, although somewhat balanced, is guardedly optimistic.

> Many states now possess the data and statistical methods that can produce teacher value-added scores and link them to preparation programs. These highlight the important responsibility that programs have to help prospective teachers learn to be effective instructors. Used thoughtfully they can inform improvements in teacher preparation. Used simplistically, they may have unfortunately, unintended consequences.
>
> *(p. 360)*

Despite their documentation of internal process measures within teacher education programs, and their favorable comparisons to other professional schools, there is still a paucity of data to illustrate that the graduates of teacher education programs develop skills, knowledge, and/or dispositions that impact students in actual classrooms. As mentioned above, whether we like it or not, teacher education programs have not provided the type of information that policy makers most want to see—evidence that teacher education graduates can increase student achievement. Further, this form of data collection and sharing has not been developed (or even started in many cases) in any systematic way.

Skills and Knowledge of Teacher Education Graduates.   One critical debate involves the skills and knowledge that teachers should possess when they enter teaching. Specifically, what knowledge and skills should teacher education programs teach and to what level of proficiency? And, what evidence exists to support the selection of particular skills and knowledge? It has long been contended that teachers go through several developmental stages as they move through pre-service programs, student teaching, beginning teaching, and career teaching (Fuller, 1969). More recently, Twiselton (2007) has suggested that in moving from novice to expert, teachers in training move through three distinct stages. These are task manager (involving students in tasks, maintaining their involvement, and helping them to complete classroom assignments); curriculum deliverer (providing information and delivering the basic curriculum); and concept/skill builder (actively focusing on students' development of concepts and skills as a way for both learning and transforming learning). If we accept these three stages, the curriculum question for teacher education programs is how to organize courses and experiences that meet these three roles? How much time should be devoted to each phase? What type of evaluation data would enable teacher educators to know if/when these goals have been addressed at least to some minimum level? And, then, in an ideal world, there would be a linkage between teacher education programs and employing school districts so that districts know the skills that beginning teachers have and those tasks that they need to develop or refine themselves. Once this communication is established, a basis would be provided so that meaningful evaluation of teachers and teaching could occur over time.

Further, if we had some sort of system to understand teachers' level of development (no matter how imperfect), then in-service training programs could be developed more strategically than they are at present. Presumably, a school district that has 100 beginning teachers, 100 teachers with 3–5 years' experience, and 100 teachers with 5 plus years of service, would need different in-service programs than a school district that had 300 beginning teachers, 100 teachers with 2–5 years' experience, and no teachers with more than 5 years of experience. Although the issue is and will remain somewhat context specific, it appears that a general problem has emerged because the teacher labor market has changed dramatically in the past 20–30 years (Marx, in press; Ingersoll & Merrill, 2012). Marx noted that along with the well-known fact that 50% of teachers stop teaching within 5 years (Ingersoll & Perda, 2012) is the new information that the rate of first-year teacher attrition is increasing (Ingersoll & Merrill, 2012). According to Marx,

> As Ingersoll and Merrill (2012) have shown, with a mode of 1 year of experience, we are approaching a time when huge numbers of America's children will be taught essentially by beginners; people with little experience and with the prospect of leaving the field quickly after beginning. For those who believe that anyone can teach, they do not likely worry much about this development. For those who believe professional teachers possess knowledge and skills that enable them to teach successfully, this development is worrisome, indeed."
>
> *(p. X)*

Thus, building on stage theorists' insights that teachers move through stages and Marx's (in press) conclusion that today's teacher has considerably less experience than was the case earlier, leads us to the conclusion that many teachers need considerable assistance with developing the skills and dispositions associated with the first two types of teachers identified by Twiselton (2007). Obviously, the distribution from district to district and from school to school might lead to different conclusions, but, on average, it would seem that superintendents and school principals might want special assurance that their teachers can manage and deliver instruction in acceptable ways. This is not to discourage interest in helping teachers to move to new levels including helping them to develop teaching abilities that challenge and assist their students to transform and to personalize information, but it is to say that if teachers do not possess well-developed skills for managing, and actively teaching, they will never reach the transformative stage. And, as shown in Chapter 3, there is abundant knowledge about classroom management and active teaching that applies to many teaching contexts. Unfortunately, little is known about how to provide teachers with the ability to help students to transform knowledge or other outcomes of schooling such as creativity. This is clearly an important research area both for teachers and teacher educators, and valuable information to help convince policy makers that students (and our future leaders) are more than just a test score.

In general, educational researchers interested in teacher education programs have endorsed considerations of value-added procedures, some enthusiastically, and others more cautiously. However, in many ways this reminds us that educational researchers have typically provided little resistance to reform mandated by policy makers. And earlier we provided this quote supporting the use of accountability:

[Forms of accountability] hold considerable promise for improving the quality of teaching and learning in U.S. schools, while simultaneously increasing the status and respect associated with the teaching profession in this country.

(Porter, Youngs, & Odden, 2001, p. 294)

The three articles we have just examined illustrate the range of opinion associated with the use of value-added procedures in evaluating teacher education. As we saw, some were guardedly positive, others were cautiously positive, and there are very few examples of anyone strongly recommending against the use of value-added procedures. And of course, there are some that are actually involved in conducting value-added procedures. Gansle, Noell, and Burns (2012) have been engaged in assessing the classroom performance of teacher education graduates to determine if variation in teacher effectiveness can be associated with the teacher education program they attended, and to some extent, the quality of the teacher education that they have attended. Interested readers can find details associated with sample selection, following teachers and students over time, data analysis, and related issues. For present purposes this study serves as a proxy that value-added analysis can be applied to teacher education programs.

It should be clear that the effects obtained in this study are very small, leaving to question the extent to which they provide useful information to programs, or for that matter, to policy makers. To begin with the issues of internal validity are enormous. For example, in many programs many students take their method courses (e.g., in math or in reading) from different instructors, that is some graduates had Professor X and others had Professor Y. *Oddly,* the premise that drives value-added analyses is that some teachers make more of a difference than other teachers. Yet, in this study, the possibility of differential effectiveness between Professor X and Professor Y is obscured. To make the situation a bit more complicated, students may also have different professors in another method concentration. Some students have Professor A and some have Professor B. We know that teachers (even university teachers) are likely to have general effects on their students (see Chapter 3) as well as subject-matter specific effects. Thus, students not only have different method instructors, but they also have different combinations of method instructors. For example, some have X and A, others have Y and A, and so forth. Moreover, for teacher candidates in secondary education, a good amount of content knowledge may come from prerequisites and content area coursework outside of a teacher preparation program. Here, too, students in secondary education have multiple teachers. This poses enormous challenges.

Further, teacher education students have different clinical experiences prior to graduation. Here too the quality of their mentor teachers likely varies in many ways including their clinical skills in providing feedback to student teachers, as well as their own ability to teach students effectively. It is not uncommon prior to student teaching that students do some clinical work that involves observations in schools and even some limited teaching. Some teacher education students do extensive observational work in third-grade classrooms that are primarily composed of students from low-income homes. Some of the candidates will do their student teaching in first-grade classrooms primarily composed of students from high-income homes. Eventually some of these teachers end up teaching fifth-grade classrooms serving heterogeneous groups of students. Other teacher graduates may have a seamless set of experiences where observation, student teaching, and first-year assignment converge. So in these analyses Gansle, Noell, and Burns (2012) reported that it appears that clinical experience and teacher education experience as a controlled, heterogeneous, and set order of courses and experiences is woefully confounded.

To take but one additional issue associated with internal validity has to do with the well-known fact that teachers' effects on students vary notably from year to year. This lack of stability has been known since the 1970s (Brophy, 1973; Emmer, Evertson, & Brophy, 1979; Rosenshine, 1970) and it has been documented consistently over time. Most recently Berliner (in press) and Konstantopolous (in press) have dramatically illustrated year-to-year variation in teachers' effects on students. Yes, some teachers are stable over time, but a number of teachers vary and in unpredictable ways (some teachers with similar profiles move up in perceived effectiveness, whereas other teachers are less effective). Even in the early research noting this phenomenon, Brophy (1973) commented:

> ... the fact that teacher effectiveness shows great individual differences and only moderate stability from year to year in an unselected sample, and the fact that yearly "class effects" were observed despite statistical controls, even in highly consistent teachers (though to a lesser degree), argue against the indiscriminate use of student gain or general achievement tests for assessing teacher accountability. Until the sources of instability become known and eliminated or controlled, this procedure is inappropriate, and certainly unfair to many teachers.
>
> *(p. 251)*

Unfortunately, not much progress has been made to address this issue, and not surprisingly, it reemerges again in the use of value-added data. When Teacher 1, a graduate of Institution B (having core method courses with Professors A and X), has high effects on student achievement (in the top 10% of comparison teachers) in year 1 and in year 2 has low–moderate effects (in the top 60% of comparison teachers), how do we use this information to compare (a) the impact of the teacher education program, (b) the impact of the method teacher or combination of method teachers, or (c) the congruence between clinical experience and initial placement. Many years ago, Lee Cronbach

(1957) reminded researchers and policy makers about the complexity involved in addressing certain types of research questions (he called it a "hall of mirrors"). We are sorry to report for those that are involved in using value-added scores to evaluate teacher education programs that the task they address is even more complex than the conditions that led Cronbach to render his pessimistic characterization.

There Is No Silver Bullet

As demonstrated above, we have illustrated teacher education's role in the arrival at today's accountability, but it is important to reiterate that this movement is not due to one single factor. The responses that teacher education has, is, and could take from this point forward are varied and also plagued by a number of complex problems. Unfortunately, teacher education is often controlled heavily by maladaptive responses in education reform. For example, one of the puzzling aspects of attempting to improve teaching is the simplistic suggestions that are often given about what to do or what not to do. This topic could be a book, but hopefully a few examples will make the point that no single variable (or magic silver bullet) is indicative of good or poor teaching. Despite the voluminous literature on teaching, many including educators, continue to argue for simple solutions. Let's consider a few of these shibboleths.

Employ Highly Verbal Teachers. Since the publication of the *Equality of Educational Opportunity* study (Coleman et al. 1966), policy makers and educational researchers have consistently concluded that one of the most important teacher characteristics for predicting teachers' ability to improve student achievement has been teachers' verbal ability. As Coleman et al. (1966) focused on this as the only teaching behavior that related to student achievement, it has been cited frequently as a valuable teacher characteristic. For example, Aloe and Becker (2009) note in a 2003 report from the U.S. Secretary of Education:

> The most robust finding in the research literature is the effect of teacher verbal and cognitive ability on student achievement. *Every study* (italics added) that has included a valid measure of teacher verbal or cognitive ability has found that it accounts for more variance in student achievement than any other measure characteristic of teachers (e.g., Greenwald, Hedges, & Laine, 1996; Ferguson & Ladd, 1996; Kain & Singleton, 1996; Ehrenberg & Brewer, 1994).
>
> *(U.S. Department of Education, 2003, p. 46)*

We emphasize that this is not an isolated sentiment as it is easy to find many educational researchers who have made similar claims. However, extant data do not support a strong relationship between teachers' verbal ability and student achievement. Aloe and Becker's review of 19 studies indicate that at best teachers' verbal ability is weakly related to student and school outcomes. In some studies, verbal ability is not related to school outcomes in any way. Thus, despite its reputed value—teacher verbal ability is not a strong predictor of student achievement.

Avoid Whole Class Teaching.   Whole class teaching, like any method, can be appropriate or inappropriate. Among its many advantages are instruction and review; a cost-effective method that can involve a large number of students. However, when done well, whole class instruction is not a teacher lecture or a one-sided conversation. It is an activity that is led by the teacher and may involve considerable teacher talk. If done appropriately, whole class teaching involves students in many ways such as asking students what they know about the topic, why it is important to learn the material, and ways the material might be useful in studying new material or in applying it in their lives.

DiCarlo, Pierce, Baumgartner, Harris, and Ota (2012) provided compelling evidence that whole class instruction can be used effectively even in preschool classrooms. Even those who believe strongly in the utility of whole class methods might have reservations—even strong ones—about using whole class instruction with very young children. However, DiCarlo and her colleagues demonstrated that it can be effective if implemented appropriately and, again, illustrating that *quality* of format always trumps the form of instruction.

The successful lessons that kept students attentive and engaged in DiCarlo et al.'s study (2012) were marked by what teachers did not do—accommodate nonparticipants—as well as what teachers did do including keeping whole class lessons focused and not overly long, acknowledging child communication and participation, providing all children with materials, and sufficient space to sit together, addresses multiple objectives/tasks, and relate whole group lesson to children's activities. These teacher actions have empirical and theoretical groundings in early work including Kounin's proactive management style, e.g., sufficient space and materials clearly is proactive management as is dealing with multiple tasks simultaneously. The use of interesting materials and connecting whole group lessons to other activities connects to earlier work on active teaching.

Use Small Group Instruction.   Throughout the 1990s, many if not most educators heavily recommended the use of small group instruction. Following constructivist thinking, small group instruction became viewed as a panacea not only for improving student achievement, but also for improving students' respect and value for other students who differed from them in important ways. For example, McCaslin and Good (1996) noted eight advantages for small group instruction that were touted by its proponents. Four of these appear below.

1. The knowledge of the group is almost always greater than the knowledge of any individual.
2. Students benefit from small group learning because more group time is spent on conceptual understanding; whereas in individual work, more time is spent on products and producing answers.
3. Tasks done in small groups tend to be more like work done at home—and in many jobs—where everyone pitches in to get a task done. Students develop an expanded understanding of self and others and learn to appreciate individual differences and become aware that everyone possesses strengths and weaknesses.
4. Students serve as models for one another, and they learn important learning-to-learn skills (e.g., how to disagree constructively).

Despite these potential advantages, McCaslin and Good (1996) identify eight problems that may prevent or minimize constructive learning. Four of these are included below.

1. Students often hold misconceptions about academic concepts, and these misunderstandings may be reinforced during small group activities.
2. Students shift dependency from teachers to peers.
3. Students enjoy differential attention and status such that in some group situations, high-achieving students may primarily perform for other students and feel pressure to do the work for the group.
4. Some students will perceive themselves as having little to contribute to the discussion and some of these students may become indebted to other group members.

It is hard to overstate the enthusiasm and the amount of material that was written advocating the importance of small group instruction. Many professional associations actively advocated for the increased use of small group instruction and the decrease of teachers teaching, especially in whole class settings. Although these either/or debates seldom ever end, the advocacy for small group instruction has abated considerably in the past few years. One notable source, The National Mathematics Advisory Panel's Report, *Foundation for Success* (2008), decried the simple straw man arguments that had been used historically in comparing teacher-directed and student-centered instruction in mathematics:

> The caricatures of teacher-directed and student-centered instruction that have sometimes emerged in debates on this subject are not validated in the versions of teacher-directed and student-centered instruction that were examined in the studies reviewed. Indeed, teacher-directed instruction involves assessment and careful attention to student progress—students were very much involved in the versions of teacher-directed instruction described in these studies. And, teachers have a key role in the versions of

student-centered instruction described here as well—they choose tasks, direct discussion, and work toward mathematical goals. The Task Group found no example of studies in which students were teaching themselves or each other without any teacher guidance; nor did the Task Group find studies in which teachers conveyed mathematics content directly to students without any attention to their understanding or response. The fact that these terms, in practice, are neither clearly nor uniformly defined, nor are they true opposites, complicates the challenge of providing a review and synthesis of the literature.

(pp. 6–12).

Essentially, the report, after reviewing many studies, reached the conclusion that neither teacher-directed nor student-centered instruction was uniformly flawed or beneficial. Depending upon the context, what was being taught, and the quality with which the instructional method was implemented, sometimes these methods were ineffective or effective. We return to our earlier point—format or form of instruction does not predict the quality of learning. What is in important is the quality of the instructional method.

In sum, we have established that teacher education has been under criticism for some time, but that current criticism has fueled teacher education accountability—demonstrate the worth of your graduates, or else. In the past, single solutions have been used in education to address "the educational problem." However, these have largely been unsuccessful because (a) classrooms are incredibly rich and complex environments, and (b) these initiatives have generally ignored the importance of quality. Carrying this belief system forward, it is clear that, as with education reform, simple and one-size-fits-all solutions that simultaneously de-skill the teacher workforce will not be the best way for teacher education to respond. Instead, we offer below a number of strategies (both global and specific) to address the accountability vise that teacher education is in.

Moving Beyond Failed Reform: General Proactive Strategies

As noted, we place a greater emphasis on teacher education in this chapter. However, we see teacher education as one of the many stakeholders. Our suggestions below reflect a more comprehensive understanding of the various groups that can take steps to modify the direction of accountability in both teacher education and K-12 settings. We also provide a number of orienting strategies that provide a framework for more specific strategies that follow below.

Adaptive Perceptions of Teachers

Teaching and teacher education have been plagued by years of criticism and negative publicity. Payne's (2008) discussion of demoralized schools included many dimensions describing teachers' lack of morale in many urban school settings including parts of the problem for which teachers are responsible. However, Payne also discussed some of the external factors that weigh heavily and negatively on teachers:

> I suspect that one of the reasons we have such persistent difficulty appreciating how damnably hard it is to change urban schools is the lack of respect we have for the people who work in them, which then predisposes us to simplistic answers. It is useful to be reminded that it is not, fundamentally, a problem that can be reduced to just the people in schools.
>
> *(p. 45)*

Another challenge is that even when criticisms or negative information about teachers and teacher education become apparent, the effects are potentially devastating and overshadow to an inappropriate extent the good that teachers and teacher educators are doing. For example, in a comprehensive review, Baumeister, Bratslavsky, Finkenauer, and Vohs (2001) illustrated convincingly that bad news is considerably stronger than good news. They noted that it takes a considerable number of good events to overcome the effects of a single bad one. If we consider the possible ramification of this for teachers in schools, it would suggest that perhaps we need to make a renewed effort to find and to report the many good things that teachers and schools do. Even little things over time might have impact from teacher of the year to teacher of the month. Teachers share this sentiment. Lortie (1975) found that 37% of teachers noted the biggest extrinsic reward they have received was respect from others.

Following the tragic shootings at a school and the heroic efforts of teachers who gallantly saved children's lives, there has been a renewed respect for teachers. For example, Patricia Alberj Graham was quoted in a news article by Armario (2012), "While it's very important that teachers assist children in learning, it's also true that they help get them in the mood for learning and protect them and care for them while they are at school." Another example of recognition for teachers came from an editorial in *The Baltimore Sun* newspaper noting that teachers are not trusted and are judged harshly on many variables outside of their control and argued that in light of the state of education we must remember the:

> … teachers leading children out of harm's way in Newtown or those half-dozen adults who died in the line of duty. Public educators deserve our respect, not just for what happened in Sandy Hook but for their extraordinary, daily devotion to the education, health and welfare of the next generation.
>
> *(Anonymous, 2012)*

However, the glow of new respect for teachers may be short lived. Armario (2012) ended her story, "Whether the courageous actions in Newtown, Conn., lead to anything more than a temporary shift in the tone of how the nation talks about teachers remains to be seen."

Support Teaching as Profession.   Consistent with lack of respect, is the failure to identify teaching as a profession and honor teachers' ability to make decisions about the work they do. Rosenholtz (1989) captures the essence of this in her book *Teachers' Workplace: The Social Organization of Schools*:

> Many of the recently passed reforms try to regulate both the content and process of education in the hopes that teacherproof instruction will increase the quality of schooling. Legislators and administrators seek to enforce hierarchical control over teachers through such routine devices as management-by-objectives, standardized curriculum packages, and minimum competency testing. These reforms live now in enormous indebtedness that is inescapably to be paid, not in money, but in wasted human potential, school mediocrity, and lost teacher commitment.
>
> *(p. 214)*

The Rosenholtz quote could have been written in 2013; these practices then and now often de-skill teachers. For example, despite the consensus that teachers matter, there is limited trust in teachers' ability to assess the outcomes of their instruction. Rather, external assessments are deemed the best measure of students' learning. However, teacher educators and citizens need to insist that teachers who see students 180 days a year also have a voice in assessing students' academic performance. Oddly, many (Kane, Wooten, Tyler, & Taylor, 2011) are asserting that students opinions matter in evaluating teachers because students know more about teachers than anyone else. Doesn't this same logic apply to teachers' knowledge of students? Yes, most assuredly it does.

Balance

For some time one of the authors has argued for a balanced approach to instruction (Good, 1996), and it was a topic included in all my graduate courses. Several years later Carrie Hummel, a talented graduate student (and now an even more talented professional—Carrie Wiley), asked me if I or we "would recognize balance if we saw it." In time, I have come to illustrate the wisdom of her question, and I came to realize that I would never see the personification of balance.

Balance as we now see it is an abstract concept that means different things in different contexts. Balanced instruction in second-grade classes and in graduate school classes varies notably. Still like other abstract concepts it has important value. Consider opportunity to learn. Opportunity to learn informs us that what students are assigned to learn both empowers and restricts learning. Opportunity to learn does not tell us what should be learned but it forcefully indicates that it correlates with student achievement.

Similarly, the concept of balance should remind us that in a democratic society schools are expected to address multiple goals and indeed, there are more goals than any school can address. But holding the concept of balance, if believed, should remind policy makers and educators that judging teachers, students, and schools solely in terms of their performance on standardized tests is unacceptably narrow. Such narrow accountability is not only a disservice to those being evaluated but also to the broader society. Teachers, students, and we as a society are more than a single test score.

As Dewey argued a century earlier, education's goals are to

> … shape the experiences of the young so that instead of reproducing current habits, better habits shall be formed, and thus the future adult society be an improvement on their own … We are doubtless far from realizing the potential efficacy of education as a constructive agency of improving society, from realizing that it represents not only a development of children and youth but also of the future society of which they will be the constituents.
>
> *(1938, p. 92)*

If teachers are to be allowed to achieve balance and to address education and need to prepare students for life in a democracy, the definitions of good teaching need to be broadened.

Going Beyond What We Know: Specific Strategies

Volumes have been written about teacher education and its future by people who have thought deeply about these issues for far longer than we have. However, as a relative newcomer to the field, and as someone working in a different but related field, we hope to bring a helpful perspective to the role of teacher education and its role in preparing teachers for today's classroom. We also believe that teacher education is only one of the many groups that can have a say in how the state of accountability moves forward. We limit ourselves to a few suggestions that both honor the work that has already been done and extends upon what is known about research on teaching. We also make these recommendations with the belief that teaching is indeed a profession and teachers hold a professional knowledge base with which they should have ownership. And, as noted, we are but two voices, so our role often is reduced to noting what should be done and starting a dialogue about how to achieve this.

Better Use of Research on Teaching: Using Videos for Learning and to Advance the Knowledge Base on Good Teaching

We described in Chapter 3 the extensive knowledge base on effective teaching and that recent work in this area has confirmed this knowledge base as still valid in understanding today's teachers, students, and learning. Although some detest the advances in technology, we believe these advances offer opportunities in research that were not widely available to researchers in the 1970s and 1980s. We see, like many others, videos as an extraordinary opportunity. However, we conceptualize the use of videos as one strategy that can address multiple accountability (and other) needs simultaneously. We describe these in detail below.

Using Videos to Prepare Teachers.   Teacher educators have long discussed the complexity of experience (Dewey, 1938) and learning from such experiences (Feiman-Nemser & Buchmann, 1985; Munby & Russell, 1994). Reflection has been a crucial part to many if not all teacher education programs. Significant amounts of reflection can occur after a teacher candidate assesses success or struggles in a given lesson or during student teaching. Unfortunately, many of these recollections of practice can be vague (Ball & Cohen, 1999), because it is difficult to remember all decisions, responses, and thought processes that occur in such a complex environment. Ball and Forzani (2009) explain:

> Teachers must decide how to use time in each lesson (Sleep, 2009), and choose tasks, examples, models or analogies, and materials. During class they must keep track of 25 or more learners as the move through content, keep their eye on the learning goals, attend to the integrity of the subject matter, manage individual student behavior and maintain a productive learning environment, pose strategically targeted questions, interpret students' work, craft responses, assess, and steer all of this towards each students' growth.
>
> *(p. 501)*

We understand that teacher education programs must necessarily be general (e.g., preparing teachers for grades 1–5); however, good programs can still establish a rich clinical awareness of good teaching by involving pre-service teachers with numerous examples of teaching drawn from various grade levels and various contexts by obtaining or creating an electronic library of teaching. These electronic and video libraries can allow for analysis of teaching prior to entering the classroom as well as during student teaching. Video analysis can create an ideal balance between research and theory and allow student teachers to interpret their own classroom practices with others and those more knowledgeable about the teaching profession. It also allows pre-service and currently practicing teachers to isolate particular interactions of aspects of teaching practice (e.g., classroom management, informal assessment) while capturing the complexity of classrooms (Brophy, 2004). At least one study has shown that pre-service teachers note more specific comments, shift their reflections more to instruction (than classroom management), and focus more on the student than themselves in video-supported than memory-based reflections (Rosaen, Lundeberg, Cooper, Fritzen, & Terpstra, 2008).

At present, at least one state is requiring the taping of new teachers, and indeed teacher educators are arguing for a return to more involvement of pre-service teaching in examining teaching behavior (Ball, Boykin, Franke, Kazemi, & Cossey, 2012). Further, states (New York, Illinois, and Tennessee, to name a few) will be adopting edTPA,[1] formerly known as the Teacher Performance Assessment, developed by Stanford University faculty and staff at the Stanford Center for Assessment, Learning and Equity (http://edtpa.aacte. org/faq#17). The edTPA is a comprehensive tool that includes the assessment of lesson plans, student work samples, analysis of student learning, reflections, and video clips of instruction of teacher candidates that will be used as part of teacher certification and for program accreditation purposes. We are not suggesting the use of edTPA (although some may want to use it) but rather we see it is a point of something to review as teacher education programs build their own assessments and evidence base. Building one's own evaluation plan is important as it helps to clarify program goals that faculty collectively pursue. Further, a program that graduates but a few teachers and those that graduate many will have different program evaluation considerations. For example, in a large program teachers in training may have several different methods teachers, whereas in a small program there may only be one teacher. In many cases smaller programs graduates tend to stay in the local areas. In contrast, graduates from larger programs may teach in many different states making follow up evaluation more difficult. We also believe that as many states adopt edTPA, video collections offer opportunities for teacher candidates to learn about what they will be expected to demonstrate in their own selected video clips and how they will be assessed by doing their own edTPA assessment on others' video-taped lessons. And, of course, many observational systems commonly used today have flaws and accordingly some teacher education programs may want to create their own systems.

The use of video has been espoused elsewhere, and there has been much advocacy for the involvement of teachers in clinical practice (classroom visits). Much can be gained in live observation especially if the opportunity involves the chance to talk with teachers or students; however, we note that increased observation in live, ongoing instruction is not likely to solve the inherent problem of teacher preparation. Going to schools can be costly and time consuming. In the time it takes to drive to a class and watch a lesson, a teacher candidate could watch five lessons drawn from different grade levels or in different contexts (rural, suburban, inner city). Further, videotapes could be collected that not only demonstrate the difficult skills of teaching, but those that address new and more complex abilities (e.g., helping students to reason mathematically, critical inquiry). It is important to note, that issues arise when using videos to make decisions about teacher certification. These issues have been illustrated elsewhere in the book (see Chapter 5).

Videos Can Provide Evidence of Teacher Education Effects.   Although we do not have room for extensive comment here, we suggest that in a time of acute policy interest in accountability throughout all aspects of education, we believe that teacher education programs should document that its graduates can teach and the evidence should come from field settings. To be valid, data collection need not be extensive but it needs to be representative (e.g., multiple observations collected on 5%–10% of graduates each year). One possibility is to observe the same graduates across multiple years in order to assess change or improvement in practices across time. Videos of graduates allow teacher education to collect data that can be analyzed and reanalyzed using different observation instruments. It can also be used to demonstrate graduates' impact on student learning more qualitatively and in ways that can offset or compliment student achievement data. Teacher education can use video data to illustrate how their graduates meet standards at the state level and at more local levels (e.g., a college of education's framework or preparation slant such as urban or social justice). Clearly, teacher education programs would want to display immediate and lasting effects of their instruction on graduates' performance in classrooms. There is no one right way to do this, but it is important for teacher education programs to collect data in meaningful and purposeful ways that fulfill the needs of teacher education, the graduates, accreditation bodies, and policy makers.

Extending the knowledge base on what is known about good teaching is a complex topic, which subsumes countless possibilities. The point here is to recognize that teacher education should apply what is known about teaching but equally important is to expand the knowledge base about good teaching. Teacher education programs have limited resources and hence may need to necessarily limit its knowledge generation to only one or two areas. Yet even limited, but focused inquiry could have strong impact in time.

Using Videos for Professional Development.   As states become acutely aware of the potential financial and time constraints of good teacher observation, videos of teachers' instruction may be a more viable solution. It is possible that videos could be used in addition to live observations or to more closely monitor a struggling teacher's progress over the course of year. As mentioned above, videos also offer better opportunities to reflect upon practice, growth, and to extend upon and learn about new practices and strategies. Research on this topic has indicated that video-aided analysis encourages teacher change (Tripp & Rich, 2012). Furthermore, participation in video clubs, professional development opportunities that include reviewing and discussing video clips from teachers' classrooms, leads to changes in instruction. Teachers were observed to allocate more time for student thinking, probing of students' understanding, and learning from students while teaching (van Es & Sherin, 2010; also see van Es, 2009).

Videos for Learning About Teaching: History Repeats Itself.   As we have noted, educational ideas often appear only to disappear and to return later in the future. Our call for extensive video libraries of teaching mirrors the once important topic of microteaching, developed at Stanford University in 1963. It was thought to be a good and realistic environment in which pre-service teachers could practice teaching skills. Indeed, teachers in training at Stanford routinely practiced teaching in microteaching settings for at least 8 weeks before assuming any classroom responsibilities (Allen & Ryan, 1969).

During the late 1960s and early 70s, microteaching was extremely popular in other universities as well. K-12 teachers in training had the opportunity to teach lessons and to be videotaped teaching those lessons, and to receive feedback from their peers and faculty. This was a mainstream activity in many universities. For one example, see the book by Emmer and Millett (1970), which outlined the procedures they followed at the University of Texas, Austin. Also, at this time, it was common for some universities to involve beginning professors and graduate students in these micro-opportunities at the college level. Albert and Hipp (1976) discussed the use of video recording in preparing college sociology teachers and they noted that graduate teachers found it a valuable opportunity and believed it should be part of the standard curriculum. Our point here is not just to note the ahistorical nature of our field, but to stress that many stakeholders would be well served by examining these past practices and learning from them. It is promising to see that others in the field are encouraging a renewed interest in attending to teaching and issues of practice (Ball & Forzani, 2009; Hiebert & Morris, 2012). But—as we have maintained throughout this book—quality counts. More use of video and digital examinations of teaching is good only if appropriate dimensions of teaching are examined.

Challenges to Using Video to Improve Practice.   One of the challenges to improving teaching (as noted in Chapter 5) is that it can be difficult for teachers to make changes in their instructional practice (Franke, Kazemi, & Battey, 2007). Teachers may possess belief systems that do not align with intended change (Forgasz & Leder, 2008) or lack the necessary resources and tools to implement change (Ma, 1999). Although video clubs have demonstrated some success (as noted above), professional development has shown to have little impact on teachers' thinking and practice (Porter, Garet, Desimone, Yoon, & Birman, 2000; Wilson, 2003). Just as we encourage the use of videos, we also encourage research exploring the ways in which videos can be used for assessment purposes, and more importantly to improve practice (and ways in which it cannot). At the risk of overstating the point, the use of videos is not the goal. The goal is to improve practice.

Using Video Libraries for Research. In alignment with the above suggestion, many are embarking on research projects that include the collection of video data. For example, the Third International Mathematics and Science Study (TIMSS) includes video samples as part of their large, international dataset in order to better able capture the differences and similarities in teaching across cultures. More recent technology has supported the data collection, storing, and sharing of large numbers of videos, an important advancement in the area of research on teaching (Stigler, Gallimore, & Hiebert, 2000). According to Stigler et al. (2000), video survey data offer a number of advantages: (1) video records of classroom lessons provide opportunities to discover unanticipated ideas and alternative analytic categories; (2) video is not as theory bound as other methods of data collection, video data, therefore, are amenable to analysis from multiple perspectives and provide a natural focal point for interdisciplinary collaboration; (3) video is not only interesting to researchers from different perspectives; it also has a longer shelf life than other kinds of data; (4) video provides concrete referents for the words and concepts used to describe instructional processes; and (5) video allows us to integrate qualitative and quantitative methods of analysis. Some ways in which this can be done are illustrated.

Other studies, such as the MET Project, which has been mentioned throughout this book, have collected a number of videos on teachers. It is important to continue this tradition alongside teacher education to extend the research on good teaching, but also on good observation and the mechanisms that occur when observers rate videos.

Videos as a Multi-Purpose Approach. We believe that teacher education, researchers, and school districts can work together to utilize videos in ways that more comprehensively respond to this current "crisis." Indeed, in ways that are both cost effective and intellectually stimulating, pre-service teachers could be coupled with principals in training to consider issues of good teaching and how it can be coded. Principals and teachers in preparation could view how current principals rated a particular video using common observation rubrics. This seems especially important given the growing demand for principals to do classroom evaluation and the fact that many principals are not well trained in this clinical research method.

We suspect that in many teacher education programs administrators trained in those same schools spend little time in the study of how to observe teaching and to provide useful feedback. This joint work would jump start both programs— teachers would get accustomed to receiving feedback, and principals in training would learn more about teaching considerations from teachers in training.

Furthermore, teacher education and school districts could work together as teacher education may hire outside observers to observe or collect additional videos of teaching practice. As noted in Chapter 5, multiple observers have the potential to help increase reliability and reduce error. If teacher education and school districts were willing to team up, these observations could be shared in ways that help better capture teachers' classroom practices.

Taken together, all of these potential video libraries can be shared in ways that help enhance research efforts exploring the psychometric properties of observation instruments, the methodological considerations of observational research, and most importantly, effective teaching practices and contextual variables. We note some of these possible directions below.

Extending the Knowledge Base on Good Teaching and Teacher Evaluation

Video libraries offer an extensive amount of opportunities to extend the knowledge base on good teaching practices and good teacher evaluation practices. It was noted in Chapter 5 that evaluators differ in their abilities to assess effective teaching. It is important to explore the underlying characteristics that result in these systematic patterns. Beyond understanding the cognitive processes that occur when an individual evaluates a lesson or video, it is important to explore the ways in which high-stakes may morph the coding processes. Do evaluators feel obligated to reach a particular quota? Are there important differences in video versus live observation? As states begin to realize the financial and practical limitations of observation plans, many may turn to having video observations collected in teachers' classrooms. The benefit of this would be that multiple individuals could score a teacher's classroom and a more informed post-conference could occur. This could also help support local and national video library collections, if made public. If not, it would allow teachers to have an extensive video collection of their own teaching. Drawbacks would be that videos can often be intrusive, and it is nearly impossible to capture on video and audio all of the learning that occurs, particularly in small groups, during a given lesson. Furthermore, it is unclear to what extent all students will be captured on video. Typically, in research, students and their parent(s) or guardian(s) are required to give consent to be present on a video, if not, non-consenting students are placed in different areas of the classroom and are not filmed. Clearly, this could result in a non-typical lesson, particularly if a teacher has purposeful seating assignments, for example, to manage classroom behavior. Second, this could become incredibly problematic if a large number of students do not consent. It will be important to watch how these issues are dealt with as states begin to implement the edTPA.

As one can see, there are a number of important questions that one can ask using video or live observation data. Furthermore, stability has been an important concern in both value-added and observation data. We believe that videos will be one opportunity to further explore this issue, in particular the variables not related to teachers (e.g., change in student characteristics, change in curriculum) that may explain significant variation in stability.

Live Observation

As we have suggested throughout the section above, video has many uses, and these uses have long been recommended for teachers to improve their teaching including the first addition of *Looking in Classrooms* (Good & Brophy, 1973). However, the use of video has many disadvantages including the need to obtain consent, and the fact that many students (and teachers too) are often constrained and behave in non-typical ways on video unless they are filmed frequently. Thus, in many situations, the use of live observation will be required or preferable.

Teachers observing their own teaching or observing their teaching with peers can be a valuable way of learning about other strategies that could have been used and ways in which teaching could be improved. As noted, in *Looking in Classrooms*, the authors have consistently advocated for the possible use of self-study groups in low-stakes environments for improving teaching. Recently, the notoriety of the Japanese use of lesson study to improve teaching (Fernandez & Yoshida, 2004) has generated considerable attention internationally. Some have moved beyond this format and have recommended learning rounds—based upon the popular practice used in medical schools in which interning physicians accompany experienced physicians on their rounds as they visit patients—for example, Scotland has seen the popular use of this technique (*Teaching Scotland,* 2010).

Given that teachers are going to receive feedback on their skills when they enter the teaching force, it seems reasonable that teacher education programs begin to allow teachers to develop those professional skills for receiving and responding to feedback about their teaching. Further, as we have noted, principals in training would also benefit from the opportunity to observe teaching, to provide feedback to teachers, and to have their clinical skills refined through feedback. Given that, in the short run, principals and teachers will be using live observations for feedback and improvement, it seems important that these skills be featured prominently in teacher education programs. There are, of course, many types of knowledge and skills that teachers in training need other than the important subject matter knowledge that they receive. For example, given the heavy use of data for value-added assessments, teachers might profitably benefit from developing expertise in understanding data that they receive from state assessments and using that information to improve instruction. However, given the attention that we have provided to observational techniques, we see this as a uniquely important role for teacher education and believe that other skills (such as analyzing and using data) can be learned on the job.

The Development of Appropriate Dispositions for Teaching

Extending the knowledge base on research on teaching also includes extending the knowledge about characteristics and dispositions that are related to good teaching practices. As noted earlier, a number of measures (e.g., education, experience) and even standardized tests (such as the SAT and ACT) are poor indicators of teacher quality (D'Agostino & Powers, 2009). This is not surprising, as illustrated in a quote by Binet and Simon (1916):

> ... in intelligence there is a fundamental faculty, the alteration or the lack of which, is of the utmost importance for practical life. This faculty is judgment, otherwise called good sense, practical sense, initiative, the faculty of adapting one's self to circumstances. A person may be a moron or an imbecile if he is lacking in judgment; but with good judgment he can never be either. Indeed the rest of the intellectual faculties seem of little importance in comparison with judgment.
>
> *(pp. 42–43)*

Clearly, Binet and Simon (1916) were aware that dispositions and characteristics not assessed in traditional standardized tests are vital, if not more important than intelligence. Thus, it is important to explore other avenues that will ultimately help teachers adapt and teach well.

The number of outcomes that teachers are expected to address in their students is so vast as to be overwhelming (see Rothstein, 2000). Smylie, Miller, and Westbrook (2008) concisely summarize these diverse expectations:

> Teachers are expected to promote students' intellectual development and academic achievement as well as their personal, social, and moral development. Teachers are to prepare students for citizenship and economic productivity. Teachers are also to perform a socialization function, passing along ways of life and culture to future generations.
>
> *(p. 4)*

There are also legal arguments that schools are about more than student achievement (*Rose v Council for Better Education*, 1989). And there is abundant information that parents and citizens want schools to develop students in ways that make them better citizens and well-rounded individuals who can respond appropriately to the social and civil demands of society (Berliner & Biddle, 1995; Rothstein, 2000). However, policy makers have used their power to distract from any outcome of schooling other than achievement. Teacher education programs have the opportunity, and perhaps the responsibility, to focus on outcomes in addition to achievement. Further, some states (e.g., Massachusetts) are now including such outcomes as part of their observational rubric, and hence, evaluation of teacher effectiveness. What these outcomes should be are clearly debatable and this debate is beyond the scope of this chapter. However, as one example, teacher education programs should address the development of appropriate dispositions for teaching.

These dispositions are, of course, disputable but some seem important. Teachers need to believe that all students can learn and that as teachers they can get better. Teachers need to be fair and sensitive to cultural differences in students. Furthermore, teachers who are cooperative, kind, considerate of the individual, patient, show an interest in pupils' problems, and possess a democratic attitude, to note a few, often find themselves in good standing with students (Witty, 1947). One can imagine that these dispositions only further support learning. Here our goal is not to recommend what needs to be developed but to suggest that teacher education programs become engaged in documenting what dispositions their teacher candidates hold and how those dispositions develop and change over time during their teacher education program and in the classroom. In the end, every teacher education program should have a list of dispositions that its graduates adhere to.

Determining Local and National Consensus about the Role of a Teacher and Desired Student Outcomes

Throughout this book, we have noted the large variation in what individuals believe that teachers should do, be, and the qualities they should possess. There is equally large variation in what is seen as important outcomes for students (Rothstein, 2000). In 1964, Rosencranz and Biddle called for a national study of teacher role. To date, no such study has been conducted. Given that different individuals hold different beliefs about teachers, a study such as this one will build consensus, but also illuminate regional and local differences. At a minimum, findings should give the evaluation of students and teachers a direction, a purpose. Without this knowledge, as Rothstein (2000) notes, "… school accountability reforms, in the absence of measurements of the broad range of publicly supported outcomes, have the potential of driving schools to change in ways that most Americans might not, upon reflection, fully support" (p. 440). In the short run teacher education programs can clarify, confirm, and convey.

Conclusion

This chapter has briefly commented upon the history of teacher and student evaluation, school reform, and what is known about instructional behavior that is associated with student achievement. We have also reminded readers of the complex and diverse ways in which states school districts and schools are responding to the current issue inherent in evaluating teachers and we have offered some modest proposals for improving these practices. We have also noted that accountability pressures have arrived on the door steps of teacher education programs.

We have spent some time documenting the evolution of interest in evaluating teacher education programs and some of the initial responses that teacher education programs are generating. We have strongly recommended that value-added assessments of teacher education graduates are an illusionary path to follow. Under some conditions value-added procedures may offer some possibility of informing teacher evaluation in public schools when supplemented with other information especially if information on outcomes other than student achievement are also included in the evaluation. In contrast, the issues of logic and confounds are so complex in following teacher education graduates into the field that it is reminiscent of the hall of mirrors that Cronbach (1957) noted.

Value-added is coming at education fast and furious. Recently, the Council for Accreditation of Educator Preparation (CAEP) released a draft of their new standards that will apply to 900 preparation programs that will participate in the CAEP accreditation system. As outlined in the draft, teacher education programs will be required to document "using value-added measures where available, other state-supported P-12 impact measures, and any other measures constructed by the provider, that program completers contribute to an expected level of P-12 student growth" (Program Impact, Standard 4.1; CAEP, 2013, p. 26).

Research has shown that there is greater variation within schools than between schools and that the teacher a student is assigned to is more important than the school a student attends (Konstantopoulos, 2006). Our concern is that similar results may emerge in evaluating teacher education using value-added data and value-added data will not offer any "value" in determining quality and ranking of teacher education programs.

This is not to suggest that teacher education programs should not collect information about what their students can do and know before they enter teacher education programs, what they learn in those programs, and how they teach in public schools. We agree with Pianta (2012) and Ginsberg and Kingston (in press) that evidence must be collected and this information must be useful not only for institutional knowledge and improvement, but also to satisfy accountability demands from policy makers and citizens.

We emphasize, again, that we do not think that value-added procedures for evaluating teacher education programs have any value for improving teacher education programs or for providing reliable and valid information about the teaching effectiveness of their graduates. Indeed, using value-added procedures will waste resources and provide meaningless data.

We have acknowledged that we do not have the solution or magic bullet to improve this complex and messy situation. We do advance considerations that in time may have useful and perhaps important consequences for improving teacher education programs. We hope that our comments stimulate discussion that improves and goes beyond the ideas that we shared.

Our recommendations include the role of teacher education programs in helping citizens to develop more positive and adaptive perceptions of teaching. These include strategies for supporting teaching as a profession and for realizing that as important as teachers are, successful learning in schools demands resources and commitments that go beyond individual teachers.

We believe that teacher education programs need to make better use of research on teaching knowledge as they prepare new teachers. This includes emphasizing what is known about effective teaching as well as new knowledge that needs to be obtained. Successful teaching is more than raising student achievement scores, although we recognize that this is one important responsibility that teachers address.

We suggest that the use of video in related clinical procedures can play an important role in preparing teachers for the classroom environments in which they will teach. Unfortunately, but for understandable reasons, we know that teacher education programs, especially at the elementary school level, are very general at the orientation. No program can prepare teachers for the specific grade level and range of students that they will teach. General principles supplemented with a range of video examples of teaching in many locations may help to improve teacher preparation for particular situations.

Teacher educators and social scientist researchers interested in teaching and learning should be actively involved in extending the knowledge base of what constitutes good teaching. And, they should be involved in building improved measures for evaluating teachers and classroom learning that are consistent with the expanding knowledge base on good teaching.

Teaching graduates should have appropriate dispositions for teaching (beliefs that all students are capable of learning, that teachers hold the responsibility for constructing safe and interesting classrooms, and so forth) and they should be able to exhibit teaching behaviors that are consistent with the knowledge base. And, of course, teacher education programs should assure that its graduates can and do utilize these strategies.

Although it is beyond the power of any teacher education program (although perhaps not beyond the combined power of all teacher education programs) to specify the outcomes other than student achievement that should be pursued at the state or national level, it is important that teacher education programs acknowledge this importance and work toward creating a local (and if possible a statewide or national) consensus on desired student outcomes. Independent of statewide or national efforts, individual teacher education programs can develop and work toward the achievement of other defined student outcomes (e.g., improving high school graduation rates and helping more students to achieve success in mathematics).

Note

1 Members of the Teacher Performance Assessment Consortium (TPAC) include Colorado, Connecticut, Delaware, District of Columbia, Georgia, Hawaii, Idaho, Illinois, Iowa, Indiana, Maryland, Massachusetts, Minnesota, New York, North Carolina, Ohio, Oklahoma, Oregon, South Carolina, Tennessee, Virginia, Washington, Wisconsin, and Wyoming (http://edtpa.aacte.org/faq#19).

References

Albert, C., & Hipp, R. (1976). Videotape recording in the preparation of college sociology teachers. *Teaching Sociology, 3*(3), 327–338.

Allen, D., & Ryan, K. (1969). *Microteaching.* Reading, MA: Addison Wesley.

Aloe, A. M., & Becker, . J. (2009). Teacher verbal ability and school outcomes: Where is the evidence? *Educational Researcher, 38,* 612–624.

Amrein-Beardsley, A., & Collins, C. (2012). The SAS Education Value-Added Assessment System (SAS® EVAAS®) in the Houston Independent School District (HISD): Intended and unintended consequences. *Education Policy Analysis Archives, 20*(12). Retrieved from http://epaa.asu.edu/ojs/article/view/1096

Anonymous. (2012, December 18). The heroes of Newton: Our view: The strength and courage of teachers and school staff—the kind of public employees so often scorned late—are the revelation of Sandy Hook. *The Baltimore Sun.* Retrieved from http://www.baltimoresun.com/news/opinion/bs-ed-educators-20121218,0,6383452.story

Armario, C. (2012, December 24). Heroic actions bring change in tone on teachers. *USA Today.* Retrieved from http://www.usatoday.com/story/news/nation/2012/12/24/connecticut-school-shooting-newtown-teachers/1788795/

Ball, D., Boykin, W., Franke, M., Kazemi, E., & Cossey, R. (2012, February). *Toward a more practice-based preparation of elementary mathematics teachers.* Forum presented at the 64th Annual Meeting of the American Association of Colleges for Teacher Education, Chicago, IL.

Ball, D. L., & Cohen, D. K. (1999). Developing practice, developing practitioners: Toward a practice-based theory of professional education. In G. Sykes & L. Darling-Hammond (Eds.), *Teaching as the learning profession: Handbook of policy and practice* (pp. 3–32). San Francisco, CA: Jossey Bass.

Ball, D. L., & Forzani, F. M. (2009). The work of teaching and the challenge for teacher education. *Journal of Teacher Education, 60*(5), 497–511. doi:10.1177/0022487109348479

Baumeister, R., Bratslavsky, E., Finkenauer, C., & Vohs, K. (2001). Bad is stronger than good. *Review of General Psychology, 5*(4), 323–370.

Berliner, D. (in press). Exogenous variables and value-added assessments: A fatal flaw. *Teachers College Record.*

Berliner, D., & Biddle, B. (1995). *The manufactured crisis: Myths, fraud, and attack on America's schools.* Reading, MA: Addison-Wesley.

Bill & Melinda Gates Foundation. (2010). *Learning about teaching: Policy brief.* Retrieved from http://www.metproject.org/downloads/Preliminary_Findings-Policy-Brief.pdf

Binet. A., & Simon, T. (1916). *The development of intelligence in children.* Baltimore, MD: Williams and Wilkins.

Brophy, J. E. (1973). Stability of teacher effectiveness. *American Educational Research Journal, 10*(3), 245–252.

Brophy, J. (2004). *Using video in teacher education.* San Diego, CA: Elsevier.

Clotfelter, C. T., Ladd, H. F., & Vidgor, J. L. (2007). Teacher credentials and student achievement: Longitudinal analysis with student fixed effects. *Economics of Education Review, 26,* 673–682.

Cochran-Smith, M., & Zeichner, K. (Eds.). (2005). *Studying teacher education: The report of the AERA Panel on research and teacher education.* Washington, DC: American Education Research Association.

Coleman, J. S., Campbell, E. Q., Hobson, C. J., McPartland, F., Mood, A. M., Weinfeld, F. D., & York, R. (1966). *Equality of educational opportunity.* Washington, DC: U.S. Government Printing Office.

Council for the Accreditation of Education Preparation. (2013). *CAEP Commission on standards and performance rating.* Retrieved from http://caepnet.files.wordpress.com/2013/02/draft_standards2.pdf

Cronbach, L. J. (1957). The two disciplines of scientific psychology. *American Psychologist, 12,* 671–684.

D'Agostino, J. V., & Powers, S. J. (2009). Predicting teacher performance with test scores and grade point average: A meta-analysis. *American Educational Research Journal, 46*(1), 146–182.

Dewey, J. (1938). *Experience and education.* New York, NY: Collier.

DiCarlo, C. F., Pierce, S. H., Baumgartner, J., Harris, M. E., & Ota, C. (2012). Whole-group instruction practices and children's attention: A preliminary report. *Journal of Research in Childhood Education, 26*(2), 154–168.

Ehrenberg, R., & Brewer, D. (1994). Do school and teacher characteristics matter? Evidence from high school and beyond. *Economics of Education Review, 13,* 1–17.

Emmer, E. T., Evertson, C. M., & Brophy, J. E. (1979). Stability of teacher effects in junior high classroom. *American Educational Research Journal, 16*(1), 71–75.

Emmer, E. T., & Millett, G. B. (1970). *Improving teaching through experimentation, a laboratory approach.* Upper Saddle River, NJ: Prentice Hall.

Feiman-Nemser, S., & Buchmann, M. (1985). Pitfalls of experience in teacher education. *Teachers College Record, 87*(1), 53–65.

Ferguson, R. F., & Ladd, H. F. (1996). How and why money matters: An analysis of Alabama schools. In H. Ladd (Ed.), *Holding schools accountable: Performance-based reform in education* (pp. 265–298). Washington, DC: Brookings Institution Press.

Fernandez, C. & Yoshida, M. (2004). *Lesson study: A Japanese approach to improving mathematics teaching and learning (studies in mathematical thinking).* Mahwah, NJ: Erlbaum.

Floden, R. (2012). Teacher value added as a measure of program quality: Interpret with caution. *Journal of Teacher Education, 65*(5), 356–360.

Forgasz, H. J., & Leder, G. C. (2008). Beliefs about mathematics and mathematics teaching. In P. Sullivan & T. Wood (Eds.), *International handbook of mathematics teacher education, Vol. I: Knowledge and beliefs in mathematics teaching and teaching development* (pp. 173–192). Rotterdam, The Netherlands: Sense.

Franke, M. L., Kazemi, E., & Battey, D. (2007). Understanding teaching and classroom practice in mathematics. In F. Lester (Ed.), *Second handbook of research on mathematics teaching and learning* (pp. 225–256). Reston, VA: National Council of Teachers of Mathematics.

Fuller, F. (1969). Concerns of teachers: A developmental conceptualization. *American Educational Research Journal, 6,* 207–226.

Gabriel, R., & Lester, J. N. (2013). Sentinels guarding the grail: Value-added measurement and the quest for education reform. *Education Policy Analysis Archives, 21*(9). Retrieved from http://epaa.asu.edu/ojs/article/view/1165

Gansle, K., Noell, G., & Burns, J. (2012). Do student achievement outcomes differ across teacher preparation programs? An analysis of teacher education in Louisiana. *Journal of Teacher Education, 65*(5), 304–317.

Ginsberg, R., & Kingston, N. (in press). Caught in a vise: The challenges facing teacher preparation in an era of accountability. *Teachers College Record.*

Good, T. (1996). Teaching effects and teacher evaluation. In J. Sikula, T. Buttery, & E. Guyton (Eds.), *Handbook of research on teacher education* (2nd ed., pp. 548–594). New York, NY: Macmillan Library Reference.

Good, T. (in press). What do we know about how teachers influence student performance on standardized tests, and why do we know so little about other outcomes? *Teachers College Record.*

Good, T., & Brophy, J. (1973). *Looking in classrooms.* New York, NY: Harper & Row.

Greenwald, R., Hedges, L. V., & Laine, R. D. (1996). The effect of school resources on student achievement. *Review of Educational Research, 66*, 361–396.

Hanushek, E. A. (1986). The economics of schooling: Production and efficiency in public schools. *Journal of Economic Literature, 24*, 1141–1177.

Hanushek, E. A. (2003). The failure of input-based schooling policies. *The Economic Journal, 113*, F64–F98.

Heilig, J. V., & Jez, S. J. (2010). *Teach for America: A review of the evidence.* East Lansing, MI: Great Lakes Center for Educational Research and Practice.

Henry, G., Kershaw, D., Zulli, R., & Smith, A. (2012), Incorporating teacher effectiveness into teacher preparation evaluation. *Journal of Teacher Education, 63*(5), 335–355.

Hiebert, J., & Morris, A. K. (2012). Teaching, rather than teachers, as a path toward improving classroom instruction. *Journal of Teacher Education, 63*(2), 92–102.

Ingersoll, R., & Merrill, L. (2012). *Seven trends: The transformation of the teaching force.* Philadelphia, PA: Consortium for Policy Research in Education, University of Pennsylvania.

Ingersoll, R., & Perda, D. (2012). *How high is teacher turnover and is it a problem?* Philadelphia: Consortium for Policy Research in Education, University of Pennsylvania.

Kain, J., & Singleton, K. (1996, May–June). Equality of education revisited. *New England Economic Review*, 87–111.

Kane, T., Wooten, A., Tyler, J., & Taylor, E. (2011). Evaluating teacher effectiveness. *Education Next, 11*(3), 55-60.

Konstantopoulos, S. (2006). Trends of school effects on student achievement: Evidence from NLS: 72, HSB: 82, and NELS: 92. *Teachers College Record, 108*(12), 2550–2581.

Konstantopoulos, S. (in press). Teacher effects, value-added models, and accountability. *Teachers College Record.*

Lortie, D. C. (1975). *Schoolteacher: A sociological study.* Chicago, IL: University of Chicago Press.

Ma, L. (1999). *Knowing and teaching elementary mathematics.* Mahwah, NJ: Erlbaum.

Marx, R. (in press). Reforming again: Now teachers. *Teachers College Record.*

McCaslin, M. M., & Good, T. L. (1996). *Listening in classrooms.* New York, NY: Harper Collins.

Munby, H., & Russell, T. (1994). The authority of experience in learning to teach: Messages from a physics methods class. *Journal of Teacher Education, 45*(2), 86–95.

Murnane, R. J., & Phillips, B. R. (1981). What do effective teachers of inner-city children have in common? *Social Science Research, 10*, 83–100.

National Council for Teaching Quality (NCTQ). (2013). *Transparency central: Our commitment to shared transparency.* Retrieved from http://www.nctq.org/transparency.do

National Mathematics Advisory Panel. (2008). *Report of the task group on instructional practices.* Retrieved from http://www.ed.gov/about/bdscomm/list/mathpanel/reports.html

Nye, B., Konstantopoulos, S., & Hedges, L. V. (2004). How large are teacher effects? *Educational Evaluation and Policy Analysis, 26*, 237–257.

Payne, C. M. (2008). *So much reform, so little change: The persistence of failure in urban schools.* Boston, MA: Harvard Education Press.

Pianta, R. (2012, May 6). Stop complaining about teacher assessments: Find alternatives. *The Chronicle of Higher Education.* Retrieved from http://chronicle.com/article/Tired-of-Debating-Teacher/131803/

Porter, A. C., Garet, M. S., Desimone, L., Yoon, K. S., & Birman, B. F. (2000). *Does professional development change teaching practice? Results from a three-year study.* Washington, DC: U.S. Department of Education.

Porter, A. C., Youngs, P., & Odden, A. (2001). Advances in teacher assessments and their uses. In V. Richardson (Ed.), *Handbook of research on teaching* (4th ed., pp. 259–297). Washington, DC: American Educational Research Association.

Rice, J. (2003). *Teacher quality: Understanding the effectiveness of teacher attributes.* Washington, DC: Economic Policy Institute.

Rose v. Council (1989) 790 S.W.2d 186, 60 Ed. Law Rep. 1289

Rosencranz, H. A., & Biddle, B. J. (1964). The role approach to teacher competence. In B. J.

Biddle & W. J. Ellena (Eds.), *Contemporary research on teacher effectiveness* (pp. 232–263). New York, NY: Holt, Rinehart and Winston.

Rosenholtz, S. (1989). *Teachers' workplace: The social organization of schools.* New York, NY: Longman.

Rosenshine, B. (1970). The stability of teacher effects upon student achievement. *Review of Educational Research, 40*(5), 647–662.

Rothstein, R. (2000). Toward a composite index of school performance. *Elementary School Journal, 100*(5), 409–442.

Rowan, B., Correnti, R., & Miller, R. J. (2002). What large scale, survey research tells us about teacher effects on student achievement: Insights from the Prospects study of elementary schools. *Teachers College Record, 104,* 1525–1567.

Smith, B. O. (1980). *A design for a school of pedagogy.* Washington, DC: U.S. Department of Education.

Smylie, M. A., Miller, C. L., & Westbrook, K. P. (2008). The work of teachers. In T. L. Good (Ed.), *21st century education handbook* (pp. 3–11). Thousand Oaks, CA: Sage.

Stigler, J. W., Gallimore, R., & Hieber, J. (2000). Using video surveys to compare classrooms and teaching across cultures: Examples and lessons from the TIMSS video studies. *Educational Psychologist, 35*(2), 87–100.

Teaching Scotland. (2010). A group perspective. *Teaching Scotland Online, 33.* Retrieved from http://www.teachingscotland.org.uk/features/33-a-group-perspective.aspx

Tripp, T. R., & Rich, P. J. (2012). The influence of video analysis on the process of teacher change. *Teaching and Teacher Education, 28*(5), 728–739.

Twiselton, S. (2007). Seeing the wood for the trees: Learning to teach beyond the curriculum. *Cambridge Journal of Education, 37*(4), 489–502.

U.S. Department of Education. (2003, June). *Meeting the highly qualified teachers challenge: The secretary's second annual report on teacher quality.* Washington, DC: Author. Retrieved from http://www.ed.gov/about/reports/annual/teachprep/2003title-ii-report.pdf

van Es, E. A. (2009). Participants' roles in the context of a video club. *Journal of the Learning Sciences, 18*(1), 100–137.

van Es, E. A., & Sherin, M. G. (2010). The influence of video clubs on teachers' thinking and practice. *Journal of Mathematics Teacher Education, 13,* 155–176. doi:10.1007/s10857-009-9130-3

Wilson, S. M. (2003). *California dreaming: Reforming mathematics education.* New Haven, CT: Yale University Press.

Wineburg, M. (2006). Evidence in teacher preparation establishing a framework for accountability. *Journal of Teacher Education, 57*(1), 51–64.

Witty, P. (1947). An analysis of the personality traits of the effective teacher. *The Journal of Educational Research, 40*(9), 662–671.

APPENDICES

Variable	Open	Traditional
1. Initiation of teacher–student	Student	Teacher interaction
2. Space	Flexible	Fixed
3. Student activities	Wide range	Narrow range
4. Source of activity interests	Students' spontaneous	Teacher or school prescribed
5. Use of time	Flexible	Fixed
6. Teacher focus	Individual student	Large or whole group
7. Content and topics	Wide range	Narrow range
8. Student–student interaction	Unrestricted	Restricted

* Adapted from information provided by Katz, L. (1972). *Developmental Stages of Preschool Teachers.* Urbana, IL: ERIC Clearinghouse on Early Childhood Education.

APPENDIX 2.2
Recommendations from Subject-Matter Study Groups*

Teaching Emphasis for Beginning Teachers

Less of This	More of This
Algorithmic worksheets	Using Chemistry to solve real-world problems
Asking primarily knowledge-level questions	Asking primarily higher cognitive-level questions

Changing Emphasis in Lesson Plans

Less Emphasis On	More Emphasis On
The "sage of the stage" approach, where the activities are all centered on the teacher	Teachers who present lessons that guide and facilitate student learning
Plans that have students working alone or in unrelated groups	Lessons that incorporate cooperative learning and collaboration among students

Changing Emphasis in Teaching Standards

Less Emphasis On	More Emphasis On
Teacher as technician	Teacher as intellectual reflective practitioner
Teacher as consumer of knowledge about teaching	Teacher as producer of knowledge about teaching

Changing Emphasis

Less Emphasis On	More Emphasis On
Assessing scientific knowledge	Assessing scientific understanding and reasoning
Development of external assessments by measurement experts alone	Teachers involved in the development of external assessments

* Tables reprinted with permission. National Research Council. (1996). *National Science Education Standards.* Washington, DC: National Academy Press.

APPENDIX 2.3
The No Child Left Behind Act of 2001

These reforms express my deep belief in our public schools and their mission to build the mind and character of every child, from every background, in every part of America.

President George W. Bush
January 2001

Three days after taking office in January 2001 as the 43rd President of the United States, George W. Bush announced No Child Left Behind, his framework for bipartisan education reform that he described as "the cornerstone of my Administration." President Bush emphasized his deep belief in our public schools, but an even greater concern that "too many of our neediest children are being left behind," despite the nearly $200 billion in Federal spending since the passage of the Elementary and Secondary Education Act of 1965 (ESEA). The President called for bipartisan solutions based on accountability, choice, and flexibility in Federal education programs.

Less than a year later, despite the unprecedented challenges of engineering an economic recovery while leading the Nation in the war on terrorism following the events of September 11, President Bush secured passage of the landmark No Child Left Behind Act of 2001 (NCLB Act). The new law reflects a remarkable consensus—first articulated in the President's *No Child Left Behind* framework—on how to improve the performance of America's elementary and secondary schools while at the same time ensuring that no child is trapped in a failing school.

The NCLB Act, which reauthorizes the ESEA, incorporates the principles and strategies proposed by President Bush. These include increased accountability for States, school districts, and schools; greater choice for parents and students, particularly those attending low-performing schools; more flexibility for States and local educational agencies (LEAs) in the use of Federal education dollars; and a stronger emphasis on reading, especially for our youngest children.

Increased Accountability

The NCLB Act will strengthen Title I accountability by requiring States to implement statewide accountability systems covering all public schools and students. These systems must be based on challenging State standards in reading and mathematics, annual testing for all students in grades 3-8, and annual statewide progress objectives ensuring that all groups of students reach proficiency within 12 years. Assessment results and State progress objectives must be broken out by poverty, race, ethnicity, disability, and limited English proficiency to ensure that no group is left behind. School districts and schools that fail to make adequate yearly progress (AYP) toward statewide proficiency goals will, over time, be subject to improvement, corrective action, and restructuring measures aimed at getting them back on course to meet State standards. Schools that meet or exceed AYP objectives or close achievement gaps will be eligible for State Academic Achievement Awards.

More Choices for Parents and Students

The NCLB Act significantly increases the choices available to the parents of students attending Title I schools that fail to meet State standards, including immediate relief—beginning with the 2002–03 school year—for students in schools that were previously identified for improvement or corrective action under the 1994 ESEA reauthorization.

LEAs must give students attending schools identified for improvement, corrective action, or restructuring the opportunity to attend a better public school, which may include a public charter school, within the school district. The district must provide transportation to the new school, and must use at least 5 percent of its Title I funds for this purpose, if needed.

For students attending persistently failing schools (those that have failed to meet State standards for at least 3 of the 4 preceding years), LEAs must permit low-income students to use Title I funds to obtain supplemental educational services from the public- or private-sector provider selected by the students and their parents. Providers must meet State standards and offer services tailored to help participating students meet challenging State academic standards.

To help ensure that LEAs offer meaningful choices, the new law requires school districts to spend up to 20 percent of their Title I allocations to provide school choice and supplemental educational services to eligible students.

In addition to helping ensure that no child loses the opportunity for a quality education because he or she is trapped in a failing school, the choice and supplemental service requirements provide a substantial incentive for low-performing schools to improve. Schools that want to avoid losing students—along with the portion of their annual budgets typically associated with those students—will have to improve or, if they fail to make AYP for 5 years, run the risk of reconstitution under a restructuring plan.

Greater Flexibility for States, School Districts, and Schools

One important goal of No Child Left Behind was to breathe new life into the "flexibility for accountability" bargain with States first struck by President George H.W. Bush during his historic 1989 education summit with the Nation's Governors at Charlottesville, Virginia. Prior flexibility efforts have focused on the waiver of program requirements; the NCLB Act moves beyond this limited approach to give States and school districts unprecedented flexibility in the use of Federal education funds in exchange for strong accountability for results.

New flexibility provisions in the NCLB Act include authority for States and LEAs to transfer up to 50 percent of the funding they receive under 4 major State grant programs to any one of the programs, or to Title I. The covered programs include Teacher Quality State Grants, Educational Technology, Innovative Programs, and Safe and Drug-Free Schools.

The new law also includes a competitive State Flexibility Demonstration Program that permits up to 7 States to consolidate the State share of nearly all Federal State grant programs—including Title I, Part A Grants to Local Educational Agencies—while providing additional flexibility in their use of Title V Innovation funds. Participating States must enter into 5-year performance agreements with the Secretary covering the use of the consolidated funds, which may be used for any educational purpose authorized under the ESEA. As part of their plans, States also must enter into up to 10 local performance agreements with LEAs, which will enjoy the same level of flexibility granted under the separate Local Flexibility Demonstration Program.

The new competitive Local Flexibility Demonstration Program would allow up to 80 LEAs, in addition to the 70 LEAs under the State Flexibility Demonstration Program, to consolidate funds received under Teacher Quality State Grants, Educational Technology State Grants, Innovative Programs, and Safe and Drug-Free Schools programs. Participating LEAs would enter into performance agreements with the Secretary of Education, and would be able to use the consolidated funds for any ESEA-authorized purpose.

Putting Reading First

No Child Left Behind stated President Bush's unequivocal commitment to ensuring that every child can read by the end of third grade. To accomplish this goal, the new Reading First initiative would significantly increase the Federal investment in scientifically based reading instruction programs in the early grades. One major benefit of this approach would be reduced identification of children for special education services due to a lack of appropriate reading instruction in their early years.

The NCLB Act fully implements the President's Reading First initiative. The new Reading First State Grant program will make 6-year grants to States, which will make competitive subgrants to local communities. Local recipients will administer screening and diagnostic assessments to determine which students in grades K–3 are at risk of reading failure, and provide professional development for K–3 teachers in the essential components of reading instruction.

The new Early Reading First program will make competitive 6-year awards to LEAs to support early language, literacy, and pre-reading development of preschool-age children, particularly those from low-income families. Recipients will use instructional strategies and professional development drawn from scientifically based reading research to help young children to attain the fundamental knowledge and skills they will need for optimal reading development in kindergarten and beyond.

Other Major Program Changes

The No Child Left Behind Act of 2001 also put the principles of accountability, choice, and flexibility to work in its reauthorization of other major ESEA programs. For example, the new law combines the Eisenhower Professional Development and Class Size Reduction programs into a new Improving Teacher Quality State Grants program that focuses on using practices grounded in scientifically based research to prepare, train, and recruit high-quality teachers. The new program gives States and LEAs flexibility to select the strategies that best meet their particular needs for improved teaching that will help them raise student achievement in the core academic subjects. In return for this flexibility, LEAs are required to demonstrate annual progress in ensuring that all teachers teaching in core academic subjects within the State are highly qualified.

The NCLB Act also simplified Federal support for English language instruction by combining categorical bilingual and immigrant education grants that benefited a small percentage of limited English proficient students in relatively few schools into a State formula program. The new formula program will facilitate the comprehensive planning by States and school districts needed to ensure implementation of programs that benefit all limited English proficient students by helping them learn English and meet the same high academic standards as other students.

Other changes will support State and local efforts to keep our schools safe and drug-free, while at the same time ensuring that students—particularly those who have been victims of violent crimes on school grounds—are not trapped in persistently dangerous schools. As proposed in No Child Left Behind, States must allow students who attend a persistently dangerous school, or who are victims of violent crime at school, to transfer to a safe school. States also must report school safety statistics to the public on a school-by-school basis, and LEAs must use Federal Safe and Drug-Free Schools and Communities funding to implement drug and violence prevention programs of demonstrated effectiveness.

APPENDIX 2.4
ELEVEN COMPONENTS OF A COMPREHENSIVE SCHOOL REFORM PROGRAM

- Employs proven methods and strategies based on scientifically based research;
- Integrates a comprehensive design with aligned components;
- Provides ongoing, high-quality professional development for teachers and staff;
- Includes measurable goals and benchmarks for student achievement;
- Is supported within the school by teachers, administrators and staff;
- Provides support for teachers, administrators, and staff;
- Provides for meaningful parent and community involvement in planning, implementing, and evaluating school improvement activities;
- Uses high-quality external technical support and assistance from an external partner with experience and expertise in schoolwide reform and improvement;
- Plans for the evaluation of strategies for the implementation of school reforms and for student results achieved, annually;
- Identifies resources to support and sustain the school's comprehensive reform effort;
- Has been found to significantly improve the academic achievement of students or demonstrates strong evidence that it will improve the academic achievement of students.

APPENDIX 3.1
SIGNIFICANT OR NEAR SIGNIFICANT PROCESS VARIABLES FROM AN ANALYSIS OF VARIANCE ACROSS THE TOP AND BOTTOM NINE TEACHERS*

Variables	p Value	X High	X Low
Number of Students	.0001	26.07	21.34
Time Teacher Taught "Whole" Class	.1001	40.47	35.83
*Time Going over Homework	.0656	4.98	8.19
*Classroom Climate[1]	.0771	2.00	2.26
*Clarity	.0135	4.06	3.53
*Average Accountability	.0424	3.46	3.15
*Average Alerting	.0350	3.90	3.59
Discipline Question[2]	.0656	0.11	0.35
Direct Question	.0113	14.07	28.26
Process Question	.0131	2.72	7.53
Correct Response	.0533	38.70	50.98
Wrong Response	.0017	5.39	11.39
No Response	.0058	1.37	3.26
Student Response Followed by Teacher Praise	.0046	2.74	14.09
Negates Wrong	.0088	1.51	3.29
Repeats Question	.0295	1.39	2.78
Student Initiated Work Related Contact: Teacher Gives Process Feedback	.0654	4.41	1.56
Student Initiated Work Related Contact: Teacher Gives Feedback	.0004	17.65	9.30
Teacher Initiated Work Related Contact: Type Feedback Unknown	.1072	0.02	0.24
Teacher Initiated Behavior Related Contact: Teacher Gives Warning	.0081	1.75	3.37
Teacher Initiated Behavior Related Contact: Teacher Gives Criticism	.0548	0.30	0.67
Total Teacher Initiated Work Related Contacts	.0383	3.01	5.97
Total Teacher Initiated Behavior Related Contacts	.0853	4.22	5.85
Total Teacher Initiated Contacts	.0129	7.23	11.83
Total Student Initiated Work Related Contacts	.0004	23.44	11.80

Variables	p Value	X High	X Low
Total Student Initiated Contacts (Work and Procedural)	.0003	25.35	13.41
Direct Questions			
Total Response Opportunities	.1089	28.13	36.54
Total Teacher Initiated Contacts			
Total Student Initiated Contacts	.0058	54.10	116.41
Process Questions			
Total Questions	.0518	7.44	14.56
Correct Responses			
Total Responses	.0051	82.80	76.17
Total Process Feedback	.1005	6.51	3.04

*This table is reprinted from Good and Grouws, 1975.

★Indicates a high inference rating.

1 This scale was reversed so the lower score on the scale implies a more relaxed learning environment.

2 The unit used in reporting the behavioral data is frequency per hour.

APPENDIX 3.2
MEAN OCCURRENCE (IN PERCENT) OF SELECTED IMPLEMENTATION VARIABLES FOR TREATMENT AND CONTROL GROUP TEACHERS AND CORRELATION OF THESE VARIABLES WITH TEACHERS' RESIDUALIZED GAIN SCORES ON SRA MATHEMATICS TESTS*

Variable	Occurrence			Correlation	
	Treatment	Control	p	R	p
1. Did the teacher conduct review?	91%	62%	.0097	.37	.04
2. Did development take place within review?	51%	37%	.16	.10	.57
3. Did the teacher check homework?	79%	20%	.0001	.50	.0001
4. Did the teacher work on mental computation?	69%	25%	.69	.20	.26
5. Did the teacher summarize previous day's materials?	28%	25%	.69	.20	.26
6. There was a slow transition from review.	7%	4%	.52	-.02	.91
7. Did the teacher spend at least 5 minutes on development?	45%	51%	.52	-.08	.65
8. Were the students held accountable for controlled practice during the development phase?	33%	20%	.20	.12	.50
9. Did the teacher use demonstrations during presentation?	45%	46%	.87	-.15	.41
10. Did the teacher conduct seatwork?	80%	56%	.004	.27	.13
11. Did the teacher actively engage students in setwork (first 1 ½ minutes)?	71%	43%	.0031	.32	.07

Variable	Occurrence			Correlation	
	Treatment	Control	p	R	p
12. Was the teacher available to provide immediate help to students during seatwork (next five minutes)?	68%	47%	.02	.28	.11
13. Were students held accountable for seatwork at the end of seatwork phase?	59%	31%	.01	.35	.05
14. Did seatwork directions take longer than 1 minute?	18%	23%	.43	-.02	.92
15. Did the teacher make homework assignments?	66%	13%	.001	.49	.004

*This table is reprinted from Good & Grouws, 1979.
SRA = Science Research Associates.

APPENDIX 3.3
THREE EXAMPLES RELATING INSTRUCTIONAL BEHAVIOR TO STUDENT ACHIEVEMENT

Visible Learning (Hattie, 2009)

- Teachers need to be directive and actively engaged in teaching and learning
- Teachers need to know how students are constructing meaning
- Teachers need knowledge of the content they teach in order to provide meaningful feedback to students
- Teachers need to be clear about intended meaning of lessons and making these success criteria explicit
- Teachers need to recognize and welcome student error and create environments where students feel safe to learn and relearn

(Based on material presented by Hattie in Visible Learning, pp. 238–239)

Teach for America (Farr, 2010)

- Communicating key ideas
- Coordinating student practice
- Checking for student understanding
- Tracking progress
- Using organization and routine to maximize efficiency
- Asserting authority by consistently following through on high expectations

Good Teaching (Ripley, 2010)

- Set big goals for their students
- Constantly reevaluated what they are doing
- Used ways to involve kids in the lesson (e.g., mental math)
- Demonstrated the learning that students were to engage in
- Implemented an "I do, we do, you do"
- Build up well-established routines

APPENDIX 5.1
FOUR OBSERVATION SYSTEMS USED FOR RESEARCH
IN THE MET PROJECT*

The MQI Protocol for Classroom Observations

Teacher-Content Relationship:

Richness of the Mathematics: This dimension pays attention to the meaning of mathematical facts and procedures, and engagement with mathematical practices.

Meaning–making includes explanations of mathematical ideas and drawing connections among different mathematical ideas or different representations of the same idea.

Mathematical practices are represented by multiple solution methods, where more credit is given for comparisons of solution methods for ease or efficiency; by developing mathematical generalizations from examples.

Errors and Imprecision: Captures whether the teacher makes major errors that indicate gaps in mathematical knowledge, and whether there is a lack of clarity in the presentation of content.

Teacher-Student Relationship:

Working with Students and Mathematics: This measures the extent to which the teacher accurately responds to students' mathematical ideas and whether teachers correct student errors thoroughly.

Student-Content Relationship:

Student Participation in Meaning–Making and Reasoning:
Captures the ways in which students engage with mathematical content, specifically whether students ask questions and reason about mathematics with adequate *mathematical* explanations.

Connections Between Classroom Work and Mathematics:
This measures whether class assignments have a mathematical point or whether instructional time is spent in nonproductive use of time including transitions and disciplines.

* These instruments appear in the Measures of Effective Teaching Project Report (October, 2010), and this project is funded by the Bill and Melinda Gates Foundation

The CLASS Protocol for Classroom Observations

Domain 1: Emotional Support

Pre-K and Lower Elementary
• Positive Climate, Negative Climate, Teacher Sensitivity, Regard for Student Perspectives

Upper Elementary and Secondary
• Positive Climate, Negative Climate, Teacher Sensitivity, Regard for Adolescent Perspectives

Domain 2: Classroom Organization

Pre-K and Lower Elementary
• Behavior Management, Productivity, Instructional Learning Formats

Upper Elementary and Secondary
• Behavior Management, Productivity, Instructional Learning Formats

Domain 3: Instructional Support

Pre-K and Lower Elementary
• Concept Development, Quality of Feedback, Language Modeling

Upper Elementary and Secondary
• Content Understanding, Analysis and Problem Solving, Quality of Feedback, Instructional Dialogue

Across grade levels, the CLASS focuses on the effectiveness of classroom interactional processes rather than on the content of the physical environment, materials, or curriculum.

DANIELSON'S FRAMEWORK FOR TEACHING FOR CLASSROOM OBSERVATIONS

FFT Domains, Components and Elements

Raters score teacher practice at the component level. For the MET project, only Domain 2 and Domain 3 of the FFT are used by raters to analyze video observations:

- **Classroom environment** (Domain 2): This scale measures general classroom atmosphere, appropriate behavioral management, the quality and effectiveness of routine and procedures, and student/teacher rapport.
- **Instruction** (Domain 3): This domain measures the general quality of instruction (including effective communication, appropriate discussion techniques, and an ability to engage students.

Domain 2: Classroom Environment

2a: Creating an environment of respect and rapport
    Teacher interaction with students
    Student interactions with one another
2b: Establishing a culture for learning
    Importance of the content
    Expectations for learning and achievement
    Student pride in work
2c: Managing classroom procedures
    Management of instructional groups
    Management of transitions
    Management of materials and supplies
2d: Managing student behavior
    Expectations
    Monitoring of student behavior
    Response to student misbehavior

Domain 3: Instruction

3a: Communicating with students
    Expectations for learning
    Directions and procedures
    Explanations of content
    Use of oral and written language
3b: Using questioning and discussion techniques
    Quality of questions
    Discussion techniques

Student participation
3c: Engaging students in learning
Activities and assignments
Grouping of students
Instructional materials and resources
Structure and pacing
3d: Using assessment in instruction
Assessment criteria
Monitoring of student learning
Feedback to students
Student self-assessment and monitoring of progress
Lesson adjustment

THE PLATO PROTOCOL FOR CLASSROOM OBSERVATIONS

PLATO Elements

The 13 PLATO Elements include:
- Purpose
- Intellectual Challenge
- Representation of Content
- Connections to Prior Knowledge
- Connections to Personal and Cultural Experience
- Modeling
- Strategy Use and Instruction
- Guided Practice
- Classroom Discourse
- Text-Based Instruction
- Accommodations for Language Learning
- Behavior Management
- Time Management

Some of the elements of the Plato Protocol appear below.

Intellectual Challenge focuses on the intellectual rigor of the activities and assignments. Activities and assignments with high intellectual challenge ask students to engage in analytic or inferential thinking. Activities and content with low challenge, basically calls only for student recall or rote thinking.

Modeling concerns the extent to which a teacher models or demonstrates strategies, skills, and processes that students will engage in as they complete the task. Modeling as defined here has a focus upon the student's completion of the classroom task (not a hypothetical or long-term task).

Strategy Use and Instruction examines the teacher's ability to teach strategies and skills associated with listening, speaking, reading, writing, and generally engaging in literature. As defined in this coding system, strategy instruction does not include the teaching of rules including such things as definitions of parts of a story or instruction related to grammar or spelling. Strategy use is reserved for teacher activities that focuses on reading for meaning, how to figure out unfamiliar words, or generating ideas for writing assignments.

Guided Practice refers to activities or strategies provided in structured and scaffolded ways that help students move toward completing lesson tasks independently. The activity must be related to a clear instructional practice and clearly provides a practice opportunity for students. For example, this might be an opportunity to practice elements of writing and reading or students might be provided with opportunities to practice asking questions about a text or ways for writing an introduction or conclusion and so forth. To be high on this dimension involves clear support from the teacher to allow students to complete tasks successfully. Teachers who are low on this dimension either provide no opportunities for guided practice or there is very little guidance from the teacher directly or through interactions with students.

Classroom Discourse examines the opportunities students have for conversations with peers or the teacher. This element focuses upon classroom talk and at the low end it indicates the extent to which a teacher accepts minimal student responses. And teachers at the high end engage students and their ideas, which enables students to clarify and specify their understandings.

Text-Based Instruction. Text-based instruction measures the extent to which texts are used in the classroom and how they are used. Texts can include published material, pieces of music, or student-generated work. The notion here is to see whether grammar (or whatever) is taught as an end in itself or whether it is taught in some meaningful context.

Behavior Management. Here the basic idea is whether students demonstrate behavior and dispositions that are appropriate for the learning task. Hence, what might be appropriate during a lecture might differ from what is appropriate during a classroom discussion or student group work. Thus given the task, are students "orderly" and appropriately engaged?

Time Management. Here the focus is on the extent to how well-paced and how effective are transitions from one activity to another. The goal here is that most time (within reason) is used for instruction and that classroom time is not squandered on other activities.

INDEX